D0984508

THE
HOMERIC ODYSSEY

THE
HOMERIC ODYSSEY

The Mary Flexner Lectures
delivered at Bryn Mawr College
Pennsylvania

BY

DENYS PAGE, F.B.A.

REGIUS PROFESSOR OF GREEK
AND FELLOW OF TRINITY COLLEGE
CAMBRIDGE

CLARENDON PRESS · OXFORD

Oxford University Press, Ely House, London W. 1

GLASGOW NEW YORK TORONTO MELBOURNE WELLINGTON
CAPE TOWN SALISBURY IBADAN NAIROBI LUSAKA ADDIS ABABA
BOMBAY CALCUTTA MADRAS KARACHI LAHORE DACCA
KUALA LUMPUR HONG KONG

FIRST PRINTED AT THE UNIVERSITY PRESS, OXFORD, 1955
REPRINTED LITHOGRAPHICALLY IN GREAT BRITAIN
FROM CORRECTED SHEETS OF THE FIRST EDITION
BY WILLIAM CLOWES AND SONS LIMITED, LONDON AND BECCLES, 1966

PREFACE

THIS book represents substantially the text of the Mary Flexner Lectures delivered at Bryn Mawr College in February and March 1954, divested only of a few improvisations and hilarities and amplified only by a number of paragraphs giving detail for which neither the time was sufficient nor the occasion suitable.

My audience included such connoisseurs of Homeric poetry as Rhys Carpenter and Richmond Lattimore: I must make it very clear from the start that I was addressing myself not to them but to their students. It was my intention to provide a general introduction to the problems which present themselves in the study of the composition of the *Odyssey*: to write (in short) the kind of book which I myself as an undergraduate should have found interesting and useful. The subject has been so much neglected in Great Britain and the United States that the student must return to D. B. Monro's Appendix to his edition of the *Odyssey*, published in 1901, to discover (in any but a foreign tongue) many of the most elementary facts.

At the beginning it seemed to me that, after taking into account the Odyssean researches of a long and distinguished line of professional scholars, it was possible to separate a little grain from a great deal of chaff and to discern amid the grain a few pieces of much greater size and higher quality than the rest. There are certain arguments, touching especially the Journey of Telemachus, the Visit to the Underworld, the last 634 lines of the poem, and a few other passages, which appeared on investigation to constitute a strong prima facie case against unity of authorship for the *Odyssey*. There was a great deal more to say; but most of it could easily be postponed until the primary questions had been answered. If the testimony of these parts of the poem does not convince, it is very improbable that the secondary witnesses will be heard with favour, however numerous and eloquent they may be.

It proved very difficult to confine myself within the limits of six lectures and to remember that I was not addressing an audience devoted to the study of the Homeric Question to the exclusion of all other interests. It was my principal object to state facts clearly and briefly in a sternly practical manner, reporting what is immediately given by the text of the *Odyssey*, and contributing little of my own except (occasionally) a glitter of rhetoric round the fringes of the self-evident. The farther I progressed, the harder I found it to be brief without being superficial, to be lucid without over-simplifying, to be persuasive without being unduly partial; and I confess that where the claims of the spoken and the written word were at variance, the former constantly prevailed.

I express most cordial gratitude to the President and Faculty of Bryn Mawr College for their abundant hospitality and great personal kindness; to Mr. G. S. Kirk, of Trinity Hall, who read a first draft of these lectures and made numerous important observations, almost all of which persuaded me; to Mr. W. A. Camps, of Pembroke College, who read and further improved the typescript after delivery of the lectures, when it was too late to make changes of substance; and, finally, to my wife, who typed the whole book and read the proofs.

D. L. P.

TRINITY COLLEGE
CAMBRIDGE

CONTENTS

I

ODYSSEUS AND POLYPHEMUS

THE story told in the *Odyssey* is a popular folk-tale of a type which recurs in different places at different times.[1] The hero has been many years away from home; his wife is surrounded by impatient suitors; his son has gone abroad in search of him; after many adventures he returns home in disguise, rescues his wife at the eleventh hour, kills her suitors, and proves by means of trials and tokens that he is what he claims to be, her husband. That, in a few words, is the main theme of the *Odyssey*, one of the two Epic poems which emerged from the Dark Ages into the dawn of Greek history, bringing with it no reliable record of the period of time within which it was composed; or of the manner of its composition—whether oral or written, whether by a single author or by several—or of the place or places where it was created.

The folk-tale adopted as the theme of the *Odyssey* has been detached from its natural setting and transferred to a person believed to be historical, Odysseus. It is therefore largely adapted to the world in which we live: in the background is the Trojan War, which the poet, if he spoke in such terms, would call the most important of all historical events; some of the places (especially Ithaca and its neighbouring islands; Pylos and Sparta) are real places; and much of the detail of social, domestic, and economic life correspond to what the earliest audiences found familiar or at least credible. But this real world is hazy on its horizon: there is no clear division between it and a very different world, a kind of fairyland where magic and mumbo-jumbo abound, a world of witches and ogres, of miraculous sea voyages, of transformations with a fairy wand.

Now the treatment of the folk-tale in the *Odyssey* is curiously complex. Into the framework of the main theme, the folk-tale of the Returning Hero, are fitted certain other folk-tales which, before their inclusion in the story of Odysseus, had nothing whatever to do with that theme. The stories of Circe and of Polyphemus, for example, are themselves (like the story of the Returning Hero) *Weltmärchen*, universal folk-tales, independent of each other and of the main theme of the *Odyssey*.

Still more remarkable, under this heading, is the transference to Odysseus of a whole cycle of Adventures which had hitherto belonged not to a more or less unidentified hero of folk-tale but to a semi-legendary person; adventures which were not merely the subject of common talk but actually fixed and glorified in an Epic poem familiar to the audience of the *Odyssey*.—I mean the Argonautic adventures recounted in the Tenth and Twelfth Books.[2]

When Odysseus left the island of Aeolus he was in the Far West of the world: quite suddenly (and without warning to the audience) he finds himself in the Far East,[3] consorting with persons whose only place in legend is the story of Jason and the Argonauts. *Circe* is sister of Aeetes, the guardian of the Golden Fleece; she lives on the remotest eastern verges of the world (12. 1 ff.), as far from Odysseus' route as possible. *The Wandering Rocks* belong only to the story of the Argonauts; they too were in that same region, the Black Sea. The *Laestrygones* have a fountain called Artakia: that is to say, they live at (or near) Cyzicus, in the Propontis, where the fountain of that name was, and still is, to be found. On the island of *Thrinakia* the companions of Odysseus kill the sacred cattle—of what god? Of Helios, the Sun, so important in the story of the Golden Fleece, quite foreign to the story of Odysseus; the arch-enemy in our poem was hitherto Poseidon, and will be again, so soon as we have finished with these Argonauts in disguise. The *Sirens* too were at home in the story of Jason long before they transferred their affections to Odysseus. In short the poet has taken a large part of the story of Jason and the Argonauts and transferred it bodily to Odysseus. And this he has done with the most disarming candour: when he comes to the Wandering Rocks he reminds his audience expressly (12. 69 ff.) that these belong to the story of the vessel Argo and its hero Jason, a tale (he says) which everybody knows, Ἀργὼ πᾶσι μέλουσα.[4]

The *Odyssey*, then, is composed of folk-tales, having little or nothing in common with each other except the fact that they are folk-tales and that they are here concentrated on the same person, Odysseus. But there are still further complexities. Examine the story of Polyphemus and you will make two discoveries. First, that there were various ways of telling that story, and our poet is not particularly careful to choose one way to the exclusion of all others; secondly, that the story of Polyphemus in the *Odyssey* is not an element but a compound—there is a basic story of Polyphemus, told with some variety of version, and to this the poet has added incidents from other folk-tales which were wholly independent of it.

This example, the story of Odysseus and the Cyclops, illustrates a general rule of considerable importance in the Homeric Question. It shows very clearly the practice of combining various versions of the same folk-tale into one version and of combining various folk-tales into one folk-tale. It may be impossible—in this example it certainly is impossible—to disentangle the threads once they are woven, except theoretically. The practice in question naturally results in inconsistencies and other imperfections; but as a general rule we may (and sometimes must) interpret such phenomena in terms of a multiplicity not of authors but of stories.

We must not press a good argument too far: we shall later inquire (with a mind still open but no longer vacant) whether there be any obstacles too high for overleaping in this way; but first let us examine the story of Odysseus and Polyphemus.[5]

The story told in the Ninth Book of the *Odyssey* is one of many versions of a folk-tale widespread throughout Europe and beyond. One hundred and twenty-five specimens were collected and published in 1904 by Oskar Hackman: for certain obvious and valid reasons, one of which will appear presently, it is quite impossible to entertain the notion that the *Odyssey* might be the common source of all or even of many. Common to these tales, in general, is the following theme: the hero is at the mercy of a giant shepherd in a cave; he blinds the giant and escapes from the cave with the help of the giant's sheep; there is a sequel, to which I shall return presently. To this outline a great variety of detail may be added. Especially popular is the following version, recorded in Spain, France, Italy, Sicily, Albania, Greece, Serbia, Hungary, Germany, Lithuania, Finland, Cappadocia, and the Caucasus, and, with only secondary variations, in several other lands. The hero, with companions, is prisoner in the cave of a one-eyed giant shepherd; some or all of the companions are cooked by the giant on a spit over a fire; the giant sleeps after his heavy dinner; the hero takes the spit, heats it in the fire, and plunges it into the giant's eye; the giant opens the door of the cave in the morning to let his sheep out and the hero escapes by walking out on all fours dressed in a sheep's skin or (less often) by clinging to the underside of a sheep: the story ends with the sequel to which I referred a moment ago.

It is evident that this is a well-constructed story. One action follows necessarily from another throughout. The fire provides the spit, the spit provides the giant's dinner and the hero's weapon; the giant's sleep follows naturally upon his heavy dinner; the fact that the giant has only one eye suggests to the hero a most simple and effective way of disabling him; and the fact that the giant is a shepherd, whose sheep must be released from the cave in the morning, gives the hero his only possible means of escape. So all that is needed is a one-eyed giant shepherd who cooks his dinner; and that, often enough, is what we find in the folk-tales.

Now consider the *Odyssey*'s narrative in equally broad outline. Odysseus and his companions are at the mercy of a one-eyed giant shepherd: that is the traditional formula; but our poet, while accepting it, rejects several of its natural consequences. Polyphemus eats his victims raw, not cooked; he is put to sleep by excessive indulgence in wine; the survivors use not a spit but a stake of olive-wood to blind him; Odysseus tells the giant that his name is *Nobody*, so when the giant's neighbours come to the rescue and ask who is killing him he answers '*Nobody* is killing me', and the neighbours go away reassured; next morning the giant opens his door to let his sheep out, and the survivors escape by clinging to the bellies of the sheep. Clearly it is the common story that is being told; but clearly too it includes some uncommon variations and at least two elements entirely foreign to the folk-tale.

It is of course this latter fact which is most remarkable in itself and most important for the understanding of the story-teller's art. Is it really the case that two incidents have been transferred to this tale from some quite independent source or sources?

I suppose that no other incidents in the tale are more amusing and memorable than the trick with the name *Nobody* and the inebriation of the giant.

1. Οὖτις ἐμοί γ' ὄνομα, Οὖτιν δέ με κικλήσκουσι. The trick with the name *Nobody* does not occur in the folk-tale versions of our story.[6] It is characteristic of another common folk-tale (represented by fifty examples in Oskar Hackman's collection)[7] concerning a contest between a human being and some sort of devil or demon: it is usually a brief tale, in which the demon, outwitted and incapacitated by the man, calls other demons to the rescue; now the man had said that his name was *Myself*,[8] so when his friends ask who has done this, he answers '*Myself did it*', and therefore gets no help or sympathy. In this folk-tale the villain is almost never a giant and almost never a man-eater; he is almost always injured by methods fundamentally different from those employed in the various versions of the story of Polyphemus. The two stories have so little in common that they could not have less without ceasing to have anything.

The facts speak for themselves. Here are 120 versions of the one story without an example[9] of this episode: in the *Odyssey*, therefore, it might be either freely invented or transferred from another tale; the choice between these alternatives is dictated by the discovery that the episode is highly characteristic of another well-known folk-tale. There is no need for further comment except the observation that our poet has not entirely reconciled, at this point, two different conceptions of the standing of Polyphemus in Cyclopean society.

Odysseus told Polyphemus that his name is *Nobody*. The giant, after his blinding, awakens the neighbours with his cries. They ask, who is killing him? And he answers, 'Nobody is killing me'.

Now clearly we cannot do without these neighbours: the Nobody device can only be employed in a conversation between the giant and bystanders; and the poet has made it clear that there were indeed many Cyclopes in the land (106 ff., 125 ff., 166 ff.), living round about in caves on the wind-swept hills (399 ff.). This is easily understood, for the Cyclopes have their own place in Greek mythology, and it was well known that they were numerous. In the First Book of the *Odyssey*, indeed, we are told of ἀντίθεον Πολύφημον ὅου κράτος ἐστὶ μέγιστον | πᾶσιν Κυκλώπεσσι (1. 70 f.), 'god-like Polyphemus, whose power is supreme among all Cyclopes': there is a whole community of them, and Polyphemus is their lord and master; when he cries out in the night it is very natural that his loyal and sympathetic subjects should emerge in their nightgowns to ask if he is in pain.

In the folk-tale, on the other hand, the giant's position is entirely different. He is a solitary rogue, living remote from men and even from other giants; and our poet, who knows very well that this is so, does not hesitate to speak in these terms when it suits his purpose. When Polyphemus is first introduced to us he is the solitary outcast of the folk-tale, not the Cyclopean king of the *Odyssey*: 'He would pasture his flocks alone, afar; he roamed not in the tracks of others, but stayed solitary, with lawlessness in his heart' (188 ff.). Here, for a brief moment, is the traditional villain of the folk-tale, the remote and lonely giant, not surrounded by other giants, not their lord and master, but living apart from them and avoiding their society.

2. Κύκλωψ, τῆ, πίε οἶνον. The second episode which is foreign to the folk-tale is the inebriation of the giant. Here again the facts are simple: this episode is not to be found in the folk-tale versions of our story; it might then be either free invention or a borrowing from some other folk-tale. The latter alternative is presumably correct, for there is a relatively small circle of folk-tales,[10] fundamentally different from our story, essentially concerned with a man who inebriates a devil or demon in order to capture and force him to reveal some knowledge or perform some act. This

episode, like the trick with the name *Nobody*, has been transferred, in our poem, to the tale of Polyphemus. I pause only to observe that herein lies one of the principal reasons why it is impossible to suppose that the *Odyssey* is the common source of the folk-tale versions: if it were so, how could it be that none of the folk-tales has adopted either of these most memorable incidents? To this simple question, first put by Wilhelm Grimm in 1857, no reasonable answer has been (or could be) given.[11]

The inebriation of the giant is exceptionally well adapted to its new surroundings. Our poet is evidently aware that his giant must either be a drinker of milk (or water), in which case Odysseus may offer him a *vin ordinaire* without special preparation; or a drinker of wines, in which case he must provide a vintage of extraordinary pedigree. The choice is made in favour of the latter alternative: there are vineyards in the land of Polyphemus (110 f.), and he himself is a drinker of wines (357 ff.). Therefore Odysseus must offer him something out of the ordinary; and so it is arranged, with uncommon care. Our attention is attracted to the presence of wines in the ship's stores at an early moment: 'All day to sunset we sat feasting on meats unlimited and red wine' (161 ff.). About this wine we are to hear some peculiar history, for soon it will be used to inebriate the giant: 'The red wine had not yet been lost out of the ships, but there was store of it; each one of us had drawn off abundance in jars, when we sacked the holy citadel of the Cicones.' It is most abnormal to make so much ado about the history of the wine consumed at dinner; but we know very well why it is done here, for the story of Polyphemus has begun. Within thirty lines Odysseus sets forth to the giant's cave and takes a pouch of wine with him—yes, it is that Ciconian wine from the celebrated vineyards of Ismarus;[12] only it is something particularly strong and sanctified, cultivated by a priest and kept secret by him, an altogether abnormal vintage, to be diluted twentyfold before drinking; and then, says Odysseus, one would not willingly hold back (211).

Only for one moment does the poet forget what he is talking about: there is a very small but very characteristic oversight in v. 297. When we are told that the giant drank *milk* with his dinner

(249, 297), the point would escape our notice altogether if the poet's subconscious mind had not expressed itself. Look again at the words: the giant was 'eating human flesh, and thereupon drinking *unmixed milk*', ἄκρητον γάλα πίνων. What in the world may this be, *unmixed milk*? That which may be mixed or unmixed for drinking is not milk but wine; ἄκρητον μέθυ πίνων. Our poet has substituted milk for wine, forgetting the unlucky adjective and forgetting, too, that in his version of the story the giant need not be, indeed is not, a drinker of milk.[13]

The success of the adaptation is the more remarkable since the episode in question does not readily lend itself to this use. Odysseus must take a pouch of strong wine when he starts for the giant's cave. At that moment, of course, he cannot possibly know that he will have any use for it; and the poet is aware that he must say something by way of apology, since heroes in the Greek Epic, when they go foraging, do not encumber themselves with pouches of preternaturally strong wine on the off-chance.[14] So Odysseus, who has not yet seen his adversary, tells us that his proud heart *had a foreboding* from the start that a strong, savage, and lawless man would come upon him (213 ff.). The listener hardly notices, and certainly does not resent, the simple subterfuge.

Moreover it may be noticed that the common folk-tale, in which the giant goes naturally to sleep after a heavy dinner, has some advantage in economy and coherence; there is no need whatever to make the giant drunk. But the poet found, as his audience still finds, particular pleasure in this incident, so humorously described, so delicately adapted to the old folk-tale. We can only wonder that the influence of the *Odyssey* was nowhere strong enough to alter the course of the common folk-tale in this direction.

So much for the two elements transferred from other folk-tales to the story of Polyphemus. Let us now consider certain variations of that story itself, made or adopted by the story-teller in the *Odyssey*.

1. *The Ring*. The common folk-tale ends with the following

episode. The hero, safely outside the cave, mocks the giant, who pretends to admit defeat and asks the hero to accept a small token of his esteem: he throws down a ring which the hero puts on a finger; at once the ring begins to shout 'Here I am!', and the blind ogre, guided by the sound, almost captures the hero, who cannot remove the ring, but escapes at the last moment by cutting off his finger. The *Odyssey* has an alternative ending, which it shares with the third voyage of Sinbad the Sailor and a few other versions of the folk-tale: the giant chases the hero to the sea; taunted by the hero he throws rocks at the ship and almost wrecks it. It is enough to observe that this version is much better suited to the *Odyssey* than the traditional sequel of the Talking Ring: the ring would be out of harmony with the tone of this realistic narrative, in which the supernatural element is deliberately suppressed and obscured; moreover Odysseus has now to sail toward further adventures, and the transition to a new place and persons is thus most easily made.[15]

2. *The Weapon.* In the common folk-tale the giant cooks his victims on a spit over a fire. When he is asleep the hero takes the spit, heats it in the fire, and plunges it into the giant's eye. The *Odyssey*, alone[16] among all versions of this folk-tale, substitutes a log of olive-wood for the spit. This variation is worth a moment's notice, for the change has obvious disadvantages which the poet does his best to gloss over.

It was a great merit of the spit that no special provision need be made for its presence in the cave: the giant's dinner is cooked, and of course there is a spit over the fire. The hero's weapon is supplied by the story itself, not by coincidence or special arrangement. Our poet (or some predecessor) has rejected the traditional weapon and substituted a wooden log: he must then consider how this is to be introduced into the story. He might either give no explanation, merely saying that the hero found a piece of wood in the cave; or he might try to make its introduction appear natural by giving some reason why this indispensable object should happen to be just where it was wanted. The *Odyssey* adopts the latter course: 'Now there was a great club belonging to the Cyclops, lying beside the sheepfold, a green one of olive-wood; he had cut it to carry when dried' (319 ff.). Here is the reason why this weapon should have been left lying about so conveniently: it was a new club, not yet seasoned, put there to dry. The element of chance is just as great as it ever was; but the poet has artfully made it seem much less.

But this was not the only matter for which the poet must make provision. The *spit* may be seized as soon as the giant is asleep: the plan may be made beforehand, its execution can be left to the last moment, since a ready-made weapon is at hand. The *wooden club*, on the contrary, must be looked for and shaped and sharpened; and when it is ready it must be carefully concealed until the time is ripe. No longer can we leave all to the last moment: for then, what if our search for a weapon should be vain? This is the last chance: there will be no more survivors after tomorrow's breakfast and supper.

In the *Odyssey* the discovery and preparation of the weapon occur, reasonably enough, during the giant's absence on the last day. Nor does the poet forget that it must somehow be concealed: 'I stored it away, hidden in the dung which was spread in great abundance through the cave' (329 f.). We are satisfied with this explanation and ask no awkward questions; we are fairly confident that the giant, when he returns, will not notice that his new club is nowhere to be seen.

Is there any trace, in the *Odyssey*, of what is certainly the older weapon, the spit? I am not sure; but I think it probable that such a trace is to be detected at one point—the description of the heating of the weapon in the fire.[17] In the common folk-tale the spit is generally made of metal, most often of iron, and is regularly heated in the fire before use. No doubt it would do its work as well cold as hot: but the iron which glows white-hot is a more picturesque and formidable weapon, an ornament of lasting quality, a memorable feature of the folk-tale. But what if your weapon is a fresh-cut log of green olive-wood? As if it were a metal spit Odysseus puts it into the embers of the fire ἧος θερμαί-νοιτο, until it should grow hot (376), and takes it out when '*green though it was*'—how conscious our poet was of the point at issue!— 'it was about to catch fire, and *glowed all through terribly*', διεφαίνετο δ' αἰνῶς. The metal spit will turn red-hot and white-hot, it will *glow all through terribly*: the fresh-cut log of green olive-wood will turn black and smoke and smoulder; in the end it may burst into flames, but there is one thing you may wait in vain for it to do—to *glow all through* like a white-hot poker. One may go so far as to suggest that this incident in general, and this description of it in particular, are much more suitable to the earlier metal spit than to the later log of wood. I do not forget that it was a common practice to apply fire to a spear-head for the purpose of hardening it; I only observe that that is not the purpose stated or implied here.

Why was the nature of the weapon changed? We can only guess. If the spit was to be used, the human victims must be cooked, as they so often are in the folk-tales, and as they are in the *Cyclops* of Euripides. Often enough they are cooked alive, and often enough the giant compels the survivors to share his dinner. The cooking might be described without these abominable details; but we may conjecture that the cooking of the human victims, whether alive or dead, was rejected as being a deed of the utmost barbarism, outside the law prescribed by tradition to the Odyssean story-teller. In many of the stories in which this action occurs it is indeed an uncommonly disagreeable tale, often told with a gusto for gruesome detail; it is not surprising that some civilized communities have rejected it and substituted other weapons for the spit.[18]

Finally, observe how clearly the poet sees the detail of his story. Odysseus' plan is wrecked if the giant should fall asleep face downwards; it is seriously hampered if he lies on his back. He must lie on his side, or at least his head must be turned sideways, so that we may have access to his eye without, as it were, putting up a scaffolding. Of course there was no need to make any provision for this point: we are more than content if the poet tells us that the giant fell asleep, in whatever position, and the hero put out his eye; the folk-tales seldom say more than this, and most of the Greek vase-painters attain the depths of indifference to realism.[19] Not so the poet in the *Odyssey*; he keeps his listeners for a moment in suspense: ἀνακλινθεὶς πέσεν ὕπτιος, the giant fell over *on his back*; but then at once rolled his head over so that it faced the audience, αὐτὰρ ἔπειτα | κεῖτ᾽ ἀποδοχμώσας παχὺν αὐχένα (371 f.).

3. *The Survivors.* At 195 ff. Odysseus set out with twelve companions. At 289 two, and at 311 two more, are devoured by Polyphemus. There are now therefore eight left; and at 335 these draw lots to select who shall assist Odysseus in the blinding of the giant. At 344 the giant devours two more, picking them, considerately enough, from among the four who were unsuccessful in the drawing of the lots. We are left to assume that Odysseus is assisted in the blinding of the giant by the chosen four while the two others watch from ringside seats; and we are tempted to conjecture that the story has been slightly abbreviated, that two more should have been devoured, leaving Odysseus with his chosen four.

Now look more closely: is not this business of the drawing of the lots an odd and ineffective affair? What is the object of it? The poet suggests that lots were to be drawn because the task of blinding the giant was one which Odysseus' companions were likely, from lack of courage, to decline: ὅστις τολμήσειεν κτλ. (332); πάντας ἑταίρους | θάρσυνον, μή τίς μοι ὑποδείσας ἀναδύη (376 f.). But then we are told that the four who drew the favourable lots were, as it happened, 'the very ones whom I should have desired to choose' (334). Then why not choose them? They are probably waiting for you to ask for volunteers; and here you take the risk of having four incompetent cowards thrust upon you by the hazard of the lot.

This episode is definitely below the level of realism attained by the poet throughout the narrative; and our feeble faith in what he tells us here may well be utterly subverted when we first conceive the idea that the drawing of the lots might have a very different purpose; that in some earlier version of this story the drawing of lots decided not *who should help Odysseus*, but *who should be eaten next.*

Two men are to be devoured at every meal. Victims with any instinct for organization will make it their first task to establish an order of precedence. There shall be no unseemly squabble at meal-times: we draw lots, and it is your turn today, mine tomorrow. That is the origin of the drawing of lots. It had nothing to do with the choosing of assistants for Odysseus: he will be glad of the help of all who survive. He will not, as the *Odyssey* would have him do, nominate four assistants, with the presumable implication that no action will be taken until the remainder have been devoured. The story will see to it that the four who draw the favourable lots are, as Odysseus says, the very ones he would have chosen if he could; and the story will also see to it (as the *Odyssey* does not) that no more than these four are alive when the moment for action comes.

I conclude this review of the story of Polyphemus with a brief comment on its two remaining features: the escape from the cave and the one-eyedness of the giant.

1. *The Escape.* In the common folk-tale the hero, with or without companions, most often escapes from the cave in the following manner: he obtains in one way or another the skin of a sheep, puts it over his head and back, and crawls out of the door; the giant feels each sheep as it passes, and often detects the fraud, but the hero slips out from under, leaving the skin in the giant's hands.

The *Odyssey* gives an alternative and much less common version:[20] the hero and his companions escape by clinging, or being tied, to the underside of sheep which carry them past the giant. This version is more suitable to the Odyssean narrative, for more than one reason.

The folk-tales are not as a rule very skilful in their methods of providing the sheepskins. Either there must be a convenient supply of these in the cave, or the survivors must themselves kill and skin some of the giant's sheep. In the first case, to account for the convenient supply of skins, the story-teller may draw attention to the fact that the giant had recently been killing sheep in the cave: thus in a Gascon folk-tale[21] 'the boy put on the golden horns and skin of the sheep *that had been killed three days before*'. This was a most natural device, for it was reasonable to suppose that the giant had been eating sheep before circumstances changed his diet; but it is not the alternative most commonly adopted. As a rule the survivors do their own killing and skinning, to the profound discomfort of the story-teller: for the killing and skinning cannot be done until the giant has been blinded, and then, since the giant is anything but inactive, there is no time to stand about skinning sheep: the folk-tales skate rapidly, and not always gracefully, over the thin ice of this episode.

We notice further that the original purpose of Odysseus' expedition had been to obtain provisions for the fleet (225 ff.) : the device employed here to extricate the survivors fulfils at the same time that expectation; they take back to the fleet the sheep which had rescued them. The entire story of Polyphemus is most carefully constructed and most firmly settled in its place among the adventures of Odysseus.

2. *The Single Eye.* The course of the story requires that the audience should know that the giant has only one eye. This fact, on which the whole action depends, is nowhere stated; nor could it be inferred from the name 'Cyclops', which might mean 'round-eyed' or 'round-faced', but not '*one*-eyed'. The fact that Polyphemus has only one eye is first implied at a late stage of the narrative when Odysseus enlists supporters to 'turn the stake in the Cyclops' *eye*' (331 ff.; the singular number recurs in 383, 394, 397) : from that moment onwards one-eyedness is presupposed by the action, but still not explicitly declared. It is probable that the story was so well known that the audience took this matter for granted from the start; but we must admit that, even. if it were not so, there was yet an infallible clue to the fact. One-eyedness, although it was not denoted by the *name* 'Cyclops', was implied by the *nature* of the persons who bore that name: everybody knew that a Cyclops had only one eye,[22] though the name 'Cyclops' did not mean 'one-eyed'.

This one-eyedness has been adopted by the *Odyssey* from the folk-tale, and there is no suggestion that there was any alternative to it. I am not at present interested in speculation about the meaning of the single eye: much has been conjectured about its ulterior significance in the regions of psychology and superstition; but we are concerned only with its place in our story. And that at least is clear enough: it is so highly convenient to the action; and it is this fact, rather than any significance derived from popular superstition or elsewhere, which established it so firmly in the folk-tale.

For the story-teller has two difficult problems. First, he must disable the giant; that may not be easy. But then he must release the hero from the cave; and that is much harder. The giant must not be able to catch the hero in the cave: yet he must be able, after his defeat, to get up and open a door, a door which is too large for anyone but the giant to open. There can be no question of killing the giant, or indeed of inflicting any injury which might impair his strength (299 ff.). It was then surely a most suitable device to make the giant blind: it is not easy to think of any other means to achieve this end, at least so naturally and economically. But of course it does not follow that the giant must be one-eyed. In the folk-tales, indeed, the two-eyed giant is common enough; but we notice what trouble he gives to his narrator. The hero's weapon is most often a metal spit; but, if the giant has two eyes, this weapon (and much that is necessarily connected with it) must be abandoned; for two weapons will then be needed, and two squads of men must operate simultaneously. It is not surprising that such grotesqueness finds no favour with the story-teller. Further, in the numerous examples of the story in which the hero is *alone*, the blinding of a two-eyed giant with such a weapon becomes practically impossible. Very different devices are therefore employed against two-eyed giants. The problem, and the artificial means employed to solve it, may be illustrated by a few examples. In *Dolopathos*,[23] a medieval collection of folk-tales, the giant *happens* to have a pain in his eyes: the hero promises to cure him and blinds him with a liniment of boiling oil, lime, arsenic, salt, and sulphur. In an Italian tale[24] the giant has two eyes, but *it happened* that one of them was defective: again, the boiling-oil treatment. In a story from the Scottish Highlands[25] the giant is most conveniently blind already in one eye: the hero undertakes to cure the blind eye and destroys the good one. In a tale from Finland[26] the giant again *happens* to be blind in one eye.

The principal defect of these devices is obvious enough: it is a fault that mere coincidence should play so large a part in a matter of such importance. By pure chance this particular giant has one blind eye or some defect of sight: this fact, essential to the development of the story, is based on nothing in the story but dragged in from outside.

A version from Finland[27] improves upon its models by making the giant *believe* that his eyes need treatment. The hero 'made believe to be sharp-sighted, and able to see all sorts of funny things ever so far off. The giant glowered for all he was worth in the same direction, but could make out just nothing at all. "Look here, young man," says he, "however did you come to be so sharp-sighted?" "Oh," says the hero, "it's in this way. I let them drip a drop of lead in my eyes. That's why I am so sharp-sighted." "Oh that's it, is it?" says the giant, "Come on, my dear fellow, and pour a little molten lead in my eyes. I should so like to be as sharp-sighted as you."' This was an amusing, though highly sophisticated, solution for the problem of coincidence. Equally effective, and much simpler, is the treatment by a Rumanian story-teller[28] whose hero succeeds in pouring oil over both eyes at once of a sleeping giant. Still the one-eyed giant has always been most popular; and it is easy to see why,—not only because the mechanics of blinding him are so much simpler, but also because he is so hideous and appalling, among the most alarming and memorable creations of universal folk-lore.

The story of Odysseus and Polyphemus exemplifies, at least as well as any other part of the poem, the general principle that minor inconsistencies and imperfections in the narrative may be readily explained in terms not of different authors but of different stories. Elements from several folk-tales are combined but not quite perfectly blended; and within one folk-tale the version adopted is not always fully to be understood except in the light of other versions not adopted. There are numerous other examples, some of them more prominent. In the course of the *Odyssey* we often come suddenly upon something which seems to imply a different story, occasionally even a different conception of the character of some person, or of the purpose of some incident. Many of the well-known inconsistencies in the narrative of the poem are, in my opinion, more easily explained in terms of one author and several stories than in terms of several authors and one story. This may be thought obvious enough: but many of the most influential writers about the *Odyssey* hold a different opinion. If one passage contradicts another, or is inconsistent with it, we are told to infer that the one version was composed by one poet, the other by another, the two being combined into their present form by a third poet or editor, at whose unlucky head hard words are flung.[29]

But let us avoid extremes: a mind free from prejudice will not, I believe, deny that there are some difficulties in the narrative of the *Odyssey* of such a nature that the burden of proof rests finally upon the person who believes in unity of authorship. We shall set forth along this path, not knowing what the end will be.

I do not know whether a lifetime of leisure and diligence would suffice for the adequate study of the Homeric Question. Of the endless array of books and essays which it is unsafe to neglect, however unprofitable to read, no man can master more than a select and relatively small proportion. I intend to do no more than define and discuss what I take to be the greatest of the obstacles to the belief that the *Odyssey* was planned and composed substantially in its present form by one person. The inquiry will be severely restricted: there is much more that might be said, and truly said; but nothing, I believe, of equal magnitude and force.

Yet even this limited ambition presupposes much work which I cannot do more than mention; much indeed which I cannot yet have done except imperfectly. Nothing solid can be built except on three foundations: first, the history of the transmission of the Homeric poems from remotest antiquity to the present day;[30] secondly, the study of the nature and origins of the Homeric dialect of Greek;[31] and thirdly, what may be summarily called the 'archaeology' of the Greek Epic.[32] When these foundations have been laid, building can begin; and the *Iliad* must come before the *Odyssey*. These lectures are one of the later chapters in

the story of the Homeric Question, one of the earlier chapters in
that part of it which deals with the making of the *Odyssey*.

I begin with the Visit to the Underworld in the Eleventh Book
of the *Odyssey*: for, if we seek unmistakable proof of the unskilful
insertion of alien matter into the framework of the poem, the
voice of scholarship, both Separatist and Unitarian, advises us to
look first in that quarter.

NOTES ON CHAPTER I

1. Numerous examples were assembled by Schnorf, *Der mythische Hintergrund im
Gudrunlied und in der Odyssee*, Zürich 1879. See also W. Spletstösser, *Der heimkehrende
Gatte und sein Weib in der Weltlitteratur*, Berlin 1899; L. Radermacher, *Die Erzäh-
lungen der Odyssee, Sitzungsberichte der Kais. Akad. der Wiss. in Wien*, phil.-hist. Klasse
178. 1 (1915) 47 ff., with further literature p. 47, n. 1; W. Crooke, *Folk-Lore* 9
(1898) 130 ff.

2. For what follows see especially K. Meuli, *Odyssee und Argonautika* (Berlin 1921)
87–115: the fact was first stated by A. Kirchhoff, *Die Homerische Odyssee* (1879)
287 ff., its proof first established by Meuli. There is much else of interest, beyond
the bounds of my present theme, in Meuli's book.

3. For the detail of this see Meuli 53 ff.; but I do not agree with his suggestion
that the move from West to East is facilitated by the fact that Aeolus' island was
mobile.

4. It is important for our purpose to remember that the Argonautic story was
originally pure *Märchen*, a folk-tale. It developed into a realistic romance, and was
presumably (like the *Odyssey*) already masquerading as romantic fiction in the
poem at which the *Odyssey* hints (Ἀργὼ πᾶσι μέλουσα). Meuli deals well with this
topic.

5. The foundations of what follows were laid by Wilhelm Grimm in a masterly
essay, *Die Sage von Polyphem* (*Abhandlung der Königl. Akad. der Wiss.*, Berlin 1857;
much of it is summarized by Merry and Riddell in their edition of the *Odyssey*,
vol. i, Appendix II). Far the most important of later works is Oskar Hackman's
Die Polyphemsage in der Volksüberlieferung (*akademische Abhandlung*, Helsingfors 1904:
few scholars name this book, and very few make use of it; the Bodleian copy was
still uncut at the end of 1953). Thirty-six specimens of the story are set out in detail
by Sir James Frazer in Appendix XIII to the second volume of his Loeb edition of
Apollodorus; I have thought it convenient to refer most frequently to this. For
further literature see Frazer, op. cit. 404 ff., and *Pausanias* v. 343 ff.; Radermacher,
op. cit. 13, n. 1; Meuli, op. cit. 66, n. 3; Crooke, *Folk-lore* 19 (1908) 172 ff.

6. See Hackman, op. cit. 179 ff., 200 f. The Nobody-trick is never combined
with the blinding of the giant with a spit (or stake); the two specimens in which it
occurs together with the blinding of the giant by other means are both late and
contaminated versions. (See now Dawkins, *More Greek Folktales* (1955) 12 ff.)

7. This is Hackman's *Group B*. He gives 125 examples of *Group A* (the Polyphemus story), 50 of *Group B*. (He adds 45 examples of *Group C*, which does not
concern us, being a relatively late and mixed folk-tale, confined to Finland and its
neighbourhood; its villain is never a giant, and never blinded by spit or stake; it
has the Nobody-device, but not the escape with the help of the sheep.)

8. The name *Nobody* is almost unexampled in the folk-tales, which use 'Myself' or 'Myself-I-did-it', or the like; Hackman, op. cit. 189 ff., Dawkins, p. 12.

9. Except the two bogus examples mentioned in n. 6 above.

10. See Meuli, op. cit. 71 f.; but his attempt to equate the giant of the Polyphemus-story with the *Naturdämonen* of the other tale is a disastrous failure.

11. See Grimm, op. cit. 23–24; Radermacher, op. cit. 7, 14. Meuli would like to believe that our poet *invented* Polyphemus, and that *all* other versions of the folk-tale are descended from the *Odyssey*: he has no answer to Grimm's objections (70), and no good argument of his own.

12. Compare Ἰσμάρῳ (40) with Ἴσμαρον (198).

13. I see only one other possibility—the far-fetched interpretation suggested by Oldfather in *Class. Phil.* 7 (1913) 195 ff.: in 246 ff. the Cyclops divided the milk into two halves, one curdled, the other in its natural state for drinking (249); ἄκρητον γάλα πίνων might then specify that he drank the uncurdled half, as well he might. What should induce our poet to point out that the milk which the Cyclops drank was *not* the curdled pail, I cannot conceive; but I suppose it must be admitted to be a possible solution, however absurd, and I shall not be surprised if something of the sort underlies the obscure words in the Scholia, ἀπαραμιγὲς ἔχον καὶ ὀρρῶδες καὶ τὸ τυρῶδες καὶ τὸ ἐλαιῶδες.

14. In 187 ff. the poet gives the misleading impression that Odysseus already knows what sort of person the Cyclops is. This is deliberately done in order that we may see nothing incongruous in the following description of the wine which he thinks fit to provide for the emergency. A moment later (216 ff.) we see through the deception: Odysseus has not yet seen the Cyclops, and has no more reason to expect trouble than he had in 175 ff., when his mind was quite open.

15. At first sight there seems to be no hint of the ring-sequel in the *Odyssey*. We may not be quite so sure if we come fresh from the numerous ring-versions to the words of Polyphemus at the end of Odysseus' adventure. In *Dolopathos* the giant drew a ring from his finger and said 'Take that for a reward, for it is not meet that a guest should go without a gift from a man like me'. In Frazer's no. 8 the giant says 'Come here and fear not; at least take a keepsake'. Compare with these (and others of the same kind) the unlikely words assigned to the Cyclops (517, cf. 229, 356): 'Come hither Odysseus, *that I may set guest-gifts before you*'. Odysseus is at this moment on the high seas; there is not the faintest possibility that he will put back to shore for a souvenir, and his reply ignores the invitation. It is an obvious possibility that the Cyclops' words are a rudiment of the ring-sequel, included here because everybody knew that the giant always said something like this at this moment in the story.

16. Or almost alone. Hackman's three examples (no. 1, Attica; no. 58, Serbia; no. 109, Magyar) are all probably dependent on the *Odyssey* in this respect; op. cit. 164.

17. The fire itself is more or less rudimentary in the Odyssean version, since its principal virtues in the folk-tale have here no scope (the spit being excluded). It is, however, singularly well employed in 251 ff.: the Cyclops returned to his cave, milked his sheep, 'and then he lit a fire, *and caught sight of us*'—the trembling victims, cowering in the shadows, were betrayed by the firelight. At first sight it appears quite rudimentary in 307 ff.: the Cyclops wakes up in the morning, *lights a fire*, milks his sheep, eats a couple of his victims (uncooked), and at once drives his flocks out to pasture for the day. We must, however, remember that the fire is needed for the heating of the weapon; the giant had no use for his fire, but the poet cannot do without it.

18. This problem of the alternative weapon admits of various solutions, some of them simpler and more organic than that of the *Odyssey*. Frazer, no. 21 (Gascon):

the hero uses a burning brand snatched from the fire—an excellent device, giving the fire an integral part to play and saving the trouble of preparing and concealing the weapon. There is a similar solution in Frazer's no. 26 (Greece). It is a Breton version which has the last word: 'The young man drew a pistol from his pocket, and firing at the giant put out his eye.'

19. See, for example, the latest additions to the vase-paintings of this scene the Proto-Argive krater (saec. VII B.C. med.) reproduced by J. M. Cook in *JHS* 73 (1953) 116, fig. 5, and the Proto-Attic example of similar date published by G. E. Mylonas in *The Illustrated London News*, 13 Nov. 1954. As a rule the Cyclops is portrayed as sitting upright (and awake); P. F. Müller, *Die antiken Odyssee-Illustrationen in ihrer kunsthistorischen Entwicklung* (Berlin 1913) 3–31; Jane Harrison in *JHS* 4 (1883) 249 ff.

20. Hackman, op. cit. 171.

21. Frazer, no. 21.

22. Hesiod, *theog.* 143, on the race of Cyclopes: μοῦνος δ' ὀφθαλμὸς μέσσῳ ἐνέκειτο προσώπῳ.

23. Frazer, op. cit. 405 with n. 3.

24. Ibid. no. 8.

25. Ibid. no. 2.

26. Ibid. no. 15.

27. Ibid. no. 13.

28. Ibid. no. 6.

29. What may happen to the Ninth Book of the *Odyssey* under this treatment may be seen in an article by Mülder in *Hermes* 38 (1903) 414 ff.: it is no longer necessary to refute this in detail, thanks to F. Focke, *Die Odyssee* (1943) 164–76.

30. This topic has been wonderfully elucidated in recent times by G. M. Bolling, especially in *The External Evidence for Interpolation in Homer* (Oxford 1925) and *The Athetized Lines of the Iliad* (Baltimore 1944). I have found myself seriously at variance with most of the tenets of Dr. Van der Valk in *The Textual Criticism of the Odyssey* (Leiden 1949).

31. The foundations of the study are laid especially by J. La Roche, *Homerische Untersuchungen*, 1869; D. B. Monro, *A Grammar of the Homeric Dialect* (1882); W. Schulze, *Quaestiones Epicae*, 1892; K. Witte, *RE* viii (1913) 2213 ff.; K. Meister, *Die Homerische Kunstsprache*, 1921; J. Wackernagel, *Sprachliche Untersuchungen zu Homer*, 1926; and we are now fortunate in having the masterly *Grammaire Homérique* of P. Chantraine. Above all, the student should be familiar with the revolutionary works of Milman Parry (for which see p. 160 below).

32. Here too the present generation is more fortunate than its predecessors, since the publication of Miss H. L. Lorimer's massive work, *Homer and the Monuments*, 1950.

II

ODYSSEUS AND THE UNDERWORLD

ODYSSEUS and his companions dwelt a year on the island of Circe, at the eastern limits of the world. From there, at the command of Circe, he sailed a day's voyage to the river Oceanus, which surrounds the earth. He discovered the entrance to Hades, and summoned the ghost of the prophet Teiresias, who should describe to him the stages of his journey home. On the threshold of Hades he saw and talked with many ghosts of the departed. There appear in succession: Elpenor, a companion lately dead; the prophet Teiresias; Odysseus' mother Anticleia; a long line of heroines of ancient legend; the great kings of the Trojan War, especially Agamemnon, Achilles, and Ajax; and finally the interior of the Underworld, where Minos is chief justice among the dead, where Orion and Heracles pursue their pleasures, and Tityus, Tantalus, and Sisyphus endure their everlasting punishments.

Two questions have been asked and answered about this Visit to the Underworld: first, is it the plan and work of a single mind? Secondly, is it an integral part of the *Odyssey*, or a later addition to it, whether specially designed for this place or adapted and transferred from a foreign source? To the former of these two questions the answer has for long been almost uniformly negative: there is no reasonable doubt that the Eleventh Book in its present form represents the expansion, by at least two or three different poets, of a briefer and simpler narrative. About the latter question there is less general agreement; we shall put aside prejudice and follow the evidence whithersoever it may lead.

The notion that ghosts in Hades might think and hear and speak, whether among themselves or in conversation with a visitor from the world above, is entirely foreign to the normal Homeric belief about the after-life. The *Iliad* and *Odyssey* present an almost uniform picture of the 'soul' and of its destiny after the body's death. *Psyche*, for which 'ghost' is a much better word than 'soul', is not to be thought of as a spiritual essence or inmate of the body, or as the sum of its intellectual and emotional faculties. It is very like what we might call a 'ghost': a shadowy figure existing independently of the body after death, having the same shape and personal appearance as the living man, but without flesh and bones and blood. It is the kind of second self which you may see in a dream; and indeed the experience of dreams is the earliest cause and justification of belief in ghosts of this type. 'While the body of the sleeper lies wrapped in slumber, motionless, the sleeper in his dream lives and sees many strange and wonderful things. It is "himself" who does this (of that there can be no doubt), and yet not the self known and visible to himself and others. . . . It follows that there lives within a man a second self, active in dreaming.' 'In the same way it is something real that appears to a man asleep as the shape of a person lately dead. Since this shape can still reveal itself to a dreamer, it must of necessity still exist . . . consequently it survives death, though only as a breath-like image.'[1] *Psyche* is a dreamlike second self, a ghost of the living man; when the body dies it leaves him, and survives apart from the body, and goes down to the Underworld. Like a reflection in a mirror, it has the same shape and appearance as the body; but apart from that body it has no substance, no power of thought or speech or feeling.

This notion of a second self, the body's image such as one perceives in a dream, is common in the thought of primitive peoples; but the Homeric poems are exceptional inasmuch as they deny to their departed ghosts all power of intervention among the living. In the Greek Epic the ghost departs from the body at death and swiftly descends to Hades, which it enters after the body has been cremated, not before. Having once entered Hades it is entirely without intelligence, emotion, and strength. It cannot ever again revisit the world of living men, and therefore has no cult or honour or worship of any kind. Such a conception of the after-life is sharply at variance both with the practice of the Mycenean civilization which preceded the rise of the Greek Epic and with that of the age which follows the dawn of history in the eighth century B.C. In the Mycenean era the dead body was interred, not cremated: the ghost was thought to survive, and must be strictly imprisoned, in the tomb; and there is evidence for a cult of the departed. This belief, that the ghost might return to earth in the region of its burial-place and have power to intervene among living men unless honoured and appeased, was widespread throughout Greece in the historical era. The Homeric poems tell (whether truthfully or not) of a period intervening in the Dark Ages between the end of the Mycenean and the beginning of the historical era, when the older custom had changed; when the dead were cremated, instead of being simply inhumed; when the ancient fear and worship of departed spirits gave way for a time to this novel and gloomy belief in feeble and forgotten ghosts remote in Hades, needing no sustenance, demanding no piety, powerless for ever to intervene in human affairs. It is remarkable that this tale of the after-life should be told so consistently; that poems of this length and variety should so uniformly suppress the fundamentally different belief and practice both of the era which they purport to represent and again of the latter period of their own development. I say, 'suppress it': for the older belief, if it was ever suspended in practice, was never quite forgotten. Hesiod testifies as much, when he tells us that in the Golden Age the spirits of the dead walked the earth taking note of right and wrong, and that in the Silver Age too the dead had honour. And the *Iliad* itself preserves the memory of the older custom in the Twenty-third Book, where the funeral rites of Patroclus are described: the slaughter of victims, the cutting of locks of hair, the pouring of wine and honey, the institution of funeral games and funeral feast, all presuppose the idea that the spirit of the dead needs and demands refreshment and respect. Yet even here it is only the incidental detail, not the central doctrine, which is contrary to Homeric custom: Patroclus is a perfectly conventional ghost who will go to Hades, never to return, so soon as his body has been cremated; you might ask, and ask in vain, of what use then were those fantastic funeral rites, all that ceremony which is appropriate only to the cult of the dead, to the belief in ghosts who have power to return and avenge neglect? 'The contradiction between Homeric belief and Homeric practice on this occasion is complete.'[2]

If ghosts in Hades have no thought or feeling, not even a voice, it is obvious that a visit by Odysseus to the Underworld will be an unpromising theme for poetry. But if only these ineffectual phantoms could be revived and given power to speak! And, however exclusive the Epic might be, there was no reason in nature or in popular belief why they should not speak. Men had long been accustomed to ideas and customs of a type which Homeric poetry keeps out of sight: in particular they were familiar with the dismal science of necromancy. It was known that certain heroes of past ages had disappeared, still living, into the gaping earth: their ghosts had not gone down to Hades, for body and ghost were still together—these persons were *alive*, beneath the earth at the place of their disappearance. If blood is poured into their caves or chasms, they will come up to drink it; and, thus replenished, will answer what you ask. The province of Boeotia is richer than most in these subterranean prophets: there is Trophonius, in a cave near Lebadea; Amphiaraus, underground in Cnopia, near Thebes; and perhaps Teiresias, at Minyan Orchomenos.[3] What more is needed than that a prophet of this kind, capable of thought and speech, should be transferred to Hades? For if he is summoned in the customary manner by blood-sacrifice, will not the feeble ghosts of the Homeric Underworld come to drink the blood, and then will they not also revive and speak?

So simple and effective is the poet's device; and no great offence is given to the customs of his craft. He is fully aware of the objection that, if Teiresias is in Hades, he must have died and become a ghost, so losing his power to think and speak. But this difficulty is easily evaded: the queen of Hades can surely make a single exception to the rule, provided that the poet tells us clearly, as indeed he does, that this is so.—'*To him alone even in death Persephone gave a mind to reason with.*'[4]

The poet who thus removed Teiresias to Hades, in order that a story of Odysseus' visit to the Underworld might begin, and who filled the empty ghosts with blood in order that they might speak, has no other conception of Hades than that which prevails throughout the Homeric poems.[5] For him too it is a region of ineffectual ghosts, devoid of thought and feeling; and extraordinary measures must be adopted to enable them for a moment to revive their faculties. Our poet is at great pains to keep within the law. In sharpest contrast stands the last scene in this Book, the description of the Hades of King Minos: there, without warning or apology, the scene is totally changed; we find ourselves suddenly in the midst of a very different Hades, such as we have not seen before and shall hardly see again[6]—a Hades in which the ghosts of the dead retain their faculties unimpaired, able to think and speak, to seek pleasure and to suffer punishment; a busy, noisy underworld, not very unlike the world above. Here is King Minos, defining law and dispensing justice for the community of ghosts. Here is Orion, pursuing his lifetime's pleasures. Here are the everlasting punishments of men who wronged the gods: Tityus, devoured for ever alive by vultures; Tantalus, hungry and thirsty amid abundant fruits and water; Sisyphus, for ever rolling uphill a stone which slips from his grasp at the summit. And here is Heracles, striding through the darkness, bow drawn and arrow stretched, impatient for a victim; or rather it is the ghost of Heracles, for his body is in heaven, lapped in Olympian luxuries.

The ancients were deeply offended by this novelty, this breach of an almost uniform tradition. The whole passage, they said, is 'spurious', however well composed. Such was the verdict of Aristarchus, and most of the modern critics have agreed. It seems indeed very improbable that one person should declare two contrary opinions about so important a matter as his own destiny after death; and that he who took so much trouble to keep within the law at the beginning should break it so openly at the end. It might still be argued that one poet, having no personal faith in either of the two doctrines, might consider both equally ornamental, and set the one beside the other for the greater pleasure of his listeners. Such is not at all the manner of Homeric poetry;

3

but it might be so. Again, it has for long been observed that this passage differs greatly from the rest in the style of the Greek. But it might be answered that since the tale here is so briefly told, taking so much for understood, it must certainly have been told before;[7] and the style of the poet here might be reflected from his model, whatever that was. What admits of no denial or palliation is rather the fact that this episode as a whole is most clumsily and carelessly adapted to its immediate surroundings. Hitherto Odysseus has been standing outside Hades, on its threshold; the ghosts, if they would drink the blood and speak, must come forth to him. But here, in the Hades of King Minos, the scene is altogether changed. Odysseus himself is deep within the Underworld, watching Orion in the meadows of asphodel, Heracles moving in the interior gloom; he sees the law court of King Minos, Tantalus in the lake, Sisyphus on the hill. Yet, so soon as this passage ends, the poet makes it clear that Odysseus never moved from his original position outside Hades: αὐτοῦ μένον ἔμπεδον, εἴ τις ἔτ' ἔλθοι (628); he stayed where he was before, waiting for new visitors.

This is careless and awkward composition; the fault is of a kind easily explained by the theory that this passage has later been inserted into the body of the poem. And if we look for confirmation of that theory, we surely find it in the lines which introduce the passage. At the end of the preceding episode the ghost of Ajax stood apart, silent and sullen, nursing resentment against Odysseus for the wrong it suffered at his hands in the world above. Odysseus implored it to forgive him and to join him in conversation: 'but it made no answer, and went after the other ghosts into Erebus' (564 f.). That surely was all: the unforgiving ghost of Ajax disappears without a word into the gloom. What drabness now intrudes upon the sombre beauty of the poet's thought, merely in order to make way for Minos and his vassal ghosts? *'And there nevertheless[8] he would have spoken to me, for all his anger, or I to him; only my heart within me desired to see the ghosts of other persons dead'* (565 f.). The silence of Ajax, then, was accidental, imposed by the requirements of a time-table. Given another moment he would have spoken. And Odysseus' plea, that

Ajax might forgive and speak to him, was nothing but formal politeness: Ajax was about to reply, but Odysseus is in a hurry, he cannot wait for the answer; another day, perhaps, but just now time is pressing. Surely we are justified in concluding with certainty that whoever conceived the image of the silent ghost of Ajax did not at once proceed to destroy his own conception?

The whole of this passage, so contrary to the Homeric idea of Hades, so ill-adapted to the story of Odysseus, and introduced at such heavy cost to the preceding episode, was beyond all reasonable doubt inserted in its present place by a later poet. Let us now turn to the beginning: how does the visit to the Underworld, as a whole, fit into the story as told before and after it? Does it follow naturally out of what precedes, and does it lead naturally to what follows?

The normal Homeric conception of the nature of ghosts in Hades is such as to exclude the likelihood of a visit by a living man to the Underworld. Odysseus cannot be allowed to wander there by chance or in a spirit of tourism. Some very strong motive must be invented for so abnormal and unpromising an adventure. And so it is done: he is sent to Hades by Circe for the purpose, expressly defined, of asking Teiresias to tell him the path and measured stages of his journey home, ὁδὸν καὶ μέτρα κελεύθου.[9] You would of course suppose two things to be certain: first, that Circe is unable herself to supply this information; secondly, that Teiresias will in fact do what she says he will do. You would then be very much mistaken, for neither expectation is to be fulfilled.

Teiresias is immediately aware that this is the reason why Odysseus has come: νόστον δίζηαι, he begins at once, 'you are looking for your journey home' (100). But he does not tell Odysseus what that journey is to be. He names one place, the island of Thrinakia; where even this may be, and how Odysseus is to make his way there, he does not tell. He warns Odysseus only of the danger which impends if he and his companions do injury to the oxen of Helios, the Sun; his vessel and companions will be destroyed, and he himself, if he escapes (even his own

escape is left in doubt),[10] will return home late and in evil case.
Now when Odysseus returns to Circe she does not pause to ask
him whether Teiresias has done what she foretold. She greets him
at once with the words: 'Tomorrow you shall sail, *and I will point
out the way and make each thing plain*, that you may not suffer by
land or sea' (12. 25 ff.). She proceeds to tell him in fullest detail
'the path and measured stages of his journey': the Sirens, the
Wandering Rocks, Scylla and Charybdis, and finally the island of
Thrinakia; she describes the oxen of Helios much more accurately
than Teiresias had done, and then repeats, word for word, what
Teiresias said about the consequences if they do injury to the
sacred cattle. It is quite obvious that this poet does not suppose
that Odysseus is already acquainted with these matters.

The strict Unitarian must suppose either that 'Homer' had no
memory from one moment to another, and no idea what was to
happen in the immediate future; or that he had the following
outline of a plan in mind: 'Circe shall be the one to tell Odysseus
what he needs to know about the journey home: but (since we
need a strong motive for sending Odysseus to Hades) she shall
say that Teiresias will do it; but a few minutes later, when we
come to Teiresias, he shall do nothing of the sort; and when
Odysseus returns to Circe we shall forget that any such motive
for the visit to Hades was ever given, and indeed that any conversation with Teiresias ever occurred. The poet Horace will say
that Homer sometimes nods: he will have no idea how fast asleep
we can be.'

Common sense suggests a much less extravagant judgement on
the evidence: that what happens is what was intended to happen
—the prophecy about the journey home was to be, as it is, given
by Circe, not by Teiresias. The statement that Teiresias should
supply this information is the work of somebody who desired to
link together the *Odyssey* and an originally independent Visit to
the Underworld. But if this is so, if Teiresias was not originally
intended to tell Odysseus about his journey home, what are we
to say about the passage in the Tenth Book, in which Circe
expressly declares that he is to do so, and that this is the reason
why Odysseus must visit Hades? How satisfactory it would be, if

we could prove beyond question that that passage, or at least a substantial part of it, was composed *later* than the events to which it refers, that is to say later than the meeting of Odysseus and Teiresias. Let us look at it closely for a moment.

10. 483–574. Odysseus says to Circe: 'Fulfil the promise which you made to send me home.' Circe (who had made no such promise) replies: 'First you must go to Hades and consult the ghost of Teiresias, the blind prophet.' Odysseus inquires how he is to find the way. Circe tells him that he will need no guide: the wind will steer his ship, and the entrance to Hades is easily found. She continues to tell him what to do when he arrives; and it is at this point that the text of the *Odyssey* presents an extraordinary problem. The lengthy passage in which Circe instructs Odysseus recurs, more or less word for word, in a few minutes' time, when Odysseus obeys her instructions in Hades. It is perfectly in accordance with custom, indeed it is of the nature of the Epic technique of oral verse-making, that the words in which an action is proposed should be repeated, so far as possible without change, when the action is executed. But of course we take it for granted that the second of two such passages was composed *after* the first. What then is to be our judgement, when we discover that in the present example the second of the two passages was composed *before* the first?—that the instructions given by Circe to Odysseus were not composed until the later passage, in which these instructions are obeyed, already existed? To establish this fact no more is needed than an elementary knowledge of the Greek language and a mind free from prejudice.

Odysseus arrives at the threshold of Hades. In accordance with Circe's instructions he digs a ditch, pours a libation to the dead, sprinkles white barley, and promises a sacrifice to Teiresias when he returns home to Ithaca. When he has finished his prayer he kills some sheep; and the dead come up from Hades eager to drink the blood. Then follow the critical words:

'Thereupon I exhorted and commanded my companions to flay and burn the sheep, which lay slaughtered by the ruthless bronze.' (11. 44 ff.)

Now look back to the instructions given by Circe, and observe how these words run in that context:

'Thither shall come many corpses of dead ghosts. Thereupon exhort and urge your companions to flay and burn the sheep *which lay slaughtered* by the ruthless bronze.' (10. 529 ff.)

Obviously the past tense, *lay*, is mere nonsense in a forecast of events which have not yet occurred; it can only be explained on the ground that this sentence, and all that necessarily coheres with it (531–7 at least), have been transplanted bodily backwards from the Eleventh Book into the Tenth.

The modern Unitarians think to evade the difficulty by reading a present tense instead of the past in their text. Uneasy rest their consciences, for the manuscript authority in favour of the past tense is decisive.[11] But the frivolity of their principles is less deplorable, or at least less important, than the failure of their practice. For present and past tenses have here one feature in common: the fact that both are impossible. Circe may say to Odysseus 'Tell your companions to burn the sheep which will be lying, or which may lie', or the like; the laws of language do not permit her to say 'Tell them to burn the sheep *which are lying*'— to state as being present, in a descriptive relative clause, a matter which will or may occur at some future time.[12]

This is not the only point at which the transference backwards is betrayed. In the Eleventh Book the preceding line runs (11. 44):

δὴ τότ' ἔπειθ' ἑτάροισιν ἐποτρύνας ἐκέλευσα.—

Transferring this to Circe in the Tenth Book, our poet was embarrassed by the end of the line. Metre forbade him to convert ἐποτρύνας ἐκέλευσα into ἐποτρύνας κέλευε, or ἐποτρῦναι καὶ κελεῦσαι. He therefore invented ἐποτρῦναι καὶ ἀνῶξαι, thereby introducing a verb form of relatively late development, ἀνῶξαι, foreign to the older Epic vocabulary.[13]

The unavoidable conclusion, that the speech of Circe was composed later than the corresponding passage in the Eleventh Book, by a poet whose vocabulary included elements foreign to the Epic tradition, is brightly illustrated by a comparison of 11. 34 ff. with 10. 526 ff. The former passage runs:

τοὺς δ' ἐπεὶ εὐχωλῇσι λίτῃσί τε, ἔθνεα νεκρῶν,
ἐλλισάμην, τὰ δὲ μῆλα λαβὼν ἀπεδειροτόμησα
ἐς βόθρον, ῥέε δ' αἷμα κελαινεφές, αἱ δ' ἀγέροντο
ψυχαὶ ὑπὲξ Ἐρέβευς νεκύων κατατεθνηώτων.

The latter part of this would have to be drastically altered to suit the context in the Tenth Book; and indeed the poet has largely reformed it,

αὐτὰρ ἐπὴν εὐχῇσι λίσῃ κλυτὰ ἔθνεα νεκρῶν,
ἔνθ' ὄιν ἀρνειὸν ῥέζειν θῆλύν τε μέλαιναν
εἰς Ἔρεβος στρέψας, αὐτὸς δ' ἀπόνοσφι τραπέσθαι
ἱέμενος ποταμοῖο ῥοάων· ἔνθα δὲ πολλαὶ
ψυχαὶ ἐλεύσονται νεκύων κατατεθνηώτων.

Indifferent, or unaware, our poet has introduced a word very common in the language of his own time but entirely foreign to the Epic vocabulary, the noun εὐχή, in place of the Epic εὐχωλή. It is not the only example of its type.[14]

What is the explanation of this transference backwards from the Eleventh Book into the Tenth? Why did a later poet transform the description of what Odysseus did in Hades into a forecast, given by Circe, of what he was to do there? There is one simple answer: to fashion a link, hitherto wanting, between the events of the Eleventh Book and those of the Tenth.

The immediate sequel in the Tenth Book, at the end of Circe's speech, does nothing but confirm our judgement of this poet's indifference to the requirements of the narrative. He proceeds from one anomaly to another. First we are told that Circe attired Odysseus and herself at daybreak: 'She dressed me in a cloak and tunic, and *the nymph* herself put on a large silver-white robe, fine and pleasing, and threw a girdle round her waist, fair and golden, and set a veil upon her head.' These lines have occurred before, in the Fifth Book (229–32), where the subject was Calypso. Here they are ill-adapted, for Circe was not, like Calypso, *a nymph*; moreover, it is alien to the style of the Greek Epic, to describe in detail the dressing of a person (or deity) who from that moment onwards is not to be seen again by mortal eyes.

Circe's next action is performed in secret, unseen. And what an action it is! While Odysseus and his companions were on the way to the shore, the goddess herself, we are told, *went and slipped past them easily and tied up beside the ship a male and a black female sheep*: why this tying-up must be performed at all; why the goddess herself must do it; why she must be invisible: our questions, which the poet could hardly answer, are interrupted by a trick of style unknown to the narrative of the older Greek Epic—the *Rhetorical Question*, addressed by the poet to his audience (10. 573-4).[15]

We have now discovered that the motive alleged for Odysseus' visit to Hades, that he might learn from Teiresias about his journey home, is flatly contradicted by the following events. Circe, who gives him this motive, is herself the person who will describe the journey; and Teiresias will do nothing of the sort. Moreover the passage in which Circe gives her instructions to Odysseus was certainly composed later than the passage in the Eleventh Book where those instructions are carried out. If our minds are honestly open to fair argument, we shall admit, as a likely consequence, that the Visit to the Underworld was originally independent of the *Odyssey*, and that it has been artificially inserted into its present place, but not very skilfully adapted to its new surroundings. Is there any other evidence in support of this conclusion? Let us examine that passage of the Eleventh Book which it will be convenient to call *The Intermezzo* (330-84), wherein Odysseus interrupts his account of the visit to Hades and converses with his host and hostess, the king and queen of Phaeacia, to whom he had been relating his adventures.

When scholars consult their calendars and clocks, constructing a chart of months, days, and hours, for the wanderings of Odysseus, I am no more patient, or less amused, than the average. But if the poet himself insists with clarity and stress upon a point of time, we must suppose that his mind is not vacant, and that he has a purpose which is to be fulfilled.

Odysseus arrives at the court of King Alcinous in Phaeacia and asks to be sent home *tomorrow* (7. 222). Alcinous promises that he shall go *tomorrow* (7. 317). When tomorrow comes, a hasty farewell feast is arranged (8. 38), the ship is launched (8. 51), and instant departure is foretold (8. 150–1). Odysseus and the king's daughter, Nausicaa, say farewell (8. 457). It is obvious and certain that this poet at this moment intends that Odysseus shall depart that night: he has repeatedly and expressly declared that this shall be so. And from start to finish of the story there is not the slightest reason why he should alter this carefully prepared arrangement. And yet in the Eleventh Book it is altered, in the oddest and most casual manner.

In the midst of the description of the visit to Hades Odysseus interrupts his narrative, saying that it is time to go to bed, whether on board with his companions (as if he had any) or here in the palace. He has entirely forgotten that he was so impatient to go home that night, and that his journey is in fact already arranged. We are left to assume that he agrees to remain in Phaeacia. When this matter is settled he resumes his narrative, and then goes to bed. Since the homeward journey is to be made *at night* he must now wait the whole of the next day, with nothing much to do. The poet himself is embarrassed by this unnecessary day; he has no plan to fill it as the former days were filled.[16]

Now it is of course true that Odysseus' story of his adventures is very long, nearly 2,500 lines; consecutive recitation, if we care to reckon so exactly, would last about five hours, or even, if you will, six hours. But why has the poet altered his clearly defined plan? He told us again and again that Odysseus was to depart that night; he even portrayed a scene of leave-taking between his hero and the princess Nausicaa. Are we seriously asked to believe that he cannot remember from one moment to another what he has so emphatically said? Or that he is now suddenly anxious about a time-table? That his listeners will object that one night is not long enough for both the narrative and the homeward journey? But, first, it is very improbable that either the poet or his audience would reckon so exactly. And secondly, if they did, the answer is easy enough: they would find that the time is sufficient, even abundant, for the purpose. When Odysseus has finished his story he and his listeners all go to bed and sleep till morning.

He might just as well have gone aboard his boat and accomplished his brief and magic voyage home. The judge of poetic art would have seen nothing amiss; and even the pedant, watch in hand, would have recorded an hour or two to spare.

It has long been recognized that this break in the story of the Visit to Hades, this Intermezzo, is a subsequent insertion, designed to be a link between the *Odyssey* and an originally independent Eleventh Book. This unwelcome interruption serves a very important purpose—to inform the listener that the story of the Visit to Hades is now and henceforth a part of the *Odyssey*, narrated (like the rest of the adventures) to the king and queen of Phaeacia. It remains to be observed that this Intermezzo is not only ruinous to the structure of the story but also of very poor quality in itself.

Odysseus says that it is time to go to bed. Now listen to the comment of the queen: 'Phaeacians, what do you think of this man's appearance and size and good sense? And again, he is my guest' (do not ask me what '*and again*' may mean in this place) 'but each of you has a share of privilege'—this inapt expression appears to mean that each has a share in the honour of entertaining Odysseus, or that each man's dignity requires that he should be no less forward than herself in hospitality to the guest. 'Therefore be not in haste to send him away, and do not stint your gifts to one whose need is so great; for many are the treasures which lie stored in your halls by the gods' favour.' After a brief comment by the aged hero Echeneus, Alcinous requests Odysseus to remain until the morrow; ending with an insensitive abasement of the celebrated words spoken by Hector to Andromache in the sixth book of the *Iliad*,

$$\pi\acute{o}\lambda\epsilon\mu\text{os } \delta\text{' } \check{a}\nu\delta\rho\epsilon\sigma\sigma\iota \ \mu\epsilon\lambda\acute{\eta}\sigma\epsilon\iota$$
$$\pi\hat{a}\sigma\iota, \ \mu\acute{a}\lambda\iota\sigma\tau\alpha \ \delta\text{' } \acute{\epsilon}\mu o\acute{\iota},$$

'Go about your work at home; war shall be the business of men, and of me above all men.' Here it runs

$$\pi o\mu\pi\grave{\eta} \ \delta\text{' } \check{a}\nu\delta\rho\epsilon\sigma\sigma\iota \ \mu\epsilon\lambda\acute{\eta}\sigma\epsilon\iota$$
$$\pi\hat{a}\sigma\iota, \ \mu\acute{a}\lambda\iota\sigma\tau\alpha \ \delta\text{' } \acute{\epsilon}\mu o\acute{\iota},$$

'Sending-home shall be the business of men, and of me above all men'; there is not much (if any) point in saying that the sending-home is *men's* (let alone *all* men's) work, in the present context. Odysseus' reply is vague and voluble: 'Lord Alcinous, renowned above all men, if you were to bid me stay here a whole year, and should speed my sending home, and give glorious gifts, that is what I should like, and much better it would be, to arrive home with a fuller hand; I should be more loved and respected by all men who see me returned to Ithaca.' It is quite clear that he looks with favour upon the suggestion that more gifts should be made to him: it is by no means clear whether he has agreed to stay until tomorrow, though it might be thought that he has agreed to stay a whole year. Alcinous answers him in the same insipid style; in the words of *Love's Labour's Lost*, 'he draweth out the thread of his verbosity finer than the staple of his argument': 'Odysseus, we who look upon you do not at all think you to be a cheat and trickster, even as [he meant *such as*] the dark earth nourishes many men, scattered far and wide, framing falsehoods *whence no man could even see.*' [This unwholesome expression may be bullied into meaning 'from sources which nobody can detect'.] 'But you have shapeliness of words'—that is more than this poet could claim; and notice the modern word μορφή, an intruder upon the Homeric vocabulary.[17] But I forbear to attempt further to demonstrate the feebleness of the style through the medium of translation.[18] If the faults of the Greek in this Intermezzo are not in themselves obvious, I can say no more to make them so. Vigilance and effort are often required to catch this poet's words in the act of meaning something.

The Intermezzo is preceded by a remarkable passage, conveniently called the Catalogue of Heroines, composed in a style unlike anything in the Homeric poems except the Catalogue of Ships in the Second Book of the *Iliad*.

The scene is filled with the ghosts of noble ladies who come forward one by one, drink of the blood of sacrifice, and recite to Odysseus their pedigree or, in some cases, part of the story of their lives. First he saw Tyro, then Antiope, then Alcmena and Megara, then the mother of Oedipus, then Chloris, then Leda,

then Iphimedeia, then Phaedra and Procris and Ariadne, then
Maera and Clymene and Eriphyle, and a host of other wives and
daughters of ancient fame.

There is beauty enough in this dream-like parade of gloomy
phantom queens; and the poet has made only the most perfunctory attempt to adapt it to the present occasion. These heroines
have nothing whatever to do with Odysseus: he has nothing to
say to them, and they have no motive for reciting to him their
pedigrees. The poet sometimes remembers, sometimes forgets,
that what they say is addressed by them to Odysseus, not by
himself to his audience.[19]

Catalogues of this type have their home in a region distinct
from that of the Homeric Epic. From time out of mind it had
been the custom in the province of Boeotia to preserve the memory
of the past in versified lists of names: catalogues of ships, catalogues of gods, catalogues of women. The Boeotian poets, of whom
the most famous was Hesiod, lived and worked remote from the
stream of the Homeric Epic. In the course of time the Catalogue
of Ships (called by the distinctive title *Boeotia*) found its way into
the framework of the *Iliad*, and settled there, however uncomfortably; and there is no doubt whatever that the source of the
Odyssean Catalogue of Heroines is the same. We notice at once
that the first six names are all at home in the legends of Boeotia,
and that all are strangers to the realm of the Homeric Epics. If
we had to guess, we should say that this passage was composed in
close imitation of a poem from the school of Hesiod; but we are
not required to guess.

The obvious sources for such an episode are the Hesiodic poems
Κατάλογος Γυναικῶν, *Catalogue of Women*,[20] a list of ladies who
founded noble families through the favour of the amorous gods;
and Μεγάλαι 'Ηοῖαι, a catalogue of similar type and theme. Now
the fact that the Odyssean list begins with six Boeotian heroines,
most of whom recite their pedigrees in the manner of Boeotian
poetry, leads at once to the conjecture that Boeotian poetry is its
model and source. But, further, we happen to know that several
of these heroines were indeed included in the Hesiodic Catalogues: Tyro in Hesiod frr. 7, 18, 130; Antiope in frr. 132-3;

Chloris in fr. 14; Iphimedeia in frr. 9–10; and we are expressly told that the pedigrees of Tyro and Chloris were recounted in the poem called *Catalogue of Women*. Further still, we now possess fragments of Hesiodic poetry, recovered from papyri, which leave us in no doubt that the Odyssean catalogue is directly indebted to Boeotian models, and is indeed at least in some points a close imitation thereof.

(1) *PSI* 1301[21]

.[....]ς· οὖ κλέος ἐσ[
ἀργαλέα[ς], μοῦνος δ' ὑπ[εδέξατο μάντις ἀμύμων·
καὶ [τὸ] μὲ[ν] ἐξε[τ]έλεσσε, [κατέσχετο δ' ἐν μεγάροισιν
δεσμὸν ἀεικες ἔχων [Νηληίδος εἵνεκα κούρης·
μνᾶτο γὰρ αὐτοκασιγν[ήτου ἐπίηρα Βίαντος,   5
ἤνυσε [δ'] ἱμερόεντα γάμ[ον, πάλιν οἴκαδ' ἐλάσσας
βοῦς ἕλικας, καὶ ἄεθλον ἀμ[ύμονα δέξατο κούρην.
Πηρὼ δ' [ἠ]ύκομος Ταλα[ὸν μέγαν ἐν μεγάροισι
γείνατο παῖδα Βίαντ[ος ἐν ἀγκοίνῃσι δαμεῖσα.—

This is a version of the story told in 11. 287 ff.,[22] how Melampus underwent an ordeal to win a bride for his brother Bias. It is clearly part of a Hesiodic poem, probably the Μεγάλαι 'Ηοῖαι. But it is by no means certain that our new fragment was itself the model for the Odyssean poet: the story is differently told in the two versions, and the verbal resemblances are slight.[23]

(2) Much more significant is our second fragment, P. Tebtunis 271[24]

].[.]..[Πο]σειδάωνα[
τέξεις δ' ἀγλαὰ τέκ]να, ἐπεὶ οὐκ ἀποφώ[λιοι εὐναὶ
ἀθανάτων· σὺ δὲ τ]οὺς κομέειν ἀτιτα[λλέμεναί τε.
].ιν ἀγλαὰ τέκνα τ[
].τα νεμεσσητοι τε[5
ὡς εἰπὼν ὁ μὲν αὖτις] ἀγα[σ]τόνωι ἔμ[πεσε πόντωι
]η ἔβη οἰκόνδε [
]..ον[

The second and third lines are identical with 11. 249–50. They are not conventional or formular phrases; it is therefore probable that the relation between the Hesiodic poem and the *Odyssey* is one of direct imitation. In both versions Poseidon is speaking to the lady of his love; the outline of the story was identical in the two poems, and so was a good deal of the detail.

(3) To the facts so far assembled we must add one more.[25] Virgil's phrase in *Georgics*, 4. 360 f., *at illum | curuata in montis faciem circumstetit unda*, is said[26] to have been taken from Hesiod's *Catalogue of Women*. Is it then merely coincidence that a perfect model for Virgil should be found in the Odyssean Catalogue and nowhere else?—243 f., κῦμα περιστάθη οὔρεϊ ἶσον, | κυρτωθέν. We had good cause to suspect that the *Odyssey* was indebted to the Hesiodic *Catalogue of Women*: now we are told that a certain unusual image[27] occurred in the Hesiodic poem; and behold, we find it in this part of the *Odyssey*.

It is obvious that there was a close kinship between the Odyssean Catalogue of Heroines and the Hesiodic *Catalogue of Women*; and there is now objective evidence that the one includes direct imitation of the other. Which is the model, which the copy? Surely the answer is simple: pedigree-catalogues of this type are at home in Hesiodic poetry, quite foreign to the Homeric tradition. Asia has innumerable tigers, our zoological gardens have only one or two, in obviously artificial surroundings. We infer that our tigers come from Asia, not that all Asiatic tigers are descended from our specimens or their ancestors.

I have dealt very briefly with this Catalogue of Heroines, since the facts are clear and the inference generally agreed. There remains a further question. The Odyssean catalogue is an imitation of Hesiodic poetry: but may it not nevertheless be an integral part of the Eleventh Book of the *Odyssey*?[28] What proof is there that it is a later insertion into its present context? There is no proof, but there is a strong probability. The episode is wholly irrelevant to Odysseus and his story; it is loosely attached and carelessly adapted to its surroundings; it separates two episodes— the meeting with Teiresias and Anticleia on the one hand, and the meeting with Agamemnon, Achilles, and Ajax on the other— which have much in common both in style and in design. There is no certainty: but we may safely conclude that the scales of evidence incline decidedly against the opinion that all was planned and composed by one person in its present form.[29]

We have now reduced the Eleventh Book more or less to its original elements. The Catalogue of Heroines and the Intermezzo in the middle, and the Hades of King Minos at the end, are later additions to the story of Odysseus' Visit to the Underworld. What now remains of the original story, to which these passages were added?

Odysseus travels to Hades and meets in turn Teiresias; his mother Anticleia; and the great heroes of the Trojan War, Agamemnon, Achilles, and Ajax. This is a most satisfactory result,[30] for all these passages are composed in a similar style of Greek, with which the remainder of the Book has little enough in common. And all the persons—except Teiresias, who serves to form the necessary link between the living and the dead—are very closely connected with Odysseus; they speak to him, and he to them, from the heart, on topics which deeply interest both parties to the dialogue.[31] The interpolator of the Catalogue of Heroines by no means solved the problem set by these surroundings. The heroines must speak to Odysseus, though what they say is of no interest to him, and he cannot, and does not, find anything to say in answer. The dialogue-form is most unsuitable, and would never have been freely chosen; it is simply imposed by the requirements of the context. Indeed, so clumsy is the technique that at one point we are required to envisage *three* persons saying the same words at the same time: 248 ff., the speech of Poseidon reported by Tyro reported by Odysseus. Nor was the composer of the Hades of King Minos more successful in this respect. The dialogue-form is again unsuitable; it is indeed abandoned until, at the end, Heracles is made to address Odysseus, in order to remind us that we are still within the *Odyssey*. But Heracles and Odysseus come from different worlds and ages: it is not surprising that when Heracles has finished speaking the scene abruptly ends; Odysseus says nothing in reply, having indeed nothing of interest to say.

What was the true purpose of the original Visit to Hades? Surely that which happens, not that which does not happen.

Teiresias does not tell Odysseus how to get home: therefore the purpose of Odysseus' visit was not that Teiresias should so tell him. What does happen is that with the help of Teiresias he meets and converses with the ghosts of his mother and his friends: that, then, was the original purpose of the visit. And it is to be noticed that almost all that is said concerns the life of these persons, and of their children, *on earth*. Again, that which occurs is that which was intended: the purpose of the visit to Hades was not to take the audience for a conducted tour of the Underworld.[32] That became a favourite theme in later poetry: it was a most unpromising theme for the poet who believed in the truly Homeric Hades of senseless and voiceless shadows. The purpose was to relate events above the earth, not below it: to tell what happened to the great heroes and their kindred after the Trojan War—the doom of Agamemnon, the great deeds of Achilles' son.

We proceed to observe further confirmation of our judgement that the original Visit to Hades had nothing to do with the remainder of the *Odyssey*. The speech of Odysseus' mother Anticleia is alone enough to show how little this poet knew or cared about the central theme of the *Odyssey*—the courting of Penelope by disorderly suitors in Ithaca.

Odysseus has asked for news of his wife and son and father, still alive in Ithaca. His mother replies (11. 181 ff.): 'Penelope your wife remains steadfast of heart in your palace, and ever sorrowful are the nights and days that pass away upon her weeping. *But nobody yet possesses the royal privilege that was yours. Telemachus rules your demesne at his ease, and feasts at equal banquets, such as the dispenser of justice should rightly enjoy; for all men invite him.*' It is perfectly obvious that this poet has no idea that Penelope is beset by impatient suitors who insult Telemachus and feast at their will in his palace, wasting the royal substance. 'Telemachus governs at his ease, and all men invite him, and he feasts at equal banquets': it is hard to see how the true state of affairs, according to our *Odyssey*, could be more grossly misrepresented. The modern Unitarians consult their calendars, and reckon that when Odysseus' mother died the suitors of Penelope had not yet begun their misbehaviour: it is true, they say, *at this time*, that all is well at home in Ithaca; and they make light of the consequence that *at that time* Telemachus would not be of an age to act as here he is said to do. This is the kind of argument which the Unitarians so fiercely, and rightly, criticize in their opponents; and here it is surely the special pleading of the advocate whose cause is lost. What conceivable motive could induce the poet to describe so fully a state of affairs which Odysseus will find *not* to exist when he returns home? And are we really required to remember what year it was when Anticleia died, what year it was when the suitors began their wooing of Penelope? Hasten to our side, O Unitarian commentator,[33] for without your help we shall certainly not know or remember anything of the kind.

But there is worse to come. For was it not but a moment ago that Teiresias told us what would truly be happening in Ithaca? '*You will find grievous things at home: proud men that devour your livelihood, seeking your wife in marriage and offering wedding-gifts*' (11. 115 ff.). What sort of poet proceeds at once to make Odysseus ask his mother whether Penelope 'remains with her son, or has the noblest of the Achaeans already married her' (11. 177 ff.)? Odysseus has just heard from Teiresias the answer to his question: his wife is not, and will not be, re-married; he will find her still beset with suitors when he returns. What sort of poet composes in this manner?

We have already seen that part of Teiresias' speech was added later in order to connect the Eleventh Book more closely with the *Odyssey*: we now conclude that the addition was a little more extensive. The original Visit to Hades was not concerned with the story of the Suitors in Ithaca. Anticleia tells Odysseus that his wife is waiting for him peacefully, however sorrowfully, and that his son is regent in his place, living at his ease, honoured by all men. If there is some other story in which these things are not so, that lies entirely outside this self-contained description of the Visit to Hades. Neither did Teiresias originally say anything about disorders in Ithaca: he may briefly forecast, as he does, the whole future course of Odysseus' life; but the details about the wooing of Penelope were added, casually or deliberately, after this Book had been attached to the *Odyssey*, without regard for the damage thus inflicted upon the structure of the whole.

If you still doubt, consider what the poet has yet in store. He tells us, as expressly as may be, that Odysseus first heard about the troubles at home *after his return to Ithaca*. Athene appeared to him and told him the truth; and he thanked her for this most important warning: 'Surely I should have been killed in my own palace, if you, goddess, had not told me all' (13. 383 ff.). This poet is obviously unaware that Odysseus has already heard from Teiresias all that Athene tells him here.

It is certain that Teiresias belongs to the original Visit to Hades: without him there would be no sacrifice, no drinking of blood, and therefore no conversation in the world below. His part has been altered and expanded, in order to adjust it to the *Odyssey*; but the figure of the prophet himself was there from the beginning. So also, we suppose, was Anticleia, the mother of Odysseus, whose part is played in close connexion with that of Teiresias. But these two were surely not the only original persons: we may continue to suppose that Odysseus' meeting with the heroes of the Trojan War formed part of the original design, unless some good reason to the contrary should appear.

This meeting with Agamemnon, Achilles, and Ajax has much in common with the narrative concerning Teiresias and Anticleia, both in style and in treatment: but there is one remarkable incongruity which has caused many to doubt whether both episodes were planned by one poet.

The Homeric conception of Hades requires that the ghosts should drink blood in order to revive their faculties: but it is not to be denied that there is a lack of clarity and consistency in the development of this motif. The ghost of Anticleia emerges, but Odysseus will not allow anyone to approach the blood until he has conversed with Teiresias. Thereupon the ghost of Teiresias appears, and at once recognizes Odysseus and speaks to him. Teiresias (so we had been told) retains his faculties even in Hades: it is therefore to be presumed that he will not drink the blood, certainly not *after* he has recognized and spoken to Odysseus. But he does drink the blood, and at the end of the dialogue he tells Odysseus that whatever ghost thereafter comes close to the blood will speak to him the truth.

The ghost of Anticleia is now allowed to approach and drink; and then at once she recognizes Odysseus and speaks to him; before, she did not even know who he was. Here for the first time we find the proper use of this motif. We pass on to the heroes of the Trojan War. First came the ghost of Agamemnon; and the manuscripts of the *Odyssey* are more or less evenly divided (11. 390): 'He knew me quickly', they all say, then some continue 'when he set eyes on me', others continue 'when he had drunk the black blood'. Which of these two was originally intended? The likelier opinion is that the phrase 'when he set eyes on me' is the earlier, altered to the phrase 'when he had drunk the blood' for the sake of consistency, since the poet has told us that these ghosts cannot speak before they have drunk. It remains possible that the order should be reversed: that the phrase 'when he had drunk the blood' was the earlier, altered in order to bring Agamemnon into line with Achilles and Ajax, neither of whom is said to drink; yet the one speaks to Odysseus and the other recognizes him.

Since the motif in question is emphasized in the episode of Teiresias and Anticleia, and largely or wholly ignored in the meeting with the great heroes, some have inferred that the two scenes were not planned in this form by a single poet. It must be admitted that it would be entirely in the manner of the Greek Epic to repeat on each occasion the phrase 'when he had drunk the dark blood'; but it is still within the region of reasonable behaviour, if a poet leaves to the understanding on a later occasion what he has expressly stated on earlier occasions. It may be that the poet here was using a motif which he had not himself invented, and which he did not care (as no doubt his predecessor did) to maintain consistently, once its principal purpose had been illustrated, as it was in the example of Anticleia. We must allow further for the chance that the text of the Book has suffered, in this as in other respects, from casual or deliberate alteration in the course of a long period of oral transmission.[34]

I have left to the end the singular incident of the death and burial of Elpenor.

Circe told Odysseus what he was to do in Hades; he went to his companions and summoned them to instant departure; then he proceeds as follows (10. 551 ff.): Elpenor was very young, not very warlike, and wanting in good sense. Being inebriated and longing for cool air he lay down to sleep alone, apart from his companions, in the palace of Circe. When he woke up, aroused by the noise and bustle of his companions, he forgot that he was on the roof of the house. (The poet too forgot to mention that that is where he was, and indeed misled us by saying that he was *in the palace* of Circe.) Instead of climbing down by the ladder, he walked straight off the roof and broke his neck.

Aimless anecdotes about insignificant persons are not at all characteristic of the *Odyssey*: we shall soon discover that this example is by no means aimless; it forms a link between the story of Circe and the story of the Visit to Hades. The question arises whether this link too was subsequently forged in order to connect two separate narratives.

Now, first, it is obvious that the description of Elpenor's death in the Tenth Book, though excellent in itself, is most uncomfortably placed in its present context. 'Let us go', said Odysseus to his companions; and they obeyed. There follows the relatively long description of Elpenor's death, ending thus: 'He forgot to return by way of the long ladder; he fell straight off the roof and broke his neck, and his ghost went down toward Hades; *and as they went their way I spoke among them . . .*' (10. 561, ἐρχομένοισι δὲ τοῖσιν, not τοῖσιν δ' ἐρχομένοισιν). The transition back to the companions of Odysseus, now on the way to their ship, is very roughly made: but the objection is by no means merely on a point of style. The Epic never steps backward in time, and never leaves intervals of time unoccupied. The death of Elpenor occurred, according to this poet, at or just after the moment when Odysseus ordered his men to depart: Elpenor was awakened by the bustle below, and, while trying to join his companions, fell off the roof and broke his neck. And then the narrative proceeds immediately as if nothing unusual had occurred: Odysseus is at once talking to his companions on the road toward the ships; the death of Elpenor is treated as if it were a commonplace occurrence calling for no action or even comment from anybody. You are not allowed to plead that Odysseus is here speaking from his later knowledge of the event. He was aware of Elpenor's death at the time when it occurred, according to our poem: for in 11. 52–54 we are told that he would have buried his companion there and then, 'only other business was pressing'. This last expression, ἐπεὶ πόνος ἄλλος ἔπειγε, presents great difficulty.

At all times of which we are aware, from the siege of Troy to the battle of Arginusae and beyond, there was no more shameful crime than neglect to bury your own dead. I do not know what business there might be so pressing that the body of a dead comrade might be left to shift for itself. And just now, when we heard of Elpenor's death, there was nothing whatever to suggest that there was any pressing business: Odysseus was not even said to be in a hurry; though the notion that you might leave a companion unburied, merely because you were in a hurry to go somewhere else, would be an outrage to Hellenic sentiment.

Our difficulties are still not at an end. Odysseus says to the ghost of Elpenor (11. 57)

Ἐλπῆνορ, πῶς ἦλθες ὑπὸ ζόφον ἠερόεντα;

Taken by itself this would naturally suggest the meaning 'How did you die?', and Elpenor, who replies by describing the manner of his death, certainly took it in that sense. But since Odysseus already knows how he died, according to our poem, a half-hearted attempt has been made to twist the meaning of 11. 57 into another shape by adding a ridiculous line:

ἔφθης πεζὸς ἰὼν ἢ ἐγὼ σὺν νηὶ μελαίνη,

'You got here quicker on foot than I in my ship'; so that the previous line may now signify not 'How did you die' but 'How do you explain the speed of your journey hither?' I say the attempt was half-hearted, because Elpenor still answers the old question, not the new one, and no attempt has been made to reconcile the question with the answer.

We are now surely in a position to diagnose the disease. In the original *Nekuia* Odysseus did not know how Elpenor died, and asked him, and was answered; in the *Nekuia*, therefore, the description of Elpenor's death was not (as it is in our *Odyssey*) narrated by Odysseus himself at the time when it occurred, though it may well have been described (in terms similar to, or even identical with, those of 10. 551–60) at the time when Odysseus met the ghost of Elpenor at the entrance to Hades. When the *Nekuia* was inserted into the *Odyssey*, the description of Elpenor's death was transferred to its proper place in the sequence of events, 10. 551 ff. Thus the body and ghost of Elpenor might serve to connect the *Nekuia* with the narrative into which it is inserted, the Visit to Circe: Elpenor now dies in the palace of Circe; his ghost encounters Odysseus at the gate of Hades; Odysseus buries him after his return to the palace of Circe;[35] the departure, the visit, and the return are, by this means, inseparably united.

The transference of the description of Elpenor's death backwards from the *Nekuia* into the *Odyssey* was both ill-conceived and ill-executed: ill-conceived, since it was now necessary to reconcile two contrary facts—Odysseus' knowledge of Elpenor's death in the Tenth Book, and his ignorance of it in the Eleventh—a task only half performed with the help of two of the silliest lines in the Greek Epic (11. 54, 58); ill-executed, for the description of Elpenor's death sits most uncomfortably in its present surroundings, as we have observed.

In summary: we have good reason to believe that there was once an independent poem on Odysseus' Visit to the Underworld, wherein the hero met and conversed with Teiresias, with his mother, and with his former comrades-in-arms. This poem was inserted into the *Odyssey*, and more or less adapted to it, especially by means of some modification of the parts of Elpenor and Teiresias; by the assignment of a speech to Circe, giving a motive for the visit; and by the insertion of the Intermezzo. Whether before or after the junction with the *Odyssey*, two extensive episodes were incorporated: the Catalogue of Heroines and the description of the Hades of King Minos.

There is one last question which suggests itself. The story of the Visit to the Underworld is told by Odysseus to the king and queen of Phaeacia, as the poem stands today: to whom was it told in the earlier independent version? There is at least one indication of an answer to this question.

The ghost of Odysseus' mother ends her last utterance with the words: 'Bear all these things in mind, *that you may hereafter tell them to your wife.*' 'The end of her speech does not seem very pointed,' observe the Oxford editors: let us frankly admit that it is a conclusion of almost comical vapidity—*unless Odysseus is in fact telling the story to his wife*; then, and then only, it is entirely natural.[36]

You may think that we have still not reached the heart of the matter. Many an Unitarian has conceded the Eleventh Book of the *Odyssey* (like the Tenth Book of the *Iliad*) to his destructive opponents: Homer composed the *Odyssey*, more or less as it stands today, all except the Visit to the Underworld, which was later inserted into the body of the poem. Is there no other concession to be made? Let us go back to the beginning and consider afresh.

NOTES ON CHAPTER II

The longer I have considered the Νέκυια the more closely I have approached the position of E. Rohde, *Rhein. Mus.* 50 (1895) 600 ff. (= *Kleine Schriften* ii. 255 ff.; very much abbreviated in *Psyche* ch. i, 8th ed. translated by W. B. Hillis, reprinted 1950). In particular his exposition of the nature of the Homeric ψυχή seems to me (as it has seemed to most students of this topic) entirely convincing. I am well aware that contrary opinions have been expressed, and that some of the detail is disputable or even untenable: but there is certainly no other way of explaining the hard facts on which the broad outline of Rohde's exposition is based. The most important point on which I am inclined to differ from Rohde is the question whether there was ever a lengthy break in the practice of worshipping the dead. As Farnell and others have said, it is possible that the Homeric poets have misled us in this respect (as in others: see Dodds, *The Greeks and the Irrational* (1951) 43 f., 70, 110). A specimen of the opposition to Rohde will be found in an article by R. K. Hack, 'Homer and the Cult of Heroes', *TAPA* 60 (1929) 57 ff.; his attack on Rohde's conception of ψυχή in the Epics seems to me to fail at all points, though he may well be right in supporting Halliday and Farnell on the point mentioned above.

I owe much to many sources, including Waser, *Myth. Lex.* s.v. Psyche 3201 ff.; Dieterich, *Nekuia* (1913) *passim*; J. A. K. Thomson, *Studies in the Odyssey* (1914) 24 ff.; Bethe, *Odyssee* (1922) 126 ff.; Cauer, *Grundfragen* (1923) 363 ff., 636 f.; Nilsson, *The Minoan–Mycenaean Religion* (1927) 514 ff.; G. E. Mylonas, *Am. Journ.*

Arch. 52 (1948) 56 ff.; Focke, *Odyssee* (1943) 199 ff.; Merkelbach, *Untersuchungen zur Odyssee* (1951) 177 ff. There is a devastating polemic by Rohde (*Rh. Mus.* l.c.) against the opinions expressed by Wilamowitz in *Homerische Untersuchungen* 140 ff., 199 ff. A different attitude, with which I am out of sympathy, is adopted by M. H. Van der Valk, *Beiträge zur Nekuia* (1935); cf. W. Büchner, *Hermes* 72 (1937) 104 ff. It may well be some deficiency in myself which prevents me from making use of K. Reinhardt's *Von Werken und Formen* (1948) 124 ff. I know that this author's *Abenteuer der Odyssee* has been much admired: yet the greatest part of his essay seems to me to consist of highly subjective opinions, incapable of proof or disproof, at a considerable distance from the realities of the text; and the opinions are almost uniformly the opposite of what I myself should hold to be probable if I thought such speculation worth while.

1. Rohde, *Psyche* 7.
2. Ibid. 16.
3. That the Eleventh Book is a νεκυομαντεία, not a νέκυια, was already observed by Schol. MV on *Od.* 24. 1. The point is agreed by most of the modern critics (e.g. Rohde, *Psyche* 36 f.; Thomson, op. cit. 25 f.; Bethe, op. cit. 132; Schwartz, *Odyssee* 137 ff.; Hartmann, *Untersuchungen über die Sagen vom Tode des Odysseus* (1917) 212 f.; Merkelbach, op. cit. 219 ff.).
4. Cf. the exceptional treatment of Menelaus in 4. 560 ff. (Rohde, *Psyche* 55 ff.; Nilsson, *Minoan–Mycenean Religion* 538 ff.).
5. But at 11. 29 ff. Odysseus promises that on his return to Ithaca he will make sacrifice to the dead, especially to Teiresias: the poet forgets that he has transferred Teiresias to a plane of existence in which he is no longer capable of intervention in human affairs, and therefore needs no such appeasement or sustenance; Rohde, *Psyche* 38.
6. I cannot do more than barely mention some of the problems presented by this extraordinary passage, which embodies so much that is foreign to the Homeric tradition, to the popular cult of the dead, and to the Pythagorean and Orphic doctrines of the sixth and fifth centuries.

(1) The ghosts here come to Minos for the settlement of disputes which occur during their life in Hades: they are therefore lively unhomeric ghosts, capable of thought and speech and action. (There is no suggestion that Minos is dispensing rewards and punishments *for conduct in the world above*, an idea observed earliest in the *Hymn to Demeter* 480 ff.; Pind. *Ol.* ii, frr. 135–7; Aeschylus, *Suppl.* 230 ff., *Eum.* 273 ff.; Democritus fr. 297; Ar. *Ran.* 145 ff., 273 ff.; for Minos as judge, cf. Plato, *Apology* 41, *Gorg.* 523; Demosthenes 18. 127; Pseudo-Plato, *Axiochus* 371. The basis of distinction was primarily the membership of a particular seot, such as Orphic or Eleusinian cult: the more elevated idea of an afterlife related to a distinction between virtuous and vicious life on earth is not observed, so far as I see, earlier than Aeschylus, who does not appear to be much interested in it.)

(2) The picture of three memorable sinners, Tityus, Tantalus, and Sisyphus, is absolutely irreconcilable with the Homeric conception of Hades: Rohde (*Psyche* 40 f., *Rh. Mus.* 629 f., cf. Dieterich, *Nekuia* 63 ff.) is clearly right in denying that they *symbolize* the punishment of sin; they are individuals, accorded highly exceptional treatment because they offended the gods. Like the ghosts who fill the law-courts of Minos, they have retained their mental and emotional faculties after death; they even have substantial bodies. The evidence concerning these and other punishments in Hades is assembled by Radermacher in *Rhein. Mus.* 63 (1908) 531 ff.

(3) The detail of the punishment of the three sinners is most extraordinary. The fate of Tantalus here contradicts what everybody knew to be the truth: he lived in perpetual danger of a rock impending overhead (in heaven, or between heaven

and earth, or on earth; not in Hades); Ἀτρειδῶν νόστος ap. Athen. 7. 281ᵇ, Archilochus fr. 55, Alcman fr. 72, Alcaeus fr. 365, Pindar, *Ol.* i. 90, *Isthm.* vii. 20, Eur. *Orestes* 4, and others (see Scheuer, *Myth. Lex.* v. 79 and *RE* iv. A 2226). Polygnotus copied *Od.* 11 for his picture in the Delphic Lesche (see Paus. x. 25. 1 ff., with Frazer's commentary, v. 356 ff.) : but ppetry ignored this aberration until the age of Propertius and Horace. Nor was the idea that Tityus was punished in Hades much more popular : he is presumably included μετὰ τριῶν in Pindar, *Ol.* i. 62; Polygnotus and Plato (*Gorg.* 525 e, cf. *Axiochus* 371 e) are directly indebted to *Od.* 11. The stone of Sisyphus was known to the vase-painters as early as the sixth century, but it is not mentioned in literature elsewhere before Aeschylus.

(4) On the ludicrous lines 11. 601–4 (the *phantom* of Heracles in Hades, but his *body* has gone to Olympus) see Rohde, *Psyche* 39: 'Whoever wrote this was practising a little theology on his own account. Such a contrast between a fully animated "self" possessing the original man's body and soul still united, and a counterfeit presentment of himself (which cannot be his psyche) relegated to Hades, is quite strange both to Homer and to Greek thought of later times.'

7. Von der Mühll (*Philol.* 93 (1938) 8 ff., approved by Merkelbach, 191) maintains that this part of *Od.* 11 is based on a *Catabasis* of Heracles; his arguments seem to me to fall far short of proof.

8. ὅμως : this word, so common in later Greek, was unknown to the Epic vocabulary; it is not found elsewhere in the *Odyssey*, and has intruded upon the *Iliad* only once (12. 393).

9. Focke, 202 : 'mit μέτρα sind die zu durchmessenden Strecken, die Abschnitte gemeint, und dazu wohl die sie begrenzenden Stationen'; cf. Becker, *Das Bild des Weges* (*Hermes*, Einzelschriften iv, 1937) 19 f.

10. The peculiar uncertainty of the prophet in this passage has often been remarked : 105 αἴ κε, 110 εἰ μέν κε, 112 εἰ δέ κε, 113 εἴ πέρ κεν : Teiresias ought to be able to do better than this.

11. According to Ludwich, the present tense is read only in Laur. conv. soppr. 52 (= F, Ludwich; L⁸, Allen; saec. xi : κατακεῖται) and in Hamburg. 15 (= T, Ludwich and Allen; saec. xiv); Allen adds only his Pˢ (saec. xv); the questionable letter is in an erasure in Ven. 613 (= M, Ludwich; U⁵, Allen; saec. xiii).

12. Kirchhoff and Blass (as one would expect) saw that the present tense was impossible here; so did Friedländer, *Analecta, Jb. class. Phil.*, suppl. iii (1858) 482. It is unfortunate that Rohde (*Rhein. Mus.* 614, n. 1) missed this important point; also Focke (203), and others. It is worth noticing further that the emphatic particle δή is properly used in the Eleventh Book (Denniston, *Greek Particles* 218 f.) but quite out of place in the Tenth.

13. First in the Hesiodic *Scutum* 479, ἤνωξε, and in the late (Shipp, *Studies in the Language of Homer* (1953) 95) passage of the *Iliad* 15. 295, where ἀνώξομεν is surely aor. subj., not future. Our poet was of course influenced by the common formula ἐποτρύνει καὶ ἀνώγει.

14. Notice especially the relatively modern word πέλας in 10. 516, foreign to the Epic tradition (elsewhere only 15. 257, in the rigmarole about Theoclymenus).

15. This device (in the narrative, as opposed to the dialogue, of the Homeric poems) recurs in *Od.* 22. 12 ff., and perhaps *Il.* 22. 202 ff., an obscure passage.

16. 13. 18 ff. : the Phaeacians bring more gifts, there is feasting and singing : the sooner it is over the better the poet is pleased, and so are we.

17. Elsewhere in the Epic only *Od.* 8. 170 (εὔμορφος is an obscure variant in *Od.* 14. 65).

18. In the language notice especially : 330 νὺξ ἄμβροτος, an aberration; the Epic says νὺξ ἀμβροσίη. 344 ἀπὸ δόξης, also *Il.* 10. 324; δόξα not elsewhere in the Homeric poems. 359 πλειοτέρῃ, a comparative form unknown to the Epic. 360 αἰδοιότερος,

also *Od.* 17. 578; the Epic elsewhere consistently avoids αἰδοῖ-. 364 ἠπεροπεύς; the Epic form is -πευτής. 381 σοι, the only example of atonic σοι in the Homeric poems (Wackernagel, *Spr. Unters. zu Homer* 54; Chantraine, *Gramm. Hom.* i. 265). 384 ἰότητι γυναικός, cf. 18. 234 μνηστήρων ἰότητι; ἰότητι elsewhere always of *divine* persons.

19. The direct speech of Poseidon (248 ff.) is obviously more suitable to the poet's own narrative than to Odysseus'. Dialogue with Odysseus is sometimes indicated by a perfunctory verb of speaking (236 f. φάτο, φῆ, 261 εὔχετο, 306 φάσκε) but more often not.

20. Alternatively called 'Or-such-as', ἠοῖαι, from the practice of introducing each new subject with the words ἢ οἵη . . ., 'or such as (e.g. Alcmena)'.

21. See the masterly treatment by Pfeiffer in *Philol.* 92 (1937) 1 ff. I have supplied new ends *exempli gratia* to vv. 3, 4, 5, 6, 9.

22. And again in 15. 228 ff., on which see Pfeiffer, l.c.

23. 11. 291 ἀργαλέας · τὰς δ' οἷος . . . is obviously related to v. 2 ἀργαλέας, μοῦνος δέ . . . . For the rest, the differences are striking: note especially βοῦς ἕλικας at the beginning of the line in v. 7, a unique position for this phrase, and a unique order for the words; 11. 289 ἕλικας βοῦς.

24. See especially Pfeiffer, l.c. I have supplemented v. 6 *exempli gratia*.

25. See Pfeiffer, l.c.

26. By Schol. Bern.

27. The verb which supplies κυρτωθέν, Virgil's *curuata*, occurs nowhere else in the Homeric poems.

28. Though 321–5, with its ladies of Athenian legend, may well be an Attic addition.

29. The proportion of linguistic anomalies is not much above the average: notice the short dative plural προχοῆς in 242; the unhomeric phrase βασίλεια γυναικῶν in 258 (and the unique position of the word βασίλεια in the line; elsewhere always at verse-end or after initial – ⌣⌣ –); βρόχος (278), a common word later, does not recur in the Epics; the use of the definite article τὴν in 298 is a relatively late development (it is remarkable that Leda should be said to have borne Castor and Pollux *to Tyndareus*, not Zeus); on the unhomeric prosody of λελογχᾶσιν (elsewhere in the Homeric poems only *Od.* 7. 114) see Wackernagel, op. cit. 169; εὖρος (312) is another word common later, unknown to the Epics; the confusion between Ὀλύμπῳ 313 (where the gods dwell) and 315 (the mountain, on which Ossa and Pelion are placed to make a ladder to the region where the gods dwell) is inelegant; φυλόπιδα in 314 is an aberration (Epic accusative is -πιν); the verb ἀνθεῖν and the adj. εὐανθής in 320 are newcomers to the Epic vocabulary, so are the abstract μαρτυρίαι and the scansion of Διόνυσον in 325.

30. It has long been remarked that when Odysseus recounts to Penelope the story of his visit to Hades (23. 322 ff.) he omits all mention of the Heroines and of the persons encountered in the realm of King Minos; he tells her of Teiresias, Anticleia, and his former comrades.

31. On this point, and what follows, see Rohde, *Rhein. Mus.* l.c. 606.

32. See Rohde, *Psyche* 38 f.

33. Van der Valk, l.c. 56 ff.; but also some of the *Analytiker*, Schwartz 140, Cauer 636 f., Merkelbach 187.

34. Focke, 220 f., ingeniously suggests that 11. 228 ff. are an adaptation of lines similarly prefixed to the episode of Agamemnon, Achilles, &c.

35. Observe (1) that Elpenor is to be buried σὺν τεύχεσιν, 11. 74: the reason is not the unhomeric belief that 'the soul . . . was capable of making use of these objects that are burnt along with its discarded envelope' (Rohde, *Psyche* 17), but that 'if . . . the body is burnt and the most treasured possessions of the dead man

consumed along with it, no tie remains that can detain the soul any longer in the world of the living' (ibid. 21). (2) That Elpenor threatens to become θεῶν μήνιμα, 11. 73; this again is consistent with normal Homeric doctrine; once burnt and buried, the ghost enters Hades and cannot interfere on earth, but so long as the funeral rites are omitted the ghost is forbidden to enter Hades, and may in the meantime haunt and harass the living; Elpenor conforms exactly to the pattern of Patroclus in *Il.* 23. 65 ff. (notice that both unburied ghosts exercise the powers of prophecy, *Il.* 23. 80 f. and *Od.* 11. 69 f.).

36. See Schwartz, *Odyssee* 139, 146. His other clue is of very slight value in itself, but still worth mentioning. In 11. 29 ff. Odysseus says: 'I promised that when I returned to Ithaca I would make sacrifice to the dead; for Teiresias a sheep, all black, the best among *our* flocks.' True, the Epic sometimes uses 'our' for 'my'; but the plural needs no apology if Odysseus is speaking to his wife.

III

THE BEGINNING OF THE *ODYSSEY*

It is becoming fashionable in some quarters to assert that the Unitarian theory of the Homeric Epic has gained ground during the present generation. Of the *Odyssey* at least that assertion is false, if *Unitarian* means what it should—one who, having examined both sides of the question carefully and without prejudice, decides in favour of at least a substantial measure of unity of authorship. The prevalent theory today is the contrary of this: the investigations of Bethe in 1922, of Schwartz in 1924, of Von der Mühll in 1940, of Focke in 1943, and of Merkelbach in 1951, however different the detail of their conclusions, all agree about certain fundamental facts which cannot be reconciled with the theory that the *Odyssey* was planned and composed, as a whole, more or less in its present form, by one poet. Their structures are built on a common foundation laid by Adolf Kirchhoff in 1879: the best statement of the case is still to be found in his edition of the *Odyssey* (Berlin 1879, esp. pp. 238–74, Excurs I, on the Telemachy); this is the bedrock on which posterity has built. Let us inquire into the matter, preserving so far as possible that patience and good humour which are so easily lost in the perusal of books on the Homeric Question.

Nobody has ever denied, what our manuscript tradition distinctly asserts, that certain additions have been made in the course of time to the text of the *Odyssey*, and it is generally agreed that at least a few of these additions are of considerable length and importance; yet it is not these which play the leading part in the debate about the composition of the poem. Our *Odyssey* is constructed, as it stands, in the following way: two threads of narrative are spun separately, one after the other, and then united. First, the poet describes the Journey of Telemachus in search of his father Odysseus; when that is more or less finished, he starts afresh and recounts the Wanderings of Odysseus; when that story too is finished he picks up the first thread and unites it with the second, twisting them into a single strand, the story of Odysseus and Telemachus in action together against the Suitors of Penelope. Here then are three episodes which are, as a matter of fact, narrated separately; and many have been led by their study of the evidence to believe that all three were originally composed separately, later conjoined into the continuous narrative which we read today by a hand which is relatively late and absolutely incompetent.

We shall first consider whether the first of these threads, the story of Telemachus, is an integral part of the *Odyssey* or a later addition to it. It seems to me, after prolonged consideration, that the strength of the case for the later addition of the story of Telemachus to the *Odyssey* lies (where one would expect it to lie) in certain faults which are found at the points where it is attached to the *Odyssey*—where it begins, in the First Book; where it breaks off, in the Fourth Book; and where it is resumed, in the Fifteenth Book. The greatest fault is found at the first point of attachment, where the goddess Athene gives Telemachus the instructions on which the action of the next three Books depends. Against this passage (1. 269–302) Kirchhoff brought weighty objections, to which no satisfactory answer has yet been given. I must say at once that I too have found no answer; and I shall now state the objections, or rather that part of them which seems to me valid, briefly and plainly, divested of the meretricious cosmetic with which they have sometimes been adorned.

1. 269–96:

σὲ δὲ φράζεσθαι ἄνωγα
270 ὅππως κε μνηστῆρας ἀπώσεαι ἐκ μεγάροιο.
εἰ δ' ἄγε νῦν ξυνίει καὶ ἐμῶν ἐμπάζεο μύθων·
αὔριον εἰς ἀγορὴν καλέσας ἥρωας Ἀχαιοὺς
μῦθον πέφραδε πᾶσι, θεοὶ δ' ἐπὶ μάρτυροι ἔστων.
μνηστῆρας μὲν ἐπὶ σφέτερα σκίδνασθαι ἄνωχθι,
275 μητέρα δ', εἴ οἱ θυμὸς ἐφορμᾶται γαμέεσθαι,
ἂψ ἴτω ἐς μέγαρον πατρὸς μέγα δυναμένοιο,
οἱ δὲ γάμον τεύξουσι καὶ ἀρτυνέουσιν ἔεδνα
πολλὰ μάλ', ὅσσα ἔοικε φίλης ἐπὶ παιδὸς ἕπεσθαι.

σοὶ δ' αὐτῷ πυκινῶς ὑποθήσομαι, αἴ κε πίθηαι·
280 νῆ' ἄρσας ἐρέτῃσιν ἐείκοσιν, ἥ τις ἀρίστη,
ἔρχεο πευσόμενος πατρὸς δὴν οἰχομένοιο,
ἤν τίς τοι εἴπῃσι βροτῶν ἢ ὄσσαν ἀκούσῃς
ἐκ Διός, ἥ τε μάλιστα φέρει κλέος ἀνθρώποισι.
πρῶτα μὲν ἐς Πύλον ἐλθὲ καὶ εἴρεο Νέστορα δῖον,
285 κεῖθεν δὲ Σπάρτηνδε παρὰ ξανθὸν Μενέλαον·
ὃς γὰρ δεύτατος ἦλθεν Ἀχαιῶν χαλκοχιτώνων.
εἰ μέν κεν πατρὸς βίοτον καὶ νόστον ἀκούσῃς,
ἦ τ' ἂν τρυχόμενός περ ἔτι τλαίης ἐνιαυτόν,
εἰ δέ κε τεθνηῶτος ἀκούσῃς μηδ' ἔτ' ἐόντος,
290 νοστήσας δὴ ἔπειτα φίλην ἐς πατρίδα γαῖαν
σῆμά τέ οἱ χεῦαι καὶ ἐπὶ κτέρεα κτερεΐξαι
πολλὰ μάλ', ὅσσα ἔοικε, καὶ ἀνέρι μητέρα δοῦναι.
αὐτὰρ ἐπὴν δὴ ταῦτα τελευτήσῃς τε καὶ ἔρξῃς,
φράζεσθαι δὴ ἔπειτα κατὰ φρένα καὶ κατὰ θυμόν,
295 ὅππως κε μνηστῆρας ἐνὶ μεγάροισι τεοῖσι
κτείνῃς ἠὲ δόλῳ ἢ ἀμφαδόν.

'*Yourself I bid take thought, how you shall drive the Suitors from your palace: come now, take notice and mark what I say. Tomorrow summon the Achaean lords to assembly, and declare your purpose to them all; and let the gods be your witnesses.*

The Suitors *you shall bid disperse, each to his own.*

For your mother, *if her heart is eager for marriage, let her go back to the palace of her mighty father; and they shall make her marriage and prepare wedding-gifts, all that rightly attend a man's own daughter.*

Yourself *shall I shrewdly counsel, if you will but obey: equip with twenty oarsmen a vessel, the best you have, and go to inquire about your father, so long abroad, if any man may tell you, or you hear a heaven-sent rumour such as oftenest brings report to mankind. First go to Pylos and question god-like Nestor, thence to Sparta to fair-haired Menelaus, for he was the last of the bronze-clad Achaeans to return. If you hear that your father is alive and coming home, then indeed though sorely oppressed endure yet a twelvemonth. But if you hear that he is dead and gone, come back to your own native land and heap a mound for him and pay him funeral honours, all that are due, and give your mother to a husband.*

And when you have finished and done all this, take thought in your mind and heart how you may kill the Suitors in your palace, whether by stealth or openly. . . .'

In this passage Athene gives Telemachus the following instructions, which are to determine the action of the Second, Third, and Fourth Books of the *Odyssey*. First (271–8) : tell the suitors to go to their own homes; Penelope, if her heart is set on marrying, is to go to her father's house, *and her family shall make her marriage* and equip her with a suitable dowry. Secondly (279–92) : go abroad in search of your father; at the end of a year (or sooner, if you learn that he is dead) come home *and give your mother to a husband.* Thirdly (293–6) : *after* you have given your mother in marriage, *kill all the Suitors in your palace.*

Now whatever judgement we may later pass upon the facts, it would be trifling with the truth to deny that this is a wonderfully incoherent series of events. The relatively inattentive reader or listener may not have time to notice much amiss: but the poet, whose story depends on what he promises here, must have some purpose and some plan in what he says. Telemachus, who is eager to know what he must do, might fairly reply as follows :

'Here is a great muddle. I need advice about my mother Penelope, and this is what you tell me. First, if she is willing, she is to go home, and her father shall bring about her marriage. That is a clear and simple instruction, however unexpected. But at once you add that nothing of the sort is to be done. She is not to begin her preparations for marriage, whether she wishes to or not, and her father is not (after all) to arrange the wedding. Nothing is to be done until I return from abroad after an interval which may be as long as a year; then, and then only, is she to be given in marriage—by me, not by her father. Obviously it is this latter course which you wish me to adopt; what then was the point of giving me the first instruction, which seemed rather foolish at the time, and which I now infer is in no circumstances to be obeyed? You might at least have left it open to me to suppose that the latter course is an alternative, to be adopted when the former fails : *if* Penelope is unwilling to go home and marry at once, *then* I am to go abroad. But you were very careful to exclude that possibility, so arranging your sentences (μνηστῆρας μέν, μητέρα δέ, σοὶ δ' αὐτῷ) that they stand on exactly the same level: one who says "A is to do this, and B is to do that, and C is to do the other", will not be understood in Greek or any other language to mean "A is to do this, and B is to do that, and *only if they will not* C is to do the other". Moreover, if you had meant this, that Penelope's surrender is merely something which I am to suggest to the Suitors, you would not have gone out of your way to exclude this part from what I am to say to them: your words were ἂψ ἴτω, not ἂψ ἴμεν; it is not something which I am to say, knowing that it will not be done, but something which she is actually to do, if she would like to. In any case it would not have been a real alternative, but mere talking for talking's sake, since you and I and our audience all know that Penelope is not, as you put it, "in a hurry to get married".

'So much for your first instruction; but there is worse to come. For you go on to tell me that I must perform my father's funeral rites, and give my mother in marriage, and when I have done all that, I am to kill all the Suitors in my house. Allow me to say that this is a remarkably foolish instruction: this story ends, as everybody knows, with the killing of the Suitors *before* the marriage of Penelope; if she should marry one of them, the *Odyssey* will have reached a premature end. I could understand and appreciate a command to kill the Suitors *before* the marriage of Penelope: but what on earth would be the point of delaying that action until after one of them has married her? Apart from that, do you not see that after the marriage there would be no Suitors left in my palace?'

At this point, as Kirchhoff says, the writer has no idea whatever what he is talking about, or to what purpose. If we wish to see the difference between good and bad, let us contrast with this rigmarole the statement of Athene at the beginning of the poem (1. 88 ff.): 'I shall go to Ithaca, and more strongly excite Odysseus' son, and put courage in his heart; that he shall summon the Achaeans to assembly, and speak his mind to all the Suitors who are slaughtering his sheep and cattle; and I shall send him to Sparta and Pylos to inquire of his father's return, and earn good repute among men.' That is what she said she would tell Telemachus: and we notice that there was not a word about Penelope, or about killing the Suitors after her marriage;

not a trace of the incoherence which disfigures the later passage. Put the one beside the other, and unless all distinction between clear thought and muddle is to be denied, the conclusion is plain enough. Kirchhoff is justified in saying that there is nothing subjective about his argument: this, and nothing else, is in the text; and, unless the Greek Epic is to be exempt from the normal laws of speech and thought, that text is, as a matter of fact, both incoherent and self-contradictory; not so much in language as in thought, not in details of secondary importance, but in matters relating to the main structure of the poem, expressly introducing all that is to happen in the next three Books. If there were any adequate answer to these arguments, it would probably have been given in the last seventy-five years; but I have not succeeded in the search for a defence that is not much weaker than the prosecution; there is no doubt about the general verdict.[1] If you ask how it can be that the world for long[2] considered this passage to be a fit beginning to one of the greatest works in the history of literature, I reply in the words of Dr. Johnson that 'one cannot always easily find the reason for which the world has sometimes conspired to squander praise'.

I see no means of avoiding the conclusion that something has gone wrong at this point; and that conclusion is strongly confirmed by the relation of what is forecast here to what actually happens later. Athene tells Telemachus what is to be done: and though the nature of her instructions is such that he cannot possibly obey them all, the least he can do is not to contradict them. Who would believe, if he had any choice in the matter, that our poet would break the most elementary laws of his craft, making *the Suitors* repeat verbatim a proposal made *by Athene* to Telemachus, and then making Telemachus reject that proposal? But that is what happens. Next day in the Assembly Eurymachus, ringleader of the Suitors, miraculously repeats word for word what Athene had said to Telemachus: 'Tell your mother to go home, to her father's house, and they shall make her marriage and equip her with a proper dowry' (2. 194 ff.)—precisely what Athene had proposed; but Telemachus will have nothing to do with it. Already, earlier in the scene, he had missed his opportunity:

Antinous said to him, 'if only your mother would marry one of us, we would leave you in peace' (2. 127 f.). This is the moment for Telemachus to repeat what Athene told him, 'Yes, she shall go home, if she is willing, and her father shall make her marriage.' Instead, as if Athene had never spoken, he abruptly rejects the proposal.

Now we notice at once that what was so absurd in the speech of Athene is entirely natural in that of the Suitors: *they* may well propose that Penelope shall choose a husband at once; *they* are not to know that there is no prospect whatsoever of the proposal being accepted. Such a proposal is for them to make, for Telemachus to reject; and that is what happens in the Second Book. Transfer it to the speech of Athene, as an instruction to Telemachus, and it becomes and always will be a piece of nonsense in itself, wholly incompatible with the rest of her instructions and wholly at variance with what happens later. It is, in short, as clear as need be that this part of Athene's address has been composed *later* than its reappearance in the speech of the Suitors, which is indeed the mine from which it was quarried: the author went to work with full knowledge of the description of the debate in the Second Book; he is not entirely at ease in handling the Epic dialect,[3] and he has not noticed that the lines which he transfers backwards from the Second Book into the First do not sit comfortably in their new surroundings.[4]

Why did he do it? Before we look for a reason, let us frankly admit two facts which seem to deepen the mystery: first, that Book I, taken as a whole, is a work of very careful construction, perfectly designed to introduce the whole story of the *Odyssey*; secondly, that the course of the action up to this point (1. 269 ff.) absolutely demands an address by Athene to Telemachus, telling him what to do; and the greater part of the instructions given here—the challenge to the Suitors in the Assembly and the journey to Sparta and Pylos—are completely in accord with what was promised earlier (1. 88 ff.) and with what is actually done hereafter.

The action of the First Book is, in broad outline, simple and coherent. The gods assemble, and agree to befriend Odysseus (all except Poseidon, who is absent). Athene says that she will go to Ithaca and send Telemachus in search of his father. To Ithaca she goes, in the guise of Mentes, king of the Taphians. She is greeted and entertained. She observes the misconduct of the Suitors, and Telemachus explains the circumstances: the absence of Odysseus; the courting of his mother; the ruin of his property. Athene expresses the wish that Odysseus may return and avenge these wrongs. Whatever fault may be found with the detail,[5] the main structure is clear and straightforward; there is no indication that it has been distorted by any later interference, except in the final address by Athene. Moreover, the First Book, as a whole, provides a remarkably good introduction to the *Odyssey*, as a whole, in its present form. We learn, within the first hundred lines, that Odysseus is detained by Calypso; that Athene befriends him, Poseidon persecutes him; that Telemachus will go in search of his father; that the Suitors of Penelope are living riotously in Odysseus' property; we even hear a summary of the forthcoming story of Polyphemus. In the sequel we meet Telemachus, and later Penelope herself, in a scene which the sternest critics have admitted to be of singular charm. Before the end of the Book the two ringleaders of the Suitors are introduced by name; so is the old nurse Eurycleia; and even Laertes, the father of Odysseus, is brought to mind. Thus the whole of the action and most of the principal persons are introduced in the course of a few hundred lines.

But the First Book, taken as a whole, is much more than merely a coherent story and a suitable preface to the *Odyssey*: it is also a work of great dramatic power, picturesque and most carefully planned.[6] The scene is set in the great hall of Odysseus at Ithaca. Here the Suitors take their pleasure, as they have done these many months, feasting as if at home, with song and dancing. They are masters in this house; and the royal prince, Telemachus, must entertain his guest, Athene, wherever he can, withdrawn from the company; they must put their heads close together and hush their voices, for there is danger if they are overheard: ἄγχι σχὼν κεφαλὴν ἵνα μὴ πευθοίαθ' οἱ ἄλλοι. So they talk low against a background of song; and imperceptibly the listener becomes aware of a third presence, haunting the scene, an image created by their thoughts and words centred on him alone—Odysseus. Whatever is said or done now, in our hearing, by wife or son or Suitors, is quickened and coloured by the invisible hand of the master who may yet return. Hence the sudden reversal of fortunes at the end of the scene. At the beginning the Suitors are masters in the royal palace, confident and secure in their pleasures, free from impediment or fear of reprisal. For Telemachus there is no comfort, and no hope; and if any danger impends, it is over him. This has been the situation for several years, and there is no apparent reason why it should not continue for several more. But by the time the scene ends, Athene has kindled a flame in the ashes of Telemachus' despair: what seemed unalterable is now suddenly in suspense, what was stagnant is now a stream in motion. For the Suitors, so long secure, the hour of reckoning is now definitely fixed, however distantly: they themselves are suddenly uneasy; they ask Telemachus who this mysterious guest may be; is there perhaps, after all, some message from Odysseus?

And now notice the most artistic touch of all. The conversation of Athene and Telemachus begins and ends with references to a song by the poet Phemius (1. 154 f., 325 ff.), a song which continues throughout the scene, forming an accompaniment to all they say; even the Suitors are listening to it in silence (1. 325). And what was the subject of that song? The most apt and ominous that could be imagined—ὁ δ' Ἀχαιῶν νόστον ἄειδε, the *Homecoming of the men who went to Troy.*

I see no escape from the following facts:

1. The whole course of the First Book, up to the point where Athene gives her instructions to Telemachus, demands that she must give him instructions; and the greater part of what she advises is indeed performed in the sequel.

2. And yet the coherence of the passage in which she gives the instructions has been broken beyond repair by somebody who, having read what follows in the next Book, incorporated into Athene's speech certain things which are said in the next Book.

There is one simple explanation: that at an earlier stage of the tradition Athene's speech contained something which was flatly contradicted by what follows in the Assembly in the Second Book; Athene's speech has therefore to some extent been refashioned; the part which was contradicted by the sequel was omitted and replaced by verses which appeared to bring the speech into conformity with the sequel.

This explanation would be the more acceptable if we could answer two further questions: first, what was there, in Athene's original instructions, which was so flatly contradicted by the sequel that some attempt must be made to reconcile the two? Secondly, how could any such contradiction ever have arisen?

A likely answer to the former question is suggested by the detail of the Second Book, in which a conflict of two contrary versions is at once apparent. We have only to ask this simple question: was the Journey of Telemachus prepared with the approval and assistance of the Suitors, or did they obstruct it? Both versions stand side by side in our text of the *Odyssey*.

Telemachus openly asks the Suitors to give him a ship and crew to take him to Pylos and Sparta in search of his father (2. 212 ff.). There is no direct reply to this request. Only one Suitor (one of the least prominent, Leiocritus) mentions the matter before the end of the Assembly. Now what he says is that Telemachus' friends shall hasten on his journey, though he himself believes it will never take place. *At once* Telemachus prays to Athene, saying that the Achaeans, especially the Suitors, keep putting off his journey! On the contrary, the only Suitor who has had a chance to mention the matter gave his permission, and that only half a dozen lines ago. This incoherence is exactly repeated later on (306 ff.): Antinous expressly says that the Achaeans shall provide a ship and crew for the voyage: *at once* Telemachus replies that he will travel as a merchant, since it is the Suitors' policy to deny him a ship and crew of his own! It is perfectly clear that two different versions of the story are being combined without the least regard for harmony: one, in which the Suitors allow Telemachus to go, and put no obstacle in his path; another, in which they pretend to agree to the journey but frustrate it by delays and hindrances.

This suggestion, that in some other version of the story the

Suitors were determined that Telemachus should stay at home, is proved beyond question by later events. It was necessary for Athene herself to provide the ship and crew (382 ff.) and to put the Suitors to sleep before Telemachus might depart, secretly after nightfall (393 ff.); and when the Suitors discover that he is gone they are alarmed and astonished. 'A proud deed insolently done', they say; 'we thought he would never accomplish it. Though all of us opposed him, this youngster has launched a ship and picked the best men in the place and is gone without a word' (4. 632 ff.). Nothing could be much more explicit than this: 'he is gone against the will of all of us', τοσσῶνδ' ἀέκητι. But in the Assembly, and after the Assembly, no Suitor said a word to oppose the journey, and two of them expressly allowed it. The poem leaves us to infer from odds and ends in the narrative that what they said was the opposite of what they intended. We are thus enabled to give a likely answer to our question, 'What was there in Athene's original instructions to Telemachus which had to be removed and replaced by something else based upon what actually happens?' It is very probable that Athene originally forecast a meeting of the Assembly in which the Journey of Telemachus was to be kept secret—though in the sequel the Suitors heard of it and tried to obstruct it.[7] All this may well have been forecast by Athene in some detail; if so, her speech would have to be altered in this respect if it were followed by a version in which Telemachus openly announced his journey, and in which the Suitors assented to it.

And now the second question. There is not yet any reason to suppose that the Journey of Telemachus has ever been absent from the Epic poem about the Return of Odysseus; or that it has ever occupied any other place in the chronological sequence of events; or that the journey itself was ever narrated in a form essentially different from what we read in the Third and Fourth Books. But it is practically certain that our text offers a version of which the beginning has been radically altered from an earlier form. Now we have no particular reason to believe that, in the era when oral recitation was the normal mode of publishing, it was an invariable practice to recite the *Odyssey* from start to finish without interruption. We must at least make allowance for the possibility that the professional reciter might choose (according to circumstances) either of two courses: the recitation of a part of the poem in isolation; or the recitation of the whole poem over a period of days.[8] If the former course was commonly adopted (and I do not know why anybody should doubt the likelihood of this), it is evident that the beginnings and ends of the parts selected would be specially exposed to alterations designed to adapt them to the requirements of separate recitation. We shall see presently what I take to be a very clear example of this general rule. In the present case our difficulties disappear so soon as we imagine a creative poet, entirely at home in the Epic tradition, giving new colour and substance to the story of Telemachus as a separate recitation, expanding the opening scene to a novel and brilliant episode, exposing the guilt of the Suitors, forecasting its punishment, and so bringing the isolated theme of the voyage to Pylos and Sparta into closest relation with the source from which it is derived—the story of the *Odyssey* as a whole. The reciter is under no obligation to take notice of anything forecast in the First Book, which lies outside the region of his part-recitation: but when in the fullness of time a standard text of the whole *Odyssey* is made, in writing, there will have to be some adjustment made in Athene's instructions if this, the best and most popular, version of the beginning of the Second Book is to be the one included.

Notice finally that the beginning of the Second Book betrays its alien and later source in its utterly unhomeric conception of the preliminaries to betrothal and marriage. The *Iliad* and *Odyssey* are aware of one custom only: *the suitor purchases the bride from her father*, the word ἔεδνα denoting the payment made by the suitor to the father. References to this practice are very common, and there is not a single exception to the rule, *except at the beginning of the Second Book*: the author of this part of the *Odyssey* is familiar with the exactly opposite custom, according to which *the father sells his daughter to the suitor*, the word ἔεδνα now denoting the dowry which accompanies the bride. In an isolated lay, intended for separate recitation, nobody would notice that this contradicts the practice elsewhere uniform throughout the *Odyssey*, wherein Penelope is to be purchased by the Suitors: this introduction to the Journey of Telemachus was evidently composed in a society which itself practised the later custom and which felt itself under no obligation to exclude it from Heroic poetry.[9]

So much for the beginning of the story of Telemachus. Let us now consider what happens when the thread is dropped, at the end of the Fourth Book, and when it is picked up again, at the beginning of the Fifteenth.

The *Odyssey* began with an assembly of the gods in heaven. Athene proposed that Hermes should be sent to command Calypso to release Odysseus, and that she herself would send Telemachus in search of his father. This latter mission is described first; and the Journey of Telemachus extends to near the end of the Fourth Book. Then we revert to the former mission, that of Hermes to Calypso, which was promised at the beginning of the poem, and which is in fact simultaneous with the mission of Athene to Telemachus. Let us look closely at this point, for the whole question of the organic unity of the *Odyssey* is at issue here.[10]

Events which occur simultaneously cannot be narrated simultaneously: they must be described one after the other, and the story-teller may or may not tell us that, although narrated in succession, they were really simultaneous; thus Virgil, at the beginning of the Ninth Book of the *Aeneid*: *atque ea diuersa penitus dum parte geruntur*, 'while these things were happening in a quite different place....' That is frank enough, however prosaic, and not at all inferior to the practice of our embarrassed novelists. From *Tom Jones* (XVI. ix): 'The reader may now, perhaps, be pleased to return with us to Mr. Jones'; from *The Mysteries of Udolpho* (I. xxii): 'Leaving the gay scenes of Paris, we return to those of the gloomy Apennine'; from *The Heart of Midlothian* (chap. xvi): 'I find myself under the necessity of connecting the branches of my story, by taking up the adventures of another of the characters, and bringing them down to the point at which we have left those of Jeanie Deans'; from *Martin Chuzzlewit* (end of chap. xvii): 'Be it the part of this slight chronicle . . . rapidly to change the scene and cross the ocean to the English shore.' Or consider the following passage of that novel: we wish to pass from Mr. Pecksniff's house in England to Martin Chuzzlewit in a train in America; this is how it is done. Chapter xx ends: 'At that moment a loud knocking was heard at the hall door'; chapter xxi begins: 'The knocking at Mr. Pecksniff's door . . . *bore no resemblance whatever* to the noise of an American railway-train at full speed. . . .' As a rule the reader is left in doubt whether the two different episodes are simultaneous or not; and as a rule it does not matter much whether they are or not.

Now the early Greek Epic observes a simple rule:[11] it is the general practice not only to narrate simultaneous events successively, but also *to represent them as if they had actually occurred successively*. It was not permissible to take a step backwards in time (or to leave any space of time unoccupied by events; though the poet might leave to the understanding an event or series of events which must have occurred in one place while he was narrating what occurred in another). In the Fifteenth Book of the *Iliad*[12] (154 ff.) Iris and Apollo stand in front of Zeus, who has a mission for both. These missions could and should be carried out simultaneously; but they cannot be described simultaneously; they are therefore described as if they had really taken place successively. First, Iris takes her message to Poseidon; not until her mission is completed (15. 222 f.) does Zeus turn to Apollo and tell him what message he must take to Hector. It is not correct to say that the poets took this particular path in order to avoid an obstacle: the truth is rather that they act as if they had no conception of an all-embracing Time to which different events might be related. They treat time simply as the measure of the duration of particular events. The idea that the duration of two events might coincide or overlap presupposes the conception of a universal Time, common to many events in different places; and of that conception there is no trace in the *Iliad*; the *Odyssey*, as we shall see, is more sophisticated in this as in other matters; let us briefly examine its methods.

When the scene and its subject change, the question whether

the new is contemporaneous with the old does not very often arise. The action throughout may be clearly continuous, or possibly continuous, and neither the poet nor his audience feels any need for special measures. In the *Odyssey*, for example, at 13. 185, the poet leaves the Phaeacians at home and passes to Odysseus in Ithaca without the slightest attempt to bridge the gap or to define the time-relation: 'Thus the leaders and rulers of the Phaeacian people stood about the altar and prayed to their lord Poseidon, *and Odysseus awoke from sleep in his native land* . . .'— whether the Phaeacians' prayer will be answered, whether we shall ever see them again, we do not know; in the middle of a line, with the utmost simplicity, we pass from one place and person to another place and person.

But, now, what happens when the poet describes events which certainly must have occurred simultaneously? The law of the Epic tradition is perfectly clear: the Journey of Telemachus (1–3) and the Wanderings of Odysseus (5–13) occurred simultaneously; but they must be (and are) narrated as if the action was continuous throughout. It was easy enough at the beginning: Athene starts Telemachus on his journey, and when that is over Hermes can start Odysseus on his; there is no need to refer openly to the times involved. It is not so easy at the other end, for after Odysseus has arrived home we must go back to Sparta and fetch Telemachus, pretending not to notice the long interval of time which must have elapsed since we last saw him. How is it actually done?

The last lines of the Fourteenth Book finish the story of Odysseus' return to Ithaca, and the first lines of the Fifteenth resume the story of Telemachus at Sparta. The one event will, according to the rule, follow immediately upon the other, as if the two were not simultaneous but successive. Now here the poet improves upon the simple methods of the past by delicately weaving the old scene and the new one together: he leaves Odysseus, *asleep at night*, in Ithaca, and passes at once to Telemachus, *asleep at night*, in Sparta. He clearly intends his listeners to imagine that this is one and the same night: the narrative is to be continuous, as the law demands; but instead of putting the one scene simply beside the other, the poet has linked them under the cover of a single space of time. You are not allowed to comment that Telemachus must have spent an unconscionable time at Sparta. What has elapsed since we left him at Sparta is not an absolute time of several weeks, for which he must be held to account, but a series of events—the Wanderings of Odysseus; and the duration of those wanderings is a quality of them only, without any wider reference whatsoever. To the Epic poet the question, 'How long is it since we last saw Telemachus?', is nonsensical: there were no events concerning Telemachus in the interval; and time, with reference to Telemachus, exists only as a measure of the duration of events in which Telemachus is engaged.

Thus the poet has observed, but also improved upon, the rules of his craft. But there is still some way to go. Telemachus must now come home from Sparta while Odysseus spends the time in Ithaca: how are these two contemporary events to be described? Very simply, we should suppose: bring Telemachus back and let him meet Odysseus; we do not inquire what Odysseus was doing in the meantime, just as we did not ask what Telemachus was doing while Odysseus returned. It is particularly to be noticed that our poet avoids this, the simple plan, and gives us a *double* change of scene, for which there is no apparent cause except the pleasure which he takes in its intricacy: from Odysseus we pass to Telemachus (14–15); back again from Telemachus to Odysseus (15. 300); and so back again from Odysseus to Telemachus (15. 494). And here is a further remarkable improvement in the poet's technique: at 15. 296 we leave Telemachus already on his way home—but we leave him at a moment of doubt and danger; the question is expressly raised, will he escape death or not? The poet deliberately leaves us in suspense, arousing our interest in a point to which we shall return, we are confident, sooner or later. Moreover, the device employed between the Fourteenth and Fifteenth Books is repeated here. When we leave Telemachus, it is night: we pass to Odysseus at Ithaca—and there too it is night, obviously the same night, spread above the separated father and son, bringing them together. Then notice how the scene changes, for the last time, back from Odysseus to Telemachus: Odysseus is awake throughout the night—that same night which is bringing his son home; he goes very late to bed, *and almost at once the dawn was there, and they, the companions of Telemachus, put into harbour at Ithaca* (15. 494 ff.).[13] It is most delicately done: the night in which Telemachus begins his journey blends imperceptibly with the night of Odysseus at Ithaca; the coming of dawn serves in one and the same phrase to end the sleep of Odysseus and to witness the arrival of Telemachus in harbour.

If you now consult your calendar you will find that you have been hoodwinked. For in the interval between the beginning of the Fifteenth Book and the arrival of Telemachus at Ithaca you will see, if you look closely, that for Telemachus two days have passed, for Odysseus only one. Our poet has advanced greatly in technique: but it is now apparent that he has strained to breaking-point the convention that one series of events in time is not to be related to another within the same time.[14]

It will, I suppose, be generally agreed that the dove-tailing in the Fifteenth Book is exceptionally smooth and artful. There can be no question of *Ordner* or *Bearbeiter*, of patchwork or compilation here: the returns of Telemachus and Odysseus are woven together with uncommon skill; they cannot be disentangled. It follows inevitably that we are obliged to regard the two main themes of the poem up to this point—the Journey of Telemachus and the Wanderings of Odysseus—as being at least in substance an integral and indivisible whole. Of course there is no reason why a poet, finding before him a story of the Wanderings of Odysseus, should not amplify it in this way, and weave the old and new together with skill and success; I only say that we have not found in the points which we have been considering any indication that this is what was done.

Finally, what about the earlier point, the transition in the Fourth Book from the Journey of Telemachus to the beginning of the Wanderings of Odysseus? Here the first thing we notice is that our poet has again made his task more complicated than was necessary. We are in Sparta with Telemachus: we must now pass to Odysseus on the island of Calypso. But are there not now three contemporary scenes, instead of two, to be held in memory? Telemachus, at Sparta; Odysseus, with Calypso; and Penelope and the Suitors at Ithaca. There was no need to go back to them and so make a double change of scene; but made it is. From Sparta we go to Ithaca, from Ithaca to the island of Calypso. All three scenes are really simultaneous; all are described, according to convention, as being successive, continuous in time. But if we now compare the technique with that of the Fifteenth Book, we find a curious mixture of like and unlike. The transition from Sparta to Ithaca is as artless as it can could well be (4. 620-5): the action is broken off sharply, incomplete; there is no moment of suspense, nothing to suggest that we must certainly return to this point, and no spreading of the same day or night over the two scenes. It is, however, imprudent to pass any definite judgement on these facts, for there is reason to believe that our text is mutilated at the critical point. Between the last mention of Telemachus and Menelaus at Sparta and the first mention of the Suitors at Ithaca there intervene four comical lines, describing an ἔρανος, or bottle-party, to which the Spartan nobles come driving their own cattle and carrying their own wine, while bread is supplied by their fashionable wives.[15]

Very different is the artifice employed at the transition from Ithaca to the Wanderings of Odysseus. Here the continuity of time is clearly marked, in the manner of the Fifteenth Book: we leave Penelope awakening from a dream by night, and the transition to Odysseus begins with the statement that night is over and a new day has broken. Moreover, the other device which we detected in the Fifteenth Book is revealed here too: both Penelope and the Suitors are left in a state of suspense; it is clearly indicated that questions are left unanswered at this point, and the listener has no doubt whatever that he will return to them later on. Penelope asks the phantom in her dream whether Odysseus is yet alive or dead, and is told that this cannot yet be known, she must wait and see: with the lightest possible touch the poet has turned us in the direction now to be followed; this question, whether Odysseus be alive or dead, we are at once to hear answered for ourselves; but we are quite sure that we shall return to Penelope, that the question may be answered for her too. And the Suitors? We shall certainly return to them; for they are lying in ambush, intending to murder Telemachus when he returns—we know then that he *will* return, and we are confident that we shall come back to this point to hear the outcome of the Suitors' designs upon his life.

Up to this point all is well and all in accord with the conventions of the poet's craft: he has improved upon the older art by connecting the old scene with the new in time and by assuring the listener that he will return to the scene which is for the time being left in suspense. We have done with Sparta and Ithaca for the moment; it only remains for the poet to continue, 'And now Zeus sent Hermes to the island of Calypso'.

What actually happens is without parallel in the Greek Epic. The action is interrupted by a second Assembly of the gods in heaven, a pale and uninteresting image of the one which begins the *Odyssey*, for no visible purpose but to go over much the same ground again and to set in motion a matter for which the first Assembly had made provision enough—the sending of Hermes to the island of Calypso.

This tedious and abnormal procedure might be excused as being merely an innovation, an unsuccessful experiment; but if we turn from the structure to the contents, we may not judge so leniently.

The gods assemble at dawn, and Athene begins to address them[16] on behalf of Odysseus. At once a most disagreeable fact obtrudes itself: Athene's speech is not a free composition naturally designed for this place and purpose; it consists of three long sentences, each one of them a fragment of another person's conversation repeated from very different surroundings in the preceding story of Telemachus.[17] Her first sentence, in five lines, was spoken by Mentor to the people of Ithaca in the Second Book; her second sentence, in four lines, was spoken by Proteus to Menelaus in the Fourth Book; and her third sentence, in three lines, was spoken by Medon to Penelope only a few minutes ago.

In the Greek Epic parts of lines, whole lines, and groups of lines are commonly repeated from one point to another; indeed the greater part of the *Iliad* and *Odyssey* consists of formular lines and phrases repeated and adapted to new contexts;[18] this is the technique of oral composition, essential to the making of such poems before the practice of writing revolutionized the art of poetry. But there were limits to what might properly be done; and it must be candidly confessed that so great an abuse of the poet's licence, so insensitive a treatment of his materials, as we find in this address by Athene, is (by good fortune) not to be found again in the Greek Epic. It is an abnormally artificial patchwork, whoever composed it. The poet desires to begin a new and very important episode with a speech by a goddess in heaven: invention and imagination fail him, as never before or again; the abundant springs of joy and resource run suddenly dry and silent; he recalls, word for word, portions of conversation recently assigned to three different persons in different circumstances, and sets them down side by side to form the opening address. They serve the purpose well enough, we admit; but I argue no further with those who think that the end justifies even these means.

It is thus established (as fact, not opinion) that both the structure and the contents of this scene in heaven are out of harmony with normal practice;[19] and it may well be thought that in both respects the poet's devices here are much inferior to what is customary. Are we to believe that this is the same poet as he who made with such artistry the change of scene from Ithaca, and who will deal so delicately with the intricate fabric of the Fifteenth Book? Surely not, since a very simple explanation is at our disposal. This fresh assembly of the gods was never intended to stand in a *continuous Odyssey*; it is a new prologue, specially designed to introduce the Wanderings of Odysseus when that part of the poem was selected for separate recitation. It may have been a normal practice, to recite the *Odyssey* in parts: and the Wanderings of Odysseus were the most attractive of all possible selections for part-recitation. But if this part is recited separately, it may well appear to need some introduction; and here, at the beginning of the Fifth Book, we find embedded in the *Odyssey*, *as a whole*, a prologue designed to introduce the recitation of the Wanderings of Odysseus *as a part*.[20]

I conclude by summarizing briefly what I take to be certain

or probable conclusions about the relation of the story of Telemachus to the *Odyssey* as a whole.

First, the weaving of the two threads into a single strand in the Fifteenth Book reveals an uncommonly skilful hand; the technique is delicate, and considerably in advance of earlier methods. It is certainly not possible to disentangle the two threads at this point; and we must conclude that the stories of Telemachus and Odysseus are organically connected in our *Odyssey*, though we cannot exclude the possibility that a poet who composed our *Odyssey* substantially as it exists today found before him a traditional version of the Wanderings of Odysseus, which he adopted as the nucleus of a much larger poem beginning with the story of Telemachus and ending with the killing of the Suitors of Penelope. That is to say, what is well enough known, that if our *Odyssey* is substantially the achievement of one poet, we cannot tell how much he took over more or less unchanged from earlier tradition.

Secondly, the transition from Ithaca to Odysseus at the end of the Fourth Book reveals the same delicate and novel artifice as that which we found in the Fifteenth Book. But here the original continuity has been broken by the inclusion in the poem of a special prologue designed to introduce the Wanderings of Odysseus as a separate recitation.

Thirdly, we have found no answer to the problems presented by Athene's instructions to Telemachus in the First Book; we were therefore obliged to conclude that the earlier part of the Second Book—the beginning of the story of Telemachus—is, in its present form, incompatible with what was originally ordered by Athene; and the detail of the Second Book revealed to us just what that point of incompatibility may have been. Here too the same explanation would be easy and sufficient: that the beginning of the Second Book was specially composed to introduce, and to endow with more substance and colour, the story of Telemachus as a separate recitation.[21]

Fourthly, we notice that these conclusions imply that the *Odyssey* took its final form, that is to say, more or less its present form, as the result of some sort of deliberate editing. This implication is at harmony with all that we know about the transmission of our poem from remote antiquity to the present day. There is little room for doubt that our *Odyssey* is ultimately derived from a standard edition, a deliberate fixation of the text, made in Athens in the sixth century B.C. If our conclusions are so far correct, it follows that the practice of reciting the *Odyssey* in parts, such parts having special prologues and prefaces, sometimes of considerable extent, materially affected the structure of the earliest standard text of the *Odyssey* as a continuous poem preserved in writing. It does not at all follow that the parts were composed by different authors; indeed we have already seen reason to believe that the parts are organically connected, though capable of being withdrawn from their contexts for separate recitation.

NOTES ON CHAPTER III

On the subjects discussed in this chapter there is still nothing to compare with A. Kirchhoff, *Die Homerische Odyssee*, Berlin 1879. Among earlier works I select for mention G. Hermann, *De interpolationibus Homeri dissertatio*, 1832 (= *Opuscula* v. 52 ff.); K. L. Kayser, *Disputatio de diversa Homericorum carminum origine*, Heidelberg 1835 (= *K. L. Kaysers homerische Abhandlungen*, edited by H. Usener (Leipzig 1881) 29 ff.); P. D. Ch. Hennings, *Ueber die Telemachie, Jb. f. Klass. Phil.*, suppl. 3 (1858) 135 ff.; E. Kammer, *Die Einheit der Odyssee*, 1873. Among later works the most important are U. von Wilamowitz-Moellendorff, *Homerische Untersuchungen*, Berlin 1884 (I should not include in this category *Die Heimkehr von Odysseus*, Berlin 1927); R. Dahms, *Odyssee und Telemachie: Untersuchungen über die Composition der Odyssee*, Berlin 1919; E. Bethe, *Homer* ii, 1922, 2nd ed. 1929, 29 ff.; E. Schwartz, *Die Odyssee*, München 1924; P. Von der Mühll, s.v. 'Odyssee' in *RE*, 1939 (also *Die Dichter der Odyssee, Jb. des Vereins Schweiz. Gymnasiallehrer*, 1940); U. Hölscher, *Untersuchungen zur Form der Odyssee, Hermes*, Einzelschriften, Heft 6, 1939; F. Focke, *Die Odyssee, Tübinger Beiträge zur Altertumswissenschaft* 37, Stuttgart 1943; F. Klingner, *Ueber die vier ersten Bücher der Odyssee, Ber. Sächs. Akad. d. Wiss. zu Leipzig*, phil.-hist. Klasse 96 (1944) 1; R. Merkelbach, *Untersuchungen zur Odyssee, Zetemata*, Heft 2, München 1951.

I take this opportunity of acknowledging a long-standing debt to one of the best of all works on the *Odyssey*, D. B. Monro's Appendix to his edition of *Od.* xiii–xxiv, first published in 1901; and of expressing my gratitude to Professor Albin Lesky for sending me copies of his invaluable *Homerforschung in der Gegenwart* (Wien 1952) and *Forschungsbericht: Homer, Anzeiger f. d. Altertumswiss.* vi (1953) 129 ff.

1. 'The gift of pleasing and persuasive exposition', says Kirchhoff, 'has not been vouchsafed to me': I doubt whether Homeric scholarship has much to show in which lucidity, intelligence, good judgement, and good manners are more perfectly combined than in this chapter of his *Odyssey*.

The ablest of the opponents of Kirchhoff among the moderns is F. Klingner: but such are his honesty of mind and clarity of judgement that he makes no attempt to palliate the sins of this passage: op. cit. 39, 'So bleibt es dabei: in dem mit Rat und Weisung vorgreifenden Teil von Athenes Rede sind die Themen, sowie sie sich beim Zustandekommen der Fabel wohl schrittweise herausgebildet hatten, *erstaunlich unbekümmert, ohne Ausgleich des sachlichen Inhalts, aneinandergesetzt.* Und dabei ist die Bewegung der Rede, auf das Ganze gesehen, schön und leuchtet ein. Auch als Teil der Erweckungsszene bringt die Rede, wieder auf das ganze Gebilde gesehen, einen Gipfel und ein Ziel, wie man es sich besser schwer wird denken können, während die Ankündigung des Künftigen im einzelnen *nur notdürftig, ja nachlässig abgetan, sagen wir ruhig: schwach und ohne volle Gegenwart des dichtenden Ingeniums weithin mit Versen bestritten ist, die &c.*' (my italics). Well worth reading is the remarkable attack on Kirchhoff's book, in the form of a Platonic dialogue, by F. Schultz, *Königl. Kaiserin Augusta-Gymnasium, Jahresbericht 1898*, Progr. 69; the opposite pole is attained by an article in *CR* 11 (1897) 290 ff., and (in my opinion) by F. Stürmer, *Exegetische Beiträge zur Odyssee* (Paderborn 1911) 64 ff.

The older editors did what they could to cure the disease by more or less extensive surgery (see, for example, Kammer, *Einheit der Odyssee*, 251–89: he thinks that he can 'remove all difficulties with the aid of excision [of 292] and the assumption of a lacuna [after 278]'). The facile assumption that the excision of v. 292 is a panacea has long been abandoned (apart from other objections, 2. 223 shows that this line is an indispensable climax to this passage as a whole). Deletion of 275–7 leaves a ridiculously meagre sequel (274) to an elaborate introduction (269–73). Deletion on a scale large enough to dispose of the main difficulties (269–78 and 293–302) would of course be a tacit admission that Kirchhoff has proved his case; but in fact such deletion is absolutely impossible except on the assumption that the deleted passages are not merely additions but substitutes for something else. See further Klingner, op. cit. 37 ff., and Ameis-Hentze, *Anhang* ad loc. On the other side, Blass, *Die Interpolationen in der Odyssee* (1904) 36 ff.

2. Some perception of the faults of 1. 269 ff. was first revealed by A. Jacob in 1856 (*Ueber die Entstehung der Odyssee* 364 ff.), and the case was well stated two years later by L. Friedländer (*Analecta Homerica, Jb. class. Phil.*, suppl. iii. 467 ff.) to whom Gottfried Hermann owed his awareness of the facts (478 f.). There is nothing to the point in Hennings's long essay on the Telemachy published in 1858. Kirchhoff's observations were made independently.

3. The threefold repetition of 'listen to what I tell you' is unusual and disagreeable (269 σὲ δὲ φράζεσθαι ἄνωγα: 271 εἰ δ' ἄγε νῦν ξυνίει καὶ ἐμῶν ἐμπάζεο μύθων: 279 σοὶ δ' αὐτῷ πυκινῶς ὑποθήσομαι). The older Epic dialect possessed no imperative-form πέφραδε (273: elsewhere only *Od.* 8. 142, a line athetized by Zenodotus, Aristophanes, and Aristarchus). ἐμπάζομαι in the Epic dialect (and everywhere else) is one of those verbs which are used only with a negative; it is noticeable that it is used twice without a negative in this passage, 271 and 305. In 275–6 μητέρα. . . ἴτω is clumsy: either μητέρα . . . ἴμεν (sc. ἄνωχθι) or simply μήτηρ . . . ἴτω would have been a great improvement.

4. The ambiguity of οἵ in 277 is awkward: the sentence as a whole would refer it to the Suitors (who are its subjects in the place where it recurs, 2. 196); but the context proves that the subject is Penelope's father and family (see further Kirchhoff, op. cit. 243 f.).

5. The most serious fault in the detail is to be found at 1. 372 ff.: Athene said to Telemachus, 'summon the Suitors to Assembly tomorrow, and tell them to leave your palace'. Telemachus would improve upon this instruction: he goes to the Suitors *at once* and says, 'Tomorrow morning let us all take our seats in the Assembly, that I may declare outright what I have to say to you'. The last thing we expect him to do is to deliver, here and now, the speech which Athene told him to deliver tomorrow, and which he is now promising for tomorrow. But that is just what he does; he gives here, word for word, the speech which, in accordance with Athene's instructions, he is to give again tomorrow: 'Depart from my palace, give your minds to banqueting elsewhere, devour what belongs to you', and so forth to

the end. This sudden outburst is (as Kirchhoff said) neither poetically nor psychologically prepared and justified. To use moderate terms: the notion that a great poet consciously planned the beginning of his poem in this way is not one which would readily suggest itself to an unprejudiced mind. It must be added that there is no possibility of merely omitting the offensive lines (374–80): μῦθον in 373 requires some definition, such as that given in the sequel; and the reply of Antinous (384–5) presupposes some very bold statement, which is not to be found unless 374–5 are retained (Kirchhoff 257). Finally, it is to be noticed that there is a serious fault in the phraseology at the very point where Telemachus begins this surprising anticipation of tomorrow's business: contrast 2. 139 ἔξιτέ μοι μεγάρων ἄλλας δ' ἀλεγύνετε δαῖτας with ἐξιέναι μεγάρων ἄλλας δ' ἀλεγύνετε δαῖτας here; the change from the infinitive ἐξιέναι (governed by μῦθον ἀποείπω) to the imperative is very abrupt, and the imperative itself is out of place, since Telemachus is here offering what he will be saying tomorrow, not what he has to say today. The case could hardly be plainer, that 1. 374 ff. was composed after (and on the model of) 2. 139 ff.; and since the offensive lines are not a mere addition (being irremovable from the context as it stands), it follows that they are substituted for something else, just as 272–8 must have been substituted for something else (see p. 81). The reason for the substitution was presumably the same in both places (see p. 72). Kirchhoff 256–7: it is a remarkable confirmation of his position, that two passages of the Second Book should bear such obvious signs of transference backwards into the First (2. 196–7 ∼ 1. 277–8; 2. 139 ff. ∼ 1. 374 ff.).

6. For what follows I am much indebted to F. Klingner, op. cit. 27 ff.

7. Relics of this version survive in 2. 255–6, the sinister prediction of Leiocritus, and in 2. 301–2, the exceptional affability of Antinous, neither of which has any meaning or motive except within the framework of a plot by the Suitors to obstruct the journey.

8. It is very important to recognize that we are wholly ignorant of the manner in which the Homeric poems were recited before the sixth century B.C. Here are some of the questions to which we do not know (and presumably never shall know) the answers:

(1) On what occasions, and before what audiences, were the Epics most commonly recited?

(2) Was there ever a recitation of continuous Epics, of the length of the *Iliad* and *Odyssey*, at particular festivals, extending over several days, before the sixth century? There is no evidence either for or against; to Professor Wade-Gery (*Poet of the Iliad* 2 ff.) it is sufficient to reply that in none of the passages on which he depends (*Il.* 2. 460 ff., 20. 403 ff.; *Od.* 6. 162 ff.) is there any hint of poetry-recital—in the first two there is not even a suggestion of a general assembly of any sort.

(3) When an early Epic poet composed (if anyone ever did) an Epic of the length of *Il.* or *Od.*, knowing (as he must have done) that it would never be recited from start to finish without interruption, did he so design it that it would be specially suitable for interrupted recitation? The technique of composition might be very much affected even if 'interruption' means no more than extension over a period of several days.

(4) Which was the commoner practice: the recitation of episodes from *Il.* and *Od.*, or the continuous recitation of the poems over a period of days? Or were both alike common? Observe that although it is true (as is commonly stated) that the *Iliad* does not fall easily apart into a succession of separate lays, it is still more obviously true that numerous episodes in the *Iliad* are exceedingly well suited to separate recitation.

(5) If it was a common practice to recite poems of this length over a period of

days, how long would each daily recitation last, and how would the poems be divided for the purpose? Or was there perhaps no common standard either for the length of time or for the division? (It is generally held that the present division into *Books* goes back no earlier than Zenodotus: I share Mazon's doubts about this; see *Introd. à l'Iliade*, 139 ff.)

The judicious reader may comment that if the answers to such fundamental questions are wholly unknown, it is very improbable that we shall ever arrive at a well-founded understanding of the development of the Homeric poems. I am inclined to agree; and I am sure that it is most important to refrain from making up the gap in our knowledge by firmly upholding one hypothesis where others would serve as well. In particular we must absolutely reject the idea that any useful purpose is served by the assumption that the Homeric poems were designed for recitation at general assemblies or festivals before the sixth century. The case is perfectly stated by Gilbert Murray (in *The Rise of the Greek Epic* 187) as follows: 'Every work of art that was ever created was intended in some way to be used. No picture was painted for blind men; no ship built where there was no water. What was to be the use of the *Iliad*? What audience would listen to the recitation of such a poem? It contains over fifteen thousand verses. It would occupy twenty to twenty-four hours of steady declamation. No audience could endure it, no bard could perform it, in one stretch. From Lachmann onward innumerable scholars have tried to break it up into separate recitations, and have all failed. It is all one— at least, as far as its composers could make it so. . . . The *Iliad* has been deliberately elaborated on a plan which puts it out of use for ordinary purposes of recitation. Yet recited it must certainly have been.' Now mark what follows (310): 'The two facts given us are: first, that the *Iliad* is a poem originally meant for recitation; second, that it does not fall into separate lays and that the whole would take some twenty-four hours to recite. Conclusion: the poem must be intended for some extraordinary occasion, demanding even greater enthusiasm and powers of endurance than the annual celebrations of tragedy at the Dionysia.' How unexpected, and (I venture to say) how improbable, is this *conclusion*! The logical conclusion, on the facts as stated, is simply this: *that the poem was intended for recitation spread over several days.* I am quite unable to understand why we must take a further step and postulate *an extraordinary occasion.* Why must we suppose the reciter incapable of doing at the court of a king or in the market-place of a city what he was capable of doing at an assembly at Delos or Mycale? Professor Wade-Gery (op. cit. 14) says that 'The *Iliad* is . . . no performance in the hall of a King or nobleman': why not? He himself tells us (n. 39) that 'Norwegian Kings listened to long sagas night after night, so that length and continuity were no bar to palace performance': why then does he say that the *Iliad* '*presupposes* [my italics] an audience gathered from many cities, a "panegyris"'? I cannot discover how or why it should *presuppose* anything of the sort. Since we have no knowledge whatever of the circumstances, we have not the slightest justification for excluding the likelihood of recitation in the market-place at Chios (or anywhere else) or at the court of Penthilus (or anyone else). Moreover, does anyone seriously suggest that, if the poems *were* recited at festivals, those were the *only*, or even the *normal*, occasions for their recitation? Were the *Iliad* and *Odyssey*, for several generations, heard only by limited numbers of persons at a few places on rare occasions? Obviously not so: recitation at festivals (if it ever occurred) cannot have been the only or even the normal mode of publication of the Greek Epic. For the norm, we have no choice (at least, I can think of none) but to look to the court or the market-place or both: but what then is the use of dragging in the abnormal, a *recitation at festivals* for which there is no foundation in evidence earlier than the Panathenaea in the sixth century?

9. The passages were collected and discussed by Cobet, *Misc. Crit.* 239 ff.; see

also Cauer, *Grundfragen* 333 ff., and Ameis-Hentze, ad loc. I take it as certain (*a*) that in *Od.* 2. 53 ἐεδνώσαιτο θύγατρα means '(the father) may furnish his daughter with a dowry', and in 2. 196 (= 1. 277) οἱ δὲ γάμον τεύξουσι καὶ ἀρτυνέουσιν ἔεδνα means '(the parents) shall make her marriage and prepare a dowry'; (*b*) that these are the only places in the Homeric poems where the dowry-custom is referred to (in *Il.* 13. 382 ἐεδνωταί means 'those who receive the ἔεδνα'; Schol. A, ad loc., Cobet 244 f., Cauer 333 f.; in effect 'matchmakers', as Leaf said).

10. For what follows I am much indebted to U. Hölscher, op. cit.; I found this part of his work important and convincing, though there is much in the remainder that is exposed to objection.

11. See H. Fraenkel, *Die Zeitauffassung in der archaischen griechischen Literatur, 4. Kongress für Ästhetik*, 97 ff.; Hölscher, op. cit. 2 ff.; and especially T. Zielinski, *Die Behandlung gleichzeitiger Ereignisse im antiken Epos*, Teil I, *Philol.* suppl. viii (1899–1901) 407 ff.

My text here is very much simplified, but not (so far as I can tell) misleading on the essential point. That the study of the treatment of parallel or simultaneous events in the Epic is, in its detail, a very complex affair (especially in the *Iliad*) may be learnt from Zielinski's elaborate essay. The most important point for my present purpose is the one summarily stated in the text—that on those occasions when it is necessary to narrate the action of two (or more) events which really occurred simultaneously, the Epic invariably represents them as if they had really occurred successively.

Among the complications of the topic I select for brief mention the following: (*a*) The general rule is not broken by the poet's practice of allowing *one of his speakers* to narrate past events, unconnected with the present action (Nestor; *Il.* 1. 365 ff.; 2. 303 ff.; 6. 152 ff.; 9. 447 ff.), or to recapitulate events within the poem (e.g. 2. 56 ff.). It is a remarkable extension of this practice, that a great part of the poem itself should take the form of a narrative of past events by a speaker therein (Odysseus in *Od.* v–xv). (*b*) As a rule, when two (or more) scenes are running parallel, and we move from scene A to scene B (as so often in the *Iliad*), we are left to assume that nothing in particular (or nothing more than we were led to believe at the moment when we left the scene) is happening in scene A while the events of scene B are being narrated (and vice versa); occasionally, however, the action in scene A (the one which is *not* being described) must be supposed to have progressed in the meantime while the action of scene B was being described (Zielinski's *zweiter Fall*, exemplified in the *Iliad* 4. 127–221, the Κόλος Μάχη, 8. 349–485, al.; not in the *Odyssey*). (*c*) Very complicated problems are set by the twelve-day intervals in the *Iliad* 1. 493 = 24. 31; Zielinski 437 ff.

12. See Zielinski, op. cit. 433 ff.

13. Hölscher (34) would have us believe that the suspense-motif occurs here too; all he can do is to allege that their going to sleep here prepares our minds for their getting up at the beginning of Book XVI!

14. My treatment of this matter (in many respects closely in agreement with Hölscher, op. cit.) represents an approach entirely different from that of Kirchhoff, whose treatment of the relation of XV init. to IV fin. is a very important part of his case for a separate Telemachy. He begins with the following observation: At the beginning of the *Odyssey* Athene demanded that Hermes should be sent as quickly as possible, τάχιστα, with an order for the release of Odysseus. But now the Journey of Telemachus intervenes: Odysseus must therefore wait a whole week for his release. Moreover, Telemachus expressly declared (4. 598) that he had no time to lose at Sparta, and must return home without delay: but since there now intervene the nine Books describing Odysseus' Adventures and Return, Telemachus must in fact remain a whole month with Menelaus in Sparta, without any apparent reason,

and without any attempt by the poet to give a motive for this delay. *Das sind Monstrositäten*, says Kirchhoff; those are monstrosities, which exclude the possibility that we may be reading a coherent narrative in its original form.

I suggest that this judgement was passed without sufficient regard for the limitations necessarily imposed upon a poet who wished to narrate simultaneous events. It was, as I have said, the practice of the Epic poets to represent such events as if they actually occurred in succession. It may be thought that this technique is naïve in itself and ill-adapted to the structure of such a poem as our *Odyssey*: here its first result is that Odysseus must wait a week for an order which was to be given with all speed. It is perhaps futile to argue about such matters: Athene said, *with all speed*; the convention for handling simultaneous events does not allow the action to follow *with all speed*—Odysseus must wait for a few days; nor does it allow any explanation or excuse to be made. I am on the side of those who find this to be not a monstrosity but a triviality; and I add that the Epic convention for handling simultaneous events, denying as it does their simultaneity, and disregarding as it does the time-relation between different series of events, renders all such criticism unstable or even wholly irrelevant.

The second result is that Telemachus must stay in Sparta for three or four weeks, although he has no reason for doing so and although he protests that he is in a great hurry. This is a more serious matter, principally because it puts a much greater strain on the technique of successive narration of simultaneous events. It is necessary at once to consider the next stage in Kirchhoff's argument.

He makes the remarkable suggestion that the narratives in the Fourth Book and the Fifteenth were once continuous; and that they have been separated and rearranged (with considerable modification) by an editor who wished to combine the Journey of Telemachus with the Adventures of Odysseus.

The facts deserve close attention. In the Fourth Book Menelaus (in the early morning) invites Telemachus to stay at Sparta for a week or two, and promises gifts, a chariot with three horses, and a fine chalice. Telemachus declines* the invitation to stay and refuses the horses because Ithaca has no plains or pasturage for them. So Menelaus promises another gift instead, a gold and silver mixing-bowl made by Hephaestus. There the narrative in the Fourth Book ends. In the Fifteenth Book, where the thread is resumed, Telemachus (also in the early morning) says that he must go home at once, and Menelaus continues the action at the point where he had left off a month or so before: he orders food to be prepared, and goes to fetch the mixing-bowl and chalice which he had promised; Telemachus receives the gifts, Peisistratus packs them, there is eating and drinking and leave-taking, and the guests depart.

The whole of this, says Kirchhoff, is the description of the events of a single day; there can be no question of a month's interval interrupting the sequence; the events of the Fourth Book clearly presuppose, as their immediate sequel, the events of the Fifteenth; the original unity of the narrative has been broken by an editor in order to frame within it the long story of Odysseus' adventures.

It would, I think, be wrong to deny that Kirchhoff's observation here is shrewd and just; and equally wrong to suppose that the inference which he draws from it is the only one possible or even the likeliest one available. We have no reason to believe that the Greek Epic poets were, in general, much concerned with chronological exactitudes, especially in the narration of simultaneous events. But the present example is an extreme one: the story of Odysseus' Adventures has filled a

* Focke (*Odyssee* 1–8) attempts to show that he does *not* decline the invitation. His argument seems to me to depend on too exact a scrutiny of the text, and too subtle an interpretation of it. Even with his observations freshly in mind I find it hard to read the passage in the sense which he desires.

large space and a long time; if it is now desired to bring Telemachus home from Sparta at the end of this enormous digression, then it might well occur to the poet that, without any breach of custom, he should create in the mind of the listener the illusion that there had been no unnecessary delay at Sparta. And this might easily be achieved by starting the narrative in the Fifteenth Book at a point which makes it *appear* to be *almost* continuous with that of the Fourth Book. Granted that the delay was long: its length could not be more artfully concealed. The resumed narrative *suggests* (as Kirchhoff demonstrated) that a very short time has passed: that suggestion is deceptive; but the ancient listener was not likely to detect an artifice which escapes the notice of most modern readers. And yet the poet has strictly observed the rule that he must not take a step backwards in time, and must not make any apology for narrating simultaneous events as if they were successive.

If this explanation is correct, there is no longer any reason to complain that Telemachus expressly said that he was in a hurry, and that no motive was given for his delay. The delay is imposed by the structure of the story: to draw attention to it, by stating and explaining it, is exactly the reverse of the poet's intention; he wishes to create the illusion that Telemachus was in a hurry, and he admits nothing that might directly suggest that a lengthy interval occurred. It is thus open to us to interpret the detail of the resumption of the story in the Fifteenth Book as a deliberate and successful device to overcome a difficulty which arose out of the limitations necessarily imposed upon a story of this structure; we are not justified in continuing to use this evidence in favour of the general theory that the Journey of Telemachus has been artificially inserted into the *Odyssey*. Further argument against Kirchhoff on these points will be found in Hölscher, op. cit. 27 ff.

There is, as usual, much subsidiary pleading, of which the following account gives only a selection, mainly from Kirchhoff 502 ff., and Wilamowitz, *HU* 98 f.

(1) 13. 440: Athene leaves Ithaca for Sparta: Book XIV intervenes before her arrival is reported (15. 1 ff.): 'It is improper', says Kirchhoff, 'to make the goddess require so long a time for her journey.' This is another example of Kirchhoff's misapprehension of the Epic rule for handling simultaneous events.

(2) 16. 23 ff.: When Telemachus arrives in Ithaca, Eumaeus greets him in his hut with the following words: 'I thought I should never see you again when you sailed for Pylos. Come in, and let me enjoy the sight of you, now that you are just come from abroad. *You do not often visit the countryside and herdsmen, but stay in the town.*' According to Kirchhoff, the earlier story told that Telemachus came to Eumaeus *from the palace in the city* (see also Von der Mühll 740, Focke 282, Merkelbach 69), not on his way home from Sparta; the italic words are suitable to that story, but unnatural in an address to one who has just come, not from the town but from a journey overseas.

The acuteness of Kirchhoff's observation is (as usual) remarkable, but the inference here is drawn from a preconceived theory. If, as Eumaeus says, Telemachus was seldom seen in the country, it is all the more surprising that he should call there so soon after his return from abroad; his comment is not at all out of place.

(3) 15. 155 f.: Telemachus promises to convey greetings from Menelaus to Nestor on his way home: but when he reaches Pylos (15. 195) he decides that he cannot afford the time, and continues his journey without a second visit to Nestor; his comrade, Nestor's son Peisistratus, of course remains in Pylos. Kirchhoff, Wilamowitz, Bethe, and others are very much offended by this 'broken promise': I am not of their opinion, particularly since there need be no 'broken promise'— Peisistratus is presumably capable of conveying the simple and formal message of greetings to his father (if we really must follow the narrative so consequentially into all its byways).

(4) 15. 44–47: More than one charge is made here. First, it is thought very objectionable that Telemachus should wake up his comrade Peisistratus λὰξ ποδὶ κινήσας, *with a kick*. The ancient critics observed that the same action and expression recur in the *Doloneia*, where Nestor thus arouses Diomedes; and they pardoned Nestor on the comical ground that the old man could not be expected to stoop down and shake the sleeper with his hand. Secondly, the tale of Telemachus' bad manners is continued: he proposes to depart without leave-taking, and does not even condescend to explain to his comrade why they must depart 'thus out of season, threading dark-eyed night'. To the first point I reply that Telemachus has just as much right, perhaps more, to arouse his young friend with a kick as Nestor had to apply the same treatment to the magnificent Diomedes; in both cases, the kicker is portrayed as being specially impatient for action, and it is for us to observe what they do, not to dictate to them what they ought to do. The second is very weak: there might be something to complain about, if Telemachus did depart in the middle of the night without taking leave of his royal host; but in fact the proposal, having served its purpose of showing Telemachus to be impatient and anxious, is instantly rejected by his friend, and all proceeds according to strictest etiquette.

(5) The speech of Athene, 15. 10–42, has been severely criticized. It is not to be denied that there are imperfections, but most of them may at least as plausibly be ascribed to the distortion of a basic text by rhapsodes over a long period of time. The end of 15. 23, οὐδὲ μεταλλᾷ, is weak. The repetition of 15. 38–39 from 13. 404–5 overlooks the fact that ὁμῶς, which made sense there, makes none here. There is something to be said for the opinion of the ancients that 15. 24–26 were a later (and unworthy) addition to the text. A few other points could be (and have been) made. More important is Kirchhoff's comment (repeated by Wilamowitz) on 15. 15 ff.: Athene bids Telemachus make haste, or he may be too late, for her father and brothers are commanding Penelope to marry Eurymachus, and she may carry away from home some property against Telemachus' will. These, says Kirchhoff, are things which she knows not to correspond to the truth; 'aimless lies', in the phraseology of Wilamowitz. 'Aimless' they are certainly not, for they serve to expedite Telemachus' departure. And if they do not correspond to the truth, they do correspond to what Telemachus expects and fears; and I do not know what further justification they need. It is not as if Athene were free to tell the truth—that Odysseus is waiting in Eumaeus' hut, and that the story cannot progress until Telemachus arrives. The poet has (or may have) planned a different way of describing Telemachus' first awareness of his father's return.

(6) I must not omit to mention the objection taken to 15. 7–9: Telemachus is awake, not dreaming, and it is very remarkable that Athene should appear to a waking mortal in her own shape. See Cauer, *Grundfragen* 397.

(7) There have probably been a number of more or less isolated interpolations: 15. 78–85, athetized by Aristarchus, lines which many have thought (and I agree) rather silly in this context. 15. 113–19 = 4. 613 ff., omitted by P²⁸ and other manuscript sources, probably rightly. See also Bethe 20, on 15. 160 ff.

15. On 4. 621–4 see Wolf, *Prolegomena* cxxxi f.; Spohn, *De extrema parte Odysseae* 9; Hennings, *Ueber die Telemachie* 212 f.

Those who believe the 'Telemachy' to represent an independent poem must, and do, attribute the remainder of Book IV (from 625) to their 'Bearbeiter'. Among its peculiar features are (i) 640: the casual reference to the συβώτης; presumably Eumaeus, though we have not yet heard of him. (ii) 735: the reference to Dolios as a friend of the family, though elsewhere (except in the last Book, which was added later) he is known only as the father of enemies of the family. (iii) 770: this is surely a silly inference from her ὀλολυγή. (iv) There are some obvious faults in the expression, especially at 740, where οἵ is unintelligible; at 758, εὔνησε γόον σχέθε δ' ὅσσε γόοιο: at 831, where θεοῖό τε ἔκλυες αὐδήν is nonsense (should be ἔκλυον). (v) Linguistic peculiarities are perhaps a little more thickly congregated than usual: the rare short dative in -οις within the line occurs at 683 and 755; the optative in -οίη (692) has only one parallel in the Homeric poems (9. 320; Wackernagel, *Spr. Unters.* 14); on ἀπαγγείλησι (775) see Wackernagel, ibid. 144; the gen. plur. πατρῶν (687) recurs in 8. 245. The word (φρένες) ἀμφιμέλαιναι (661) does not recur in *Od.*, nor does the phrase (841) νυκτὸς ἀμολγῷ; the adj. ἀμαυρόν (824, 835) does not recur in *Il.* or *Od.*

This sort of evidence proves nothing about authorship or time of composition; though of course it might be used in confirmation of a theory, if only that theory is first firmly based on evidence of a different kind.

16. She does so in very conventional verses: *Od.* 5. 1–2 = *Il.* 11. 1–2; *Od.* 5. 3 = partly *Il.* 4. 1, 7. 443, partly *Il.* 13. 689, 18. 494; *Od.* 5. 4 = *Il.* 14. 54, al., +2. 118, al.; *Od.* 5. 7 = 8. 306, 12. 371, 377. But, granted that this scene was to be portrayed, the lines are apt to the context; there is therefore no fault to be found on this score.

17. *Od.* 5. 8–12 = 2. 230–4; 5. 14–17 = 4. 557–60; 5. 18–20 = 4. 700–2. Reinhardt's interpretation of these repetitions as deliberate *Rückverweisungen* (*Von Werken und Formen* 38) seems to me to reach the extreme of special pleading. *Od.* 5. 13 = *Il.* 2. 721: as the Scholia say, κρατέρ' ἄλγεα πάσχων is suitable there, but not here (νῦν δὲ ἔδει τετιημένος ἦτορ εἶναι).

18. See C. E. Schmidt, *Parallel-Homer*, p. viii: he reckons 1,804 lines wholly repeated, their occurrences amounting altogether to 4,730 lines, about one-sixth of *Il.* and *Od.*; including repetitions slightly modified, his figures are 2,118 lines, with 5,612 occurrences. Adding lines repeated not as a whole but separately in both halves (or lesser divisions), the figures amount to 9,253 repetitions, about one-third of the whole of *Il.* and *Od.*

19. This second Divine Assembly has long been a thorn in the flesh of the strict Unitarian. Only Reinhardt, who finds no problem anywhere, finds none here; his comment (which reads as though frivolous, but may have been seriously intended) on the scene is gently and properly condemned by Lesky, *Homerforschung in der Gegenwart* 66. Zielinski, op. cit. 444, says that the technique in 5. 1 ff. is 'wholly analogous' to that in *Il.* 15. 56 f. ~ 220 f. That it is 'wholly analogous' is patently untrue; that there is any resemblance at all is not evident to me.

20. It is disputable how far this new preface extends. I find no good reason to deny that we are in good company again from 5. 50 onwards. Of the intervening lines (21–49), 44–49 are much better adapted to the situation in *Il.* 24. 340–5, where they recur; and Kirchhoff's argument against 32–40 deserves consideration —the main point is that Zeus here foretells things which are soon to be represented as arising from causes for which Zeus makes, and perhaps could make, no allowance: things which are not within his will and purpose, being partly unpremeditated and fortuitous, partly caused by the intervention of Poseidon, of which Zeus here makes no reckoning. The observation is just, but may well be thought to fall short of proof that the lines in question were added later by a composer ignorant of the normal technique.

21. The primary source of trouble is 269–78. 279–92 are free from difficulty so long as they are not combined with the nonsense which precedes and follows; they may well be a relic of that address which must always have stood in this place within the framework of the First Book, and which must always have given the command to go to Pylos and Sparta. Of the second difficult passage, 293–302, no clear account has been given. Its addition here is not obviously related to the cause which led to the substitution of 272–8 for something else; and nothing connects the two passages except the very curious fact that both take the liberty (never repeated, so far as I know, in Greek literature) of using the verb ἐμπάζομαι without a negative.

IV

THE MIDDLE OF THE *ODYSSEY*

THE Wanderings of Odysseus are over. He and his son are home again, in Ithaca. Somehow they must overthrow the Suitors of Penelope, who are numerous and powerful: that is to be the subject of the remainder of the poem.

Let us reconsider for a moment what it is that we are trying to do. Here is a poem, over twelve thousand lines in length, emerging ready-made from the darkness which goes before the dawn of European history. Twenty-five hundred years have passed since then; and it is questionable whether the art of poetry has often attained an equal height of excellence. We should naturally like to know who composed the *Odyssey*: and we recognize from the start that we do not even know whether this word, 'who', should be singular or plural. That question has long been debated, whether the *Odyssey* is the work of a single author or not. It is a problem of many aspects; and I have confined these lectures to that one which I believe to yield the most certain results—the study of the *structure* of the story. If we are disposed to be guided by factual evidence, by observations made directly from the text of the poem itself, we quickly discover that the whole of the Visit to the Underworld was inserted, as a kind of afterthought, into its present place in the poem; and that the story about Odysseus which it presupposes is very different from that which is told in the rest of our *Odyssey*. We have further observed that the beginnings of the first two episodes, the Journey of Telemachus and the Wanderings of Odysseus, fall far below the level of their surroundings, and afford objective evidence which would be very hard to reconcile with a theory that these parts of the poem were planned and executed in their present form by a single poet of high quality. Let us now proceed to consider the next part of the poem which, when we come to it and read it with impartial eyes, forces upon our attention certain facts which have an obvious bearing on the question of unity of authorship. I refer to a region in, or a little beyond, the middle of the poem, in which we begin the story of the destruction of the Suitors of Penelope. Some careful preparation is made for this; but the more we have admired the story-teller's art so far, the more bewildered we shall be. For surely there are questions to be asked, if the poet chooses to tell us how certain things will be, if he raises in us definite expectations and makes definite statements of fact, and then proceeds to tell us a tale at variance with such promises. Let him start without stating the detail of his plan; let him leave much to the understanding; and we are more than content. But what if he attracts our attention at this time to a number of expectations, not one of which is to be fulfilled? Here are three facts which, if our minds are not closed to criticism, we may reasonably judge to be in need of explanation:

1. The poet now introduces, with quite extraordinary elaboration, a new character in his story, for whom he will hereafter find (to his manifest embarrassment) no useful employment.

2. He tells us here, at the beginning, that Odysseus was transformed by the magic wand of Athene into a form and appearance other than his own; he is physically so altered that nobody could possibly recognize him until he is changed back, by means of the magic wand, into his natural shape. But hereafter the poet will require us consistently to suppose that no such transformation ever took place.

3. In the Sixteenth Book Odysseus describes in detail his plan of action against the Suitors: but the action which follows takes no account whatever of the greater part—perhaps of any part—of what is so carefully prepared on this occasion.

The role of Theoclymenus[1]

Telemachus, about to return home by sea from the coast near Pylos, offers sacrifice to Athene beside his ship; and there he is approached by a person whom the poet distinguishes with an introduction of thirty-two lines (15. 223 ff.), by far the longest and most elaborate preparation of its kind in the *Odyssey*. This person, whose name is Theoclymenus, is in flight from Argos, having killed a man; he is a diviner by profession, of the prophetic family of Melampus. We listen to the story of Melampus and a long genealogy; both assume that we know much more than is stated here.

It is natural to presume that a person whose introduction is so long and loudly trumpeted will say or do something of some importance, either now or hereafter; but the truth turns out to be the reverse. His part is very small, and wonderfully unimportant. The very first words he utters are offensive to the custom of the Greek Epic: he is in flight, pursued by the kindred of the man he killed, and he throws himself upon the mercy of Telemachus: 'O friend,' he begins, 'since I come upon you sacrificing in this place, I implore you by your burnt offerings[2] and by the god you worship,[3] and then again by your own head and by your companions', tell me the truth without concealment.' Now what is this truth that 'roars so loud and thunders in the index'? Is it 'Save my life', perhaps, or 'protect me from my enemies'? No: τίς πόθεν εἰς ἀνδρῶν, πόθι τοι πόλις ἠδὲ τοκῆες, 'what is your name, and where is your home?' Great is the descent from the moderately sublime;[4] all the more offensive, since ancient custom would frown upon a suppliant who began his prayer by asking the name and address of his protector; it is for Telemachus to ask Theoclymenus, not vice versa.

Arrived at Ithaca, Theoclymenus inquires what roof shall shelter him. Telemachus regrets that he cannot invite him to the palace, since he himself will not be there, and his mother (he says) spends most of her time upstairs. But let Theoclymenus take comfort: 'I will tell you of another man to whom you may go—*Eurymachus, whom the Ithacans look upon as a god; he is a prince among men, and the most eager to marry my mother and to rule in my father's place.*'

Now what (if anything) is the meaning of these words? You cannot stay with me, says Telemachus to his new friend, but I can strongly recommend the hospitality of my most dangerous enemy; not that you will often find him at his home—he spends his time in my palace, being easily the foremost competitor for my mother's hand and for the place that is my father's.

There follows at once an omen: a hawk was observed holding a dove in its talons, plucking it and shedding its feathers to the ground, midway between Telemachus and his ship. Theoclymenus accepts the challenge to his professional skill, and interprets the omen as follows (first calling Telemachus to stand apart from his companions, nobody knows why). 'Telemachus, not without divine agency came the bird on our right; I knew, when I looked full upon it, that it was a bird of omen' (so far, it needed no prophet come from Argos to tell us this). Now the interpretation: 'Among the people of Ithaca there is no race more kingly than yours, but you are supreme forever.' That is not the work of a man who has gone far in his profession; he might, without excessive intellectual effort, have interpreted the killing of a dove by a hawk as symbolizing the killing of the Suitors by Odysseus. That is presumably what the hawk in fact intended: away it flies, disgusted by this drab *non sequitur*.

Telemachus replies: 'I wish this word might be fulfilled; you would then find me grateful, and I would make you rich.' Turning to a companion named Peiraeus, he continues: 'Peiraeus, you are the most obedient of all who accompanied me to Pylos: please take my friend and entertain him honourably in your house until I come.' And so it is done, and Theoclymenus is the guest of Peiraeus thereafter (17. 55; 20. 372).

There is no need to dwell on this. One moment Telemachus proposes that his friend shall stay with his arch-enemy Eurymachus; the next moment, without another word about that fantastic proposal, he commits him to the hospitality of his most loyal companion, Peiraeus. What the poet had in mind is beyond our comprehension: 'his words are like spilt water; the thought that he had in him remains conjectural to this day.'[5]

The next appearance of Theoclymenus is in the Seventeenth Book. Penelope asks Telemachus, seeing him for the first time since his return from Sparta, to tell her how he met Odysseus.[6] Telemachus replies that he cannot possibly stop to answer now; he must first go to the market-place and fetch Theoclymenus. Why, we learn neither now nor later. He goes, and after more important transactions, fetches Theoclymenus. Then at last he tells Penelope the story of his travels; and, when he has finished, the modern text offers us a speech by Theoclymenus: he assures Penelope that Odysseus is in Ithaca, 'either sitting or moving' (an absurd expression), plotting death and doom for the Suitors. Such, he asserts, was the omen which he saw on board ship and declared to Telemachus. It is fair comment that he did not see it 'on board ship', and that the interpretation which he offers to Penelope is quite different from what he 'declared to Telemachus'. But it is not worth while to pursue this unhappy man further at this point, for the ancient critics inform us that the whole of Theoclymenus' speech was, in their opinion, a later addition to the text;[7] and here, as so often elsewhere, we find good reason to accept their verdict. No doubt the interpolator thought that, if Theoclymenus is brought to the palace with so much ado, he must say something, however false and foolish; and there is a long time to wait before he speaks again. His next and last appearance is in the Twentieth Book; it is brief but memorable, some compensation for the dismal past:

'Thus spoke Telemachus: but among the Suitors Pallas Athene aroused laughter unquenchable, and turned their wits astray; and at once they were laughing with unnatural lips. Defiled with blood were the meats they ate; and their eyes filled with tears, and their hearts foreboded lamentation. Then godlike Theoclymenus spoke among them: "Unhappy men, what evil is amiss with you? In darkness your heads are shrouded, and your faces, and your knees below. A sound of mourning rises like a flame, and your cheeks are wet with tears. Blood lies spattered on the walls and the fine rafters; full of phantoms is the doorway, and full the courtyard, rushing down to darkness, the road to Erebus. And the sun has perished out of heaven, and a foul mist is spread above." So he spoke; but they all laughed at him.' (20. 345 ff.) After this impressive exhibition of 'second-sight' (a faculty wholly unfamiliar to Homeric persons) Theoclymenus goes back to his lodging and disappears from our sight for ever.

Such are the facts about Theoclymenus in the *Odyssey*. He is introduced at great length and with much ado; thereafter the part he plays is very small and confused until the end, when he sees and describes a vision of doom impending on the Suitors.

It is quite clear that there was once a much fuller story about him; and it is highly probable that the connexion of that story with the story of Odysseus was once much closer and stronger than it is in our *Odyssey*. But the facts are so few and shapeless that they could be forced to fit a variety of patterns. There are two principal clues: they may be misleading, if indeed they lead anywhere, but they are worth a moment's attention in default of any better guide.

1. It is tenable that nobody would be so foolish as to make Telemachus propose that his friend should be the guest of his arch-enemy, the ringleader of the Suitors, unless he knew a version of the story in which the fact was so. Telemachus sent Theoclymenus to stay with Peiraeus only for the time being, 'until I come', εἰς ὅ κεν ἔλθω (15. 543=17. 56); then perhaps he put him in the charge of his enemy Eurymachus. It is easy enough to imagine a good reason for such a proposal: but I say no more about it, since it is vain for us to speculate about the nature of that which has left no traces.

2. I draw attention especially to the incompleteness of the action at the beginning of the Seventeenth Book. Here is the first meeting of Penelope with Telemachus after his return from abroad: yet Telemachus instantly refuses to reply to her question, what he has to tell of Odysseus. He bids her take a bath, and put on clean clothes, and make sacrifice to Zeus—for what purpose? And he adds that he must be off to the market-place to fetch Theoclymenus—again, for what purpose? He fetches him; and when they have bathed and dressed and eaten and drunk, at last Penelope may hear the story of his travels. But why must Penelope bathe and put on clean clothes before meeting this shabby outlaw Theoclymenus; and why was it necessary to make such ado about fetching Theoclymenus before speaking to Penelope? What is Theoclymenus going to do when he arrives? According to the true text, he preserves the stoniest of silences; according to our interpolated text, he does nothing but give, very briefly, an inaccurate reminiscence of an omen already known to us. For the

second time in the history of Theoclymenus elaborate introduction leads to nothing whatever. Obviously he did something of importance, if the story were known: we can say no more than that, in some other version of the story, his presence was indispensable, particularly at the moment when Telemachus gave Penelope an account of his travels; if, in that version, Theoclymenus were Odysseus himself in disguise, much that is now obscure would be instantly clear as day, but much too would remain inscrutable.

The transformation of Odysseus[8]

In the second half of the *Odyssey* the hero returns home unrecognized after many years; he overthrows his enemies; and proves to his faithful wife that he is indeed Odysseus. Of course there must be some reason why he is not recognized as soon as he arrives in his kingdom; and the answer given or implied by universal folk-lore is simple and sufficient—the hero is said to be disguised, or so altered by time and sufferings that he not only escapes recognition but even has to prove, in the end, by means of tokens and trials, that he is what he claims to be.[9]

This is not an incidental detail, but a matter on which the credibility of the narrative depends; and the great poet of the Greek Epic has no advantage in this respect over the nameless story-teller of folk-lore. He must either tell us why Odysseus passes unrecognized or, if he prefers, leave us to assume that some disguise, or the mere passage of years, has altered him enough.

Now the facts may be simply stated as follows. In the Thirteenth Book (429 ff.) Odysseus is transformed by supernatural means into the shape of an entirely different person. We are not allowed to guess, or to take anything for granted. The poet is eager to tell us, at the start, the answer to our question. So soon as Odysseus has landed on the coast of Ithaca, Athene visits him, and toward the end of their conversation she says (13. 397): *'But come, I will make you unrecognizable to all men.'* And so she does. She touched him with her wand; she withered all the flesh on his limbs, made his hair to perish from his head, and clothed his body in the skin of an old, old man; she dimmed his eyes, and dressed him in rags, all tattered and foul, grimy with soot, and cloaked him in a shabby deerskin; and she gave him a staff and a miserable pouch, full of holes, hanging from a twisted cord. In the Sixteenth Book this transformation is first undone in order that his son may recognize him, and then renewed in order that his servant may not. Thereafter it is never undone: from that moment onwards the remainder of the *Odyssey* is composed on the assumption that no such transformation ever took place. There is abundant evidence, from the end of the Sixteenth Book onwards, that Odysseus is simply altered by the passage of time and disguised by his dress.

In 18. 67, when Odysseus prepared himself for the boxing-match with the beggar Irus, *'you could see'*, the poet tells us, *'his huge thighs and broad shoulders and chest and strong arms'*: where then was the withered and wrinkled beggar, the old, old man dim of eye and bald, heavy with age, whom Athene's wand created? Athene here, it is said, 'gave growth to his limbs': but that does not mean, or imply, that she transformed him back to his proper shape; nor does anybody notice any such alteration. Odysseus here is simply Odysseus, unrecognized because the passage of years has altered him. He considers whether he should kill his opponent or be content to knock him down, and decides in favour of the latter course: for otherwise, we are told, the people might recognize him for what he really was—how could they, if he was transformed as Athene transformed him? Later his old nurse, Eurycleia, is about to bathe his feet (19. 380 ff.): 'many a long-suffering stranger', she says to him, 'has come to this house; *but never one who resembled Odysseus in shape and voice and feet as you do'*; a poor testimonial to Athene's powers of transformation. Then Penelope describes him; to her he is no dilapidated scarecrow, but just such a man as Odysseus might be (21. 334): *'this stranger is tall and well-compacted; he claims to be son of a noble father'*. A faithful servant, Philoetius, agrees (20. 194): *'truly he has the build of a lord and king'*. He is dressed like a beggar, but his form and features are those of a king among men. When he wishes to make himself known to his servants, he has only to show them a

7

scar, which they will recognize; and they need no further proof; they are not aware of anything in his physical appearance which might require explanation. When at last he is recognized by Penelope, there is no question of a transformation back to his proper shape. He may take a bath,[10] and Athene may beautify him: but the poet has left us in no doubt whatever that the man who conversed with Penelope *before* the bath was one whom she might well admit to be Odysseus, certainly not a withered, wrinkled, bald, and blear-eyed mooncalf. She did not recognize him, we hear, dressed as he was in rags (23. 95); she admits that he may very well be her husband, but he must prove it by some token or trial (107 ff.). There is not the slightest suggestion that Odysseus is at present unrecognizably transformed: on the contrary all parties, even Penelope, understand that there is no physical impediment to immediate recognition.

Thus the whole of the remainder of the *Odyssey*, from the end of the Sixteenth Book onwards, draws a clear and consistent picture:[11] Odysseus is Odysseus in disguise, altered by the passage of time. But our poet began by assuring us, with equal clarity and with much emphasis, that these things would not be so: he transformed his Odysseus, by supernatural means, into a shape which could not possibly be taken, or mistaken, for that of Odysseus; and he reminded us that this was so, when he changed Odysseus back into his proper shape for a moment in order that his son might recognize him.

In ordinary affairs of life, common sense and the law maintain that a man must be presumed to have intended the natural consequences of his own actions. If the poet had, at the time when he composed the transformation of Odysseus, any thought at all in his mind about the sequel of his own story, he cannot have been unaware of certain obvious consequences.

Since Odysseus is in fact going to be recognized by several persons in the course of the action, this transformation will give more trouble than it is worth. Athene will have to intervene twice, on each occasion, first to undo and then to renew her magic. The machinery is not of the lightest; and where it is employed, to enable Telemachus to recognize his father, it seems out of place in an otherwise realistic setting, and it does nothing to improve a scene which, it appears, has given more dissatisfaction, as a whole, than any other of comparable length and importance in the *Odyssey*. Moreover, the interest of the action is surely much better maintained if Odysseus has not this great advantage over his opponents—if the enemies (and indeed the friends) with whom he converses *might* recognize him at any moment.

We, however, are concerned at present with matters not of taste or judgement but of fact: and the fact is this, that the transformation of Odysseus is contradicted by the whole of what follows. You cannot combine recognition by means of tokens and trials with recognition by means of alteration from one shape to another. The two are mutually exclusive alternatives: and indeed our poet makes no attempt to reconcile them. He begins with an Odysseus who can only be recognized by the one means, and continues with an Odysseus who can only be recognized by the other. Let us ask the simple question: How is Penelope to recognize Odysseus? If he has been transformed, she cannot recognize him until he resumes his original shape: then of course she must recognize him at once, for there was no point in transforming him if she cannot recognize him in his proper shape. There is, then, no use whatever for tokens and tests and trials: so long as he remains transformed, she will not recognize him no matter what examinations he may pass. If, on the other hand, he is simply Odysseus, altered in appearance by time and troubles, he will need some means of proving that he is what he claims to be; he will have to undergo some trial, produce some token.

We pay the poet no compliment if we suppose him unaware of this most simple and obvious consequence of what he has done. Whatever the explanation may be, the fact is certain: first the poet transforms Odysseus, and thereafter he requires us consistently to reflect and remember, not that he has been transformed, but that he has not.

The removal of the armour[12]

16. 281–98: Odysseus and Telemachus are in the hut of the faithful swineherd Eumaeus. Neither has yet visited the palace since returning to Ithaca. Odysseus concerts with Telemachus a means of action against the Suitors. He says: 'Go tomorrow morning and mingle with the Suitors in the palace. I will come later disguised as a beggar. Do not intervene, except by protesting, if the Suitors treat me roughly.' Now there follow some definite instructions: (1) 'at a suitable moment I will give you a sign; when you see me nod my head, transfer all weapons from the main room to a store-room; (2) when the Suitors notice the change, here are some explanations which you are to give them; (3) leave behind in the main room a pair of swords, spears, and shields for our own use.'

The subject is important and the narrative is full and clear: all weapons are to be removed from the dining hall, except just sufficient for Odysseus and his son; when the Suitors observe what has been done, two plausible excuses will be given to them. It is a natural presumption that what is here promised will be later fulfilled; at least that it will not be left entirely out of sight. But whether we like to call ourselves Unitarians or Separatists, we must all admit that of the three instructions given here, two are not fulfilled, and the third, if indeed it is carried out at all, is most oddly distorted.

Most remarkable is the fact that the very natural and sensible precaution, that weapons for their own use should be left in the hall, though essential to the plan, and expressly ordered here, is totally neglected. Not that the need for it lapses or is overlooked: when the time comes, the poet makes it clear that it is a pity that nobody thought of taking this precaution. When the battle begins, attention is drawn to Odysseus' need of armour, and Telemachus must repair the omission by departing, at a moment when his presence would be useful, to fetch spears and shield and helmet from the store-room to which he had taken them. Less important in relation to the action, but not less significant as breaches of custom, are the facts (1) that the lengthy and detailed explanations prepared for the Suitors are never given, and indeed never required, for the Suitors do not notice the sudden bareness of the walls (at least until it is too late for explanations); and (2) that the circumstances in which the armour is actually removed from the hall are entirely different from those to which this pre-concerted plan was intended to apply.

Let us consider the passage at the beginning of the Nineteenth Book, where the armour is actually removed from the dining hall.

At the end of the Eighteenth Book the Suitors go to their own homes for the night. The next Book begins thus: '*Now godlike Odysseus was left behind in the hall, planning death for the Suitors with the help of Athene.*' He says to Telemachus, 'we must store all the weapons of war inside'; and he continues to repeat word for word the excuses to be given to the Suitors when they notice the change. Telemachus commands the nurse Eurycleia to keep the maidservants locked away; Athene lights the path with a golden lamp; Odysseus and Telemachus convey all weapons from the dining hall to an inner room. Telemachus goes to bed and Odysseus remains in the hall. The episode ends as it began, with the words '*Now godlike Odysseus was left behind in the hall, planning death for the Suitors with the help of Athene.*' It is proper to notice, however leniently we may judge the aberration, that it is not the practice of the Epic poets to frame an episode within identical lines or groups of lines of a non-formulary character; and this couplet does not recur elsewhere.

Now it has long been observed that although this episode presupposes the plan made in the Sixteenth Book, it does almost everything in its power to make nonsense of that plan. It frustrates one half of the purpose thereof by forgetting to leave in the dining hall a pair of weapons for the use of Odysseus and Telemachus. Those weapons, which *will* be required, are entirely overlooked; yet the lengthy explanations prepared for the Suitors, which will *not* be required, are repeated in full. Moreover, the situation here is entirely different from that which Odysseus envisaged when he first devised the plan: indeed, it is now clear that the poet is unaware, at this point, that a plan has been pre-arranged.[13] There is no place here for the signal agreed upon, νεύσω κεφαλῇ, 'I will nod my head to you': there is no question here, as formerly, of the action being performed by Telemachus, in the presence of others, as the result of a pre-concerted plan. Odysseus himself, in the absence of all other company, openly declares to Telemachus what is to be done, describes it in detail, and does it himself, assisted by Telemachus. That is certainly not what the poet intended in the Sixteenth Book; and it is his fault, not ours, if awkward questions are asked about his state of mind. He began with a clear picture, of good and appropriate design: at the first opportunity it is drastically altered, and one of its most important features is simply blotted out.[14]

The problems set by this passage, both in itself and in its relation to the Sixteenth Book, are complex[15] and perhaps insoluble. I confine myself here to a single point: the significance of the non-fulfilment of the action promised in the Sixteenth Book. The established fact, the inference to be drawn from it, and the problem created by it, remain to be stated thus:

The *fact* is that the plan described in the Sixteenth Book is not carried out in our *Odyssey*, being superseded by a very different plan. In the Sixteenth Book the poet promises, with much detail, the following version of the story. Odysseus, in the presence of other company, will choose his time and make a secret signal to Telemachus, who will thereupon remove the armour from the hall, all except two sets for his own and his father's use; and when the Suitors complain Telemachus will give them the pre-arranged excuses: 'I have stored the weapons away from the smoke, since they are no longer like those which Odysseus left behind when he went to Troy, but are all befouled, so far as the breath of fire has reached them. . . . And lest it happen that you Suitors should get drunk and start fighting and injure one another.' It may well be thought that this plan is superior in design to that which is adopted in the *Odyssey*; it must certainly be admitted that what it promises is not fulfilled.

The *inference* is that there must have existed some other poem in which the action did develop in accordance with what is promised in this plan; a poem, therefore, very different from the

Odyssey in these respects. This inference is supported in general by our other discoveries—there must have been a version (or versions) of this part of the *Odyssey* in which Odysseus was magically transformed into a different shape, and in which Theoclymenus actually performed whatever part his introduction may have been designed for. The last Book of the *Odyssey*, when we come to it, will reinforce our argument at this point; indeed it will convert what is now a high probability into an absolute certainty.

The *problem* is: how are we to account for the inclusion in our *Odyssey* of this substantial fragment (or these substantial fragments) of a different version of the slaying of the Suitors? And here we come to a full stop. It is easy to detect what has happened: it is impossible, for lack of direct evidence, to discover for certain how it happened. The part of Theoclymenus, the transformation of Odysseus, the plan for the removal of the armour, all prove beyond reasonable doubt the general conclusion that extensive and important parts of the middle of the *Odyssey* were not planned and executed in their present form by a single poet. Substantial fragments of entirely different versions of the story are here embedded in our text. The matters which we have been considering cannot be explained away as being merely incidental, of minor importance: they are cardinal points, upon which the progress of the action and the credibility of the story revolve. Whoever introduced Theoclymenus into this poem intended him to say or do much more than he says or does. Whoever transformed Odysseus into a different shape, in the Thirteenth and Sixteenth Books, intended that transformation to play its natural part in the sequel. Whoever composed the plan for the removal of the armour, in the Sixteenth Book, intended, at the time when he composed it, to carry that plan out into action. It is something, indeed much, to be certain of these facts: in this region of the poem, as elsewhere, we find that Unity of Authorship is a concept not only not suggested by the evidence but in some respects plainly contrary to it. If we try to proceed beyond the full stop, and ask how it happened, we are in a region of thought where one guess may be as good, or as bad, as another; if by chance we hit

upon the truth, we should not know that we had done so: εἰ γὰρ
καὶ τὰ μάλιστα τύχοι τετελεσμένον εἰπών, αὐτὸς ὅμως οὐκ οἶδε.

One step we may perhaps safely take. If we ask, *who* introduced
these disjointed fragments of alien versions into a more or less
coherent narrative, it is hard to imagine more than three theoretically possible answers: (1) 'Homer'; (2) The professional
reciters; (3) The person (or persons) who made the standard text
(in writing) from which our manuscripts are ultimately derived.

1. It is theoretically possible that the *Odyssey* was composed
substantially by one person, who had no clear conception of his
story, not even in broadest outline, but lapsed into incoherence
at several most important points of his narrative: a poet capable
of introducing, with elaborate preparation, a new character for
whom he will find no useful employment thereafter; and of pre-
fixing to the Slaying of the Suitors a detailed plan of which
thereafter he will take no account. Such a possibility seems absurd
to those of us who recognize in the *Odyssey* at large a supreme
master of the art of story-telling; I leave it out of account and
look further afield.

2. In the period preceding (and for long after) the fixation of
the text in writing, professional reciters knew the traditional
poems and lays by heart, one learning from another; and they
repeated them from memory, substantially as they remembered
them, but with many an addition and subtraction and considerable variety of phrase on various occasions. A reciter who was
familiar with more than one version of the story of Odysseus, for
example, the version followed in our *Odyssey*, and the version in
which the removal of the armour was carried out as forecast in
16. 281 ff., might include in his recitation of the one version
incidents and details supplied to him by his memory of the other
version. It would be easy to illustrate this encroachment of one
poem upon another with examples from the history of recited
poetry both ancient and modern: but here, in the *Odyssey*, we
do not find what we need—some good motive[16] for the interpolation, some virtue which might explain at once both why it
entered and why it stayed.

3. The third of our three candidates is the most promising. It

has already been proved in the transition from the Tenth Book to the Eleventh, and will be still more clearly proved when we reach the Continuation (pp. 101 ff. below), that the present form of the *Odyssey* owes something to what may fairly be described as a rather perfunctory and mechanical editorial activity: common sense suggests that we need look no farther for the cause of those serious faults which obtrude themselves in the middle of the poem. I do not inquire precisely how or why the first editor did what he did; for we know nothing whatever about the conditions under which he worked. We do know that the story of Odysseus circulated in divergent versions; we do know that our manuscripts presuppose a standard Athenian text made in the sixth century B.C.; we infer that some of the faults in our text are due to that first editor.

It is probable enough that his task was one of great complexity. It is not as if we had any reason to assume that there existed, earlier than the Athenian standard edition, a canonical text of the *Odyssey* in writing. We do not even know that there were *any* written texts of it before the sixth century B.C. If we are to make assumptions, let us start from the likeliest: that the first editor worked with the materials available at the time and customary at the time, i.e. the versions offered by contemporary reciters. Whatever part the practice of writing may have played in the composition of an Epic poem, its true text, at any time in the archaic era, was the spoken word, not the written word: the Greek Epic was then always developing, in speech, not static in a written form. We must imagine the first editor, the maker of our standard text, taking down what the great professional bards of his day recited to him, not copying and collating manuscripts like an Aristarchus or an Allen. Not that it would help us much to suppose that the first editor used written copies of the *Odyssey*: the texts of such copies, if indeed any existed, may have varied greatly from time to time and from place to place. Our editor, if he was acquainted with written copies, must presumably have obtained them from contemporary reciters or guilds of reciters; and we have no reason to suppose that he had any reliable means of judging the age and authority of the text represented in any particular copy; he could not possibly have known how far it might have been altered, for better or worse, in the course of the generations before him. If his task involved the recovery of a uniform continuous *Odyssey* from the discrepant versions of a dozen rhapsodes (or their written texts, if they had any), the wonder will be that his faults and failures are so few.[17]

NOTES ON CHAPTER IV

1. The principal facts have long been observed. There is a good discussion including some shrewd observations which I have not seen elsewhere, by Merkelbach, op. cit. 69 ff.

2. This use of ὑπέρ c. gen. with verbs of beseeching is rare, and not free from awkwardness in this context.

3. καὶ δαίμονος is inelegantly vague in this context.

4 See Merkelbach, op. cit. 69.

5. The standard explanation (see, for example, Blass, *Die Interpolationen &c.* 245 f.) is that Telemachus is induced to change his mind in favour of Theoclymenus because the latter has given him, in the meantime, a complimentary interpretation of an omen. I should not understand how anybody could be satisfied with such an explanation, even if it did not entirely miss the point at issue—the absurdity of committing the suppliant, for whose protection you are responsible, to the hospitality of your most dangerous enemy. The omen might (in a feeble poet) explain the *change* of intention; it cannot possibly explain the intention itself.

6. 17. 44 ὅπως ἤντησας ὀπωπῆς: not that Penelope has the least reason to suppose that he *has* seen his father.

7. For the detail see Bolling, *External Evidence &c.* 214: Aristarchus athetized 147–65 (to which three lines have been added since Aristarchus' time, probably 152 and 155–6).

8. The expositions which I have found most satisfactory are those of Kirchhoff, *Homerische Odyssee* 538 ff., and Bethe, *Homer* ii. 68 ff. (The difficulties of 13. 187 ff. should be considered in relation to this problem; there is an interesting discussion in Focke, *Odyssee* 272 ff.) Hölscher, op. cit. 79, writes: 'Von Verzauberung—und dazu gehört immer Erlösung—ist in der Odyssee nichts'—that is simply a false statement: by 'Verzauberung' here he means the magical transformation of Odysseus' body into a different and unrecognizable shape; and that is explicitly attested by the text at 13. 439 ff. (cf. 16. 172 ff., 456 ff.). When Hölscher continues (as he does forthwith, as if it were not a quite different matter), 'Nie ist Odysseus so verwandelt dass er nicht mehr Odysseus wäre', we agree; Odysseus remains, as a personality, Odysseus; it is only his physical appearance which has been transformed. The whole of this section of Hölscher's work (§ 7, 'Die Verwandlung des Odysseus') is vitiated by his refusal to look the facts of 13. 439 ff. plainly in the face. He leaves us to wonder how he would reconcile with the alleged absence of 'Verzauberung' such expressions as 'withered the skin of his limbs', 'put the skin of an aged man on all his limbs', 'destroyed the hair from his head', 'dimmed his two eyes' (13. 439 ff.); 'once more he became dark in colour, and his cheeks filled out', 'smote him with her wand and again made him an aged man' (16. 175 f.; 456 f.).

9. I have seen it stated (by Bethe, among others, op. cit. 57) that there is no exception to the rule in folk-tale versions of the story.

10. On this subject see pp. 114 f. below.

11. But 18. 355 appears to be an exception to this general statement: Eurymachus' joke about Odysseus' bald head seems to presuppose the transformation scene, 13. 431, where Athene 'destroyed the hair from his head'.

12. In addition to my usual sources see Woodhouse, *The Composition of Homer's Odyssey* (1930) 158 ff.

13. Woodhouse, op. cit. 161, puts the point very clearly: 'the impression conveyed by this passage, taken by itself, is that the plan has flashed into his mind then and there (i.e. at 19. 3), as the outcome of his silent pondering whilst waiting in the great hall'.

14. Kirchhoff argues from certain points in the phraseology that the Nineteenth Book is dependent on the Sixteenth in this matter. If so, the fact is of course consistent (in itself) with unity of authorship; the difficulties begin when the contents of the two are examined. He observes further that the intervention of 19. 1–50 makes the timing of Penelope's arrival on the scene very artificial (19. 53); and that the maidservants might have been expected to comment on the extraordinary experience of being locked up (19. 60 ff.).

15. In the sequel there are two references to the removal of the armour, both after the killing of the Suitors has begun. Odysseus kills Antinous, and then (22. 21) 'the Suitors made uproar throughout the house, when they saw the man fall; and from their seats they leapt, bestirred throughout the house, *looking on all sides toward the well-built walls; but there was no shield or mighty spear to seize*'. Here at last is surely a little comfort: two of the original instructions were neglected, but at least the third was carried out; the weapons really were removed, and the removal has here a moment of prominence. Yet the strength of Kirchhoff's attack on these lines should not be underestimated. Odysseus has shot an arrow, killing Antinous. The Suitors leap up from their seats. If now they look to the wall for weapons, they presumably do not suppose the death of Antinous to have been an accident; if they still think that Odysseus is a mere vagabond, and that he has killed one of their company with a stray shot, why do they look to the wall for weapons? If they wish to punish him, they need no special equipment: they have swords (22. 74, 79 f., 90, 98) and are both confident and capable of dealing with him, as they themselves assert even after they have observed that the weapons have been taken from the walls (22. 27 ff.). Either this looking at the wall for weapons has, in the context, no meaning whatever; or it has. And if it has, it can only signify that the Suitors at once realize that they too are in danger. But nothing is farther from their thoughts: they tell Odysseus that he will pay for his deed with his life, and the text continues, '*for they thought that he had killed the man without intending it*'. (Lines 31–33 are said by Eustathius to have been considered 'spurious' by the ancients; and it is not surprising, if some attempt was made to clarify the passage. But the point is not one of much importance at present, for these lines do nothing more than make explicit what is already clearly implied—that the Suitors have not recognized Odysseus, and therefore have no reason to believe that they are in any danger, whatever accident may have befallen their comrade.) It certainly looks as though whoever composed or inserted 23–25 in their present place was either not thinking what he was doing or had in mind a version of the story in which the Suitors did, at this point, suspect or know the identity of Odysseus.

There remains one other reference to the removal of the armour (22. 140–1): Melanthius says that he will fetch armour for the Suitors 'from the store-room; *for inside, and nowhere else, I suppose, Odysseus and his son have put the armour*'. About these lines we should admit with equal candour that there is little or no fault to be found in them, and that (on the other hand) they are not bound to their context by any tie; their removal would leave no trace. (Kirchhoff, 584 ff., attacked 22. 141 vigorously; I have not found enough substance in his arguments to be worth repeating here. There is, however, considerable force in his observation—typically acute—that 22. 109, θάλαμόνδ' ὅθι οἱ κλυτὰ τεύχεα κεῖτο, would naturally signify 'the inner chamber *where his weapons were normally kept*'; if the weapons were there merely because someone has recently removed them thither, the form of expression is, in the context, unnatural and even misleading. But it must not be overlooked that, whether the explicit references to the removal of the armour in 22. 21 ff. and 140 f. are later additions or not, the fact that weapons have to be brought for the Suitors from a store-room presupposes the deliberate removal of the armour from the walls of the main hall, their customary place.)

16. I cannot accept the reason given by Kirchhoff, and still sometimes quoted with approval, in respect of the transformation of Odysseus. The alleged editor is said to have introduced the transformation because he thought that the handsome and vigorous Odysseus of the Phaeacian scenes must otherwise have been instantly recognized at Ithaca. As if it were not enough for the poet to tell us, as he does (from the end of the Sixteenth Book onwards), that his Ithacan Odysseus is disguised, unrecognizable because dressed in beggar's rags.

17. The whole of the passage in the Sixteenth Book describing the plan for the removal of the armour was believed by Zenodotus and Aristarchus, the great Homeric editors of the third and second centuries B.C., to be a later addition to the text of their 'Homer'; their judgement (together with our own) is confirmed by the fact that the passage both begins and ends with the formula '*Now I will tell you another thing, and do you take it to heart*'—a formula never elsewhere used twice within the same speech, let alone twice in successive sections of a speech. Whatever their reasons may have been for the condemnation of the passage, their conclusion is precisely that which most modern critics are agreed upon; the result is particularly pleasing to those (including myself) who agree with G. M. Bolling at least so far as to believe that the commonest reason for the condemnation of a passage by the great Alexandrians is that it appeared insufficiently supported by their manuscript tradition.

The Scholia indicate that Aristarchus did not reject 19. 1–50: since that passage clearly presupposes 16. 281–98, it would be interesting to know how he reconciled rejection of the latter with retention of the former. Notice too that 24. 165 f. (pp. 121 ff. below) presuppose the action described in 19. 1–50, not the plan promised in 16. 281 ff. I am inclined to believe that both 19. 1–50 and 17. 147–65 were added later under the influence of 16. 281 ff. and the introduction of Theoclymenus, after these had become firmly established in the recitation of the *Odyssey*; but there are difficulties here which I have neither solved myself nor seen solved by others.

V

THE END OF THE *ODYSSEY*

THE greatest of the ancient critics, Aristophanes and Aristarchus, maintained that the *Odyssey* of Homer ended at 23. 296: τοῦτο τέλος τῆς ᾿Οδυσσείας φησὶν Ἀρίσταρχος καὶ Ἀριστοφάνης (Schol. HMQ); Ἀριστοφάνης δὲ καὶ Ἀρίσταρχος πέρας τῆς ᾿Οδυσσείας τοῦτο ποιοῦνται (Schol. MVVind. 133). 'Aristarchus and Aristophanes say that this is the end of the *Odyssey*'; 'Aristophanes and Aristarchus make this the limit of the *Odyssey*.' There is no doubt about the meaning of these simple words:[1] they believed that the poem up to this point was the *Odyssey* of Homer, and that all that follows was added by some other poet or poets.

We do not know what reason they had for this belief. It may be that some record of the fact had survived into their time; it may be that they were acquainted with manuscripts of the *Odyssey* which did not go beyond this point;[2] or it may be simply that they drew the natural inference from the sudden change for the worse in technique, style, and quality.

This appendix to the *Odyssey*, hereafter called *The Continuation*, consists of four episodes. First, Odysseus gives Penelope a brief and in some respects tactful account of his adventures abroad. Next morning he sets out for the country-side to find his father Laertes (23. 297–end). While he is on the way, the scene shifts to the ghosts of the Suitors, who go down to Hades, where Achilles and Agamemnon converse, and one of the Suitors recounts the whole story of the return and revenge of Odysseus (24. 1–204). Thirdly, the meeting of Odysseus and Laertes is described at some length (24. 205–411). Finally, there is a pitched battle between Odysseus and his supporters on the one side and the kinsmen of the slain Suitors on the other (24. 412–end).

To the question, whether the ancients were correct in their judgement of this Continuation, an affirmative answer may be given with the utmost confidence. The objective proof of the fact is given by a study of the language and versification of the third episode. It is a generally true statement that abnormalities of vocabulary, syntax, and style, and tokens of relatively late composition, occur sporadically throughout the *Odyssey*. No passage of considerable length is free from them. Now of the four scenes which comprise the Continuation, none except the third is exceptional in this respect; but of the third scene, the meeting of Odysseus and Laertes, it may be confidently asserted that there is no other passage of comparable length in the Homeric poems in which linguistic evidence of relatively late composition is to be observed in such profusion. The evidence is indeed overwhelming, and leaves no room whatever for doubt: that scene as a whole was composed by a poet familiar with the idioms, syntax and vocabulary of an era not earlier than the sixth century B.C.; a poet whose understanding of the older Epic language and versification is very imperfect.

I append a summary and abbreviated catalogue of the principal abnormalities in all four scenes.

(1) 23. 297–end.

23. 316 ἦην: see on 24. 343 below.

326 Σειρήνων ἀδινάων φθόγγον: Σ. ἀδιναί is an almost, if not quite, meaningless expression; the author has misunderstood the Epic usages of this adjective (Spohn 183, Merry and Ameis-Hentze ad loc., Ebeling s.v.).

330 ψολόεντι κεραυνῷ, cf. 24. 539 ψ. κεραυνόν: this adjective and its cognates are foreign to the Homeric vocabulary. The formula ψ. κεραυνός, for which there is abundant scope in the Homeric poems, never occurs there (Hes. *Theog.* 515).

347 χρυσόθρονον ἠριγένειαν: ἠριγένεια in the Homeric vocabulary is an adjective (and a common one) for ἠώς; here and in the similar verses at 22. 197 it is misused, as if it were a substantive capable of being qualified by another adjective.

361 ἐπῑτελλω: as Monro said, 'This scansion is indefensible by Homeric rules'. (Stanford's reference to *Od.* 16. 297 ἐπῖθυω is irrelevant; that is from ἐπ-ιθύω, cf. *Il.* 12. 443 ἴθυσαν ἐπὶ τεῖχος, al.). Some manuscripts offer ἐπιστέλλω, a valiant conjecture introducing a modern verb (first attested in Aeschylus).

Among other points notice especially the new abstract formation πολυμηχανίη in 321; a singularly unsuccessful novelty, not to be found again before Plutarch.

(2) 24. 1–204.

1. On the form Ἑρμῆς and the adj. Κυλλήνιος see p. 117 below. 40 λελασμένος ἱπποσυνάων: from *Il.* 16. 776, where the subject is, as it should be, a charioteer; to apply such an expression to *Achilles* would be unthinkable in the older Epic. Our poet's thought here is in harmony with the glib poetaster Tryphiodorus, in whom Deiphobus is given the same description (Tryph. 629). (106 τί παθόντες . . .: see Wackernagel, *Spr. Unters. zu Homer* 158. The Attic idiom τί παθών . . ., 'what possessed you to do so and so?', occurs in the *Iliad* at 11. 313 only, in the *Odyssey* here only if at all. Many, including Monro, Ameis-Hentze, and LSJ, are content to take it here in its non-idiomatic sense, 'what befell you, that you descended, &c.'; since this possibility is open to choice, it is more prudent not to use this piece of evidence here.)

111 ff.   ἦ που ἀνάρσιοι ἄνδρες ἐδηλήσαντ' ἐπὶ χέρσου
         βοῦς περιταμνομένους ἠδ' οἰῶν πώεα καλά,
         ἦε περὶ πτόλιος μαχεούμενοι ἦε γυναικῶν;

This is a clumsy copy of *Od.* 11. 401–3 (itself athetized by Aristarchus): there the object of the verb ἐδηλήσαντο was singular, here it is plural; metre forbids, what the sense demands, that the form μαχεούμενον (itself a unique monster) should be changed to μαχεουμένους. Hence μαχεούμενοι here, agreeing with the *subject* of the main verb, to the great confusion of the whole sentence.

In addition notice the *Nine Muses* in 60, a numeration alien to the Homeric tradition (first in Hes. *Theog.* 50 ff.). Some have alleged that our poet need not be charged with believing that the number of the Muses was nine: out of an unspecified total number (they suggest), nine are mentioned here merely because nine is a convenient and favourite number in Epic verse. It is difficult to imagine how special pleading could go further. Notice too ὅτε κεν ζώννυνται in 88–89, an unlikely subjunctive-form (ῥήγνυται in Hipponax fr. 25 is not the kind of evidence one willingly admits in support of an Epic usage).

(3) The above two scenes are not at all exceptional in either number or nature of abnormalities. The following scene, 24. 205–411, stands in sharpest contrast:

237 εἰπεῖν ὡς ἔλθοι: this use of the optative in *oratio obliqua* is the idiom of a much later era; it never occurs in the Homeric poems.

240 ἐπέεσσῖν πειρηθῆναι: a unique breach of the law observed throughout some 28,000 Homeric verses, *that νῦ ἐφελκυστικόν cannot be added to assist the lengthening of a naturally short vowel before the fifth dactyl of the line*. It is a special case of a breach of Wernicke's law that no naturally short syllable may be lengthened by 'position' in that place (see the discussion in *CR* 11, 1897). A composer less out of touch with the Homeric tradition might have ended his line ἔπεσιν διαπειρηθῆναι, which is actually found in a late papyrus-text (Allen's P²⁸, saec. 3–4 A.D.): whoever wrote that was guided by a true instinct, but his lonely voice is shouted down by the unanimous outcry of our manuscript tradition—a unanimity altogether unintelligible if ἔπεσιν διαπ. is anything but a conjecture or oversight.

242 κατέχων κεφαλήν: κατέχων here, contrary to the normal usages of this verb at all times, means κάτω ἔχων, 'holding his head down'. This usage is not recognized by LSJ, but I notice that it recurs in Eur. *Ino* fr. 410. 3 τὰ δ' αἰσχρὰ μισεῖ καὶ κατ' ὀφθαλμοὺς ἔχει.

245 εὖ τοι κομιδὴ ἔχει: εὖ ἔχει τι, *bene se res habet*, is another idiom of later Greek, not elsewhere in the Homeric poems (not even yet in Pindar, Bacchylides, or Aeschylus, and very rare in Sophocles).

247 οὐκ ογχνη‾ ου‾ πρασιη: synecphonesis of this type in the Homeric poems is elsewhere almost confined to the monosyllables δή, ἦ, μή, with a following long vowel or diphthong; also ἐπεῖ ου‾. The only places which serve to illustrate ογχνη‾ ου‾ are (1) *Il.* 17. 89 ασβεστω‾ι· ου‾δ' υιον λαθεν Ατρεος; (2) *Il.* 18. 458 υιει εμω‾ι ωκυμορωι, where however some manuscripts have υι' εμωι ωκυμορωι, which may be right; and (3) *Od.* 1. 226 ειλαπινη‾ ηε γαμος. (*Il.* 2. 651 ενναλιωι ανδρειφοντηι is capable of other treatments than ενναλιω‾ι αν.)

250 ff.   αὐχμεῖς τε κακῶς καὶ ἀεικέα ἕσσαι·
                  οὐ μὲν ἀεργίης γε ἄναξ ἕνεκ' οὔ σε κομίζει,
                  οὐδέ τί τοι δούλειον ἐπιπρέπει εἰσοράασθαι
                  εἶδος.

The author's vocabulary is not that of the old Epic. αὐχμεῖν and its cognates are foreign to the Homeric poems; so are δούλειος (Homeric δούλιος)* and ἐπιπρέπειν. The new formation ἀεργίη, itself no more remarkable than κακοεργίη in *Od.* 22. 374, is thus seen to be in congenial company. ἀρτίφρων in 261 is another of the same type, not to be found in the Homeric poems (in which ἀρτι-compounds are very rare: ἀρτιεπής *Il.* 22. 281, ἀρτίπος *Il.* 9. 505, *Od.* 8. 310).

267 f.   κaὶ οὔ πώ τις βροτὸς ἄλλος
                  ξείνων τηλεδαπῶν φιλίων ἐμὸν ἵκετο δῶμα.

Compare 19. 350 f.

                  οὐ γάρ πώ τις ἀνὴρ πεπνυμένος ὧδε
                  ξείνων τηλεδαπῶν φιλίων ἐμὸν ἵκετο δῶμα.

It is obvious that φιλίων in 19. 351 is the genitive plural of the adjective (though φίλιος does not recur in the Epics): the sense is, as Monro said, 'no man so wise has ever come to my house', not (as some contortionists have taken it) 'no man *so wise* has ever come *more welcome* to my house'. The imitation in 24. 268 shows that our poet thought that φιλίων was nominative singular of a comparative adjective: φίλος φιλίων, like κακὸς κακίων; no Greek ever repeated this blunder.

273 καί οἱ δῶρα πόρον ξεινήϊα οἷα ἐῴκει: our poet was unaware that ξεινήϊον is established in use in the Epic as a substantive, not as an adjective. (It would be most awkward and artificial here to take ξεινήϊα as standing in apposition to δῶρα: how much better it is done in the *Battle of the Frogs and Mice* 16, δῶρα δέ τοι δώσω, ξεινήϊα πολλὰ καὶ ἐσθλά.)

---

* δοῦλος and cognates are very rare in the Epics: δοῦλος itself does not occur, δούλη only in *Il.* 3. 409 (athetized) and *Od.* 4. 12; δουλοσύνη only in *Od.* 22. 423; δούλιος in *Il.* 6. 463, *Od.* 14. 340, 17. 323.

8

278   γυναῖκας ἀμύμονα ἔργα ἰδυίας
       τέσσαρας εἰδαλίμας:

κῦδος κυδάλιμος, therefore εἶδος εἰδάλιμος; this unpromising neo-
logism recurs only once (despite the authority of 'Homer') in
Greek literature; *Anth. Pal.* 7. 491 (Mnasalcas). It is not as if
there were any lack of Homeric epithets meaning 'beautiful'.

286 ξενίη ἀγαθῇ: cf. 314 μείξεσθαι ξενίη. The prosody ξεῖν- for
ξειν- is confined to the *Odyssey*, as opposed to the *Iliad*; adj.
ξένιος, six times. But the substantive ξενίη, apart from the question of prosody, is a word of relatively late time, unattested before
the fifth century; though there is wide scope for its use, if it had
existed, in the Homeric poems and elsewhere. Wackernagel,
op. cit. 120 f.

286 ἡ γὰρ θέμις, ὅστις ὑπάρξῃ: the use of ὑπάρχειν is characteristic of the fifth century, unattested before; especially common
in Attic.

288 ποστὸν δὴ ἔτος ἐστίν: ποστός is a very rare, and so far as
we know very late, formation; again apparently Attic (Aristophanes fr. 163, Xenophon *Cyr.* 4. 1. 16, Philippides fr. 22; see
Wackernagel, op. cit. 158).

299 ποῦ δαὶ νηῦς ἕστηκε: δαί is peculiar to fifth-century Attic;
frequent in Comedy, rare in Tragedy (Eur. *Med.* 339 n.). The
manuscript evidence clearly attests its presence here; in *Od.* 1.
225 it was read by Aristarchus, obviously against the weight of
manuscript evidence, in order to obviate hiatus; in the *Doloneia*
408 it is one of several well-attested variants. 'A colloquial particle', as Denniston says (*Greek Particles* 263).

318 ff.   ἀνὰ ῥῖνας δέ οἱ ἤδη .
       δριμὺ μένος προὔτυψε φίλον πατέρ᾽ εἰσορόωντι,
       κύσσε δέ μιν περιφὺς ἐπιάλμενος:

The vocabulary here shows the greatest insensitivity to the asso-
ciations of words: προτύπτω is elsewhere used only in the phrase
Τρῶες δὲ προὔτυψαν, 'the Trojans *thrust forward*', i.e. pressed forward to battle; ἐφάλλομαι in the Epic is used of leaping on to a
horse or leaping on to an enemy. More unsuitable words for the
present context would be hard to find.

341 ff.   ὄρχους δέ μοι ὧδ᾽ ὀνόμηνας

δώσειν πεντήκοντα, διατρύγιος δὲ ἕκαστος

ἤην· ἔνθα δ᾽ ἀνὰ σταφυλαὶ παντοῖαι ἔασιν

ὅππότε δὴ Διὸς ὧραι ἐπιβρίσειαν ὕπερθεν:

Here again we find ourselves in a realm of language remote from that of the old Epic. This is a poet who could use the verb ὀνομαίνω to mean 'promise', and make it govern a future infinitive; neither the sense nor the construction of the verb (whether ὀνομαίνω or ὀνομάζω) is found in the Epics. His διατρύγιος is, as one might hope, unique: '*diuersis temporibus fructus ferens*' (Ebeling) gives the intended meaning well enough, '(each) separately harvestable'. ἤην, for ἦεν, which recurs in 23. 316 above, is another monster: but there is one other place where it stands, as here, before a vowel, *Od.* 19. 283; in *Il.* 11. 808 the manuscript variant ἦεν is at our disposal. See Chantraine, *Gramm. Hom.* i. 289, and Bolling, *Language* 13 (1937) 306 ff. The adverbial use of ἀνά is very rare, except *in tmesi*: here it is modelled on *Il.* 18. 562 ἀνὰ βότρυες ἦσαν. The greatest offence is given by the sequence ἔασιν ... ἐπιβρίσειαν: 'the optative cannot be explained unless we look upon it as connecting the clause with the past tenses of the narrative, δῶκας, ὀνόμηνας, etc. If so, the words ἔνθα–ἔασιν are parenthetical. On this view however the arrangement of the clauses is very unsatisfactory', Monro. The alleged parenthesis is surely out of the question: even Stanford, who defends what he can, finds it 'hardly satisfactory'. Of Schwartz's conjecture ἔησαν, for ἔασιν, it is sufficient to say that the whole of Greek literature affords not a single example of that potentially useful form. (In the papyrus text of part of *Od.* 9, edited by Guéraud in *Rev. Ég. Anc.* i (1927) 88 ff., we are offered (at v. 425) οἶες ἔησαν for οἶίες ἦσαν, 'a barbarism and forgery', as Guéraud says.)

348 f.   τὸν δὲ ποτὶ οἷ

εἷλεν ἀποψύχοντα:

Another unique abuse of Homeric vocabulary. ἀποψύχοντα here means 'breathing out his life', a sense of the verb normal in the fifth century (Aeschylus fr. 104, Soph. *Ai.* 1031, Thuc. 1.

134. 3) but contrary to Epic usage (the verb occurs only in the phrase ἱδρῶ ἀπεψύχοντο *Il.* 11.621, 22. 2, ἱδρῶ ἀποψυχθείς 21. 561).

360 προΰπεμψ᾽ : 'The only Homeric instance of a compound of προ- in which we cannot write the uncontracted form προε-', Monro. It is just in such refinements that the hand of the later poet betrays itself: in a short space he breaks rules instinctively observed by his predecessors throughout two long Epics. Cf. 24. 240 n.

386 δείπνῳ ἐπεχείρεον : cf. 395 σίτῳ ἐπιχειρήσειν. This poet is far from the main stream of Epic tradition : the common formulas are forgotten or despised—not οἱ δ᾽ ἐπ᾽ ὀνείαθ᾽ ἑτοῖμα προκείμενα χεῖρας ἴαλλον, or the like, but δείπνῳ ἐπεχείρεον : the verb, and this construction with the dative case, are common in the prose and poetry of the fifth century (esp. Attic) ; they will not be found earlier (unless Theognis 75 is a little earlier : there, however, the verb governs the accusative case).

388 ἐξ ἔργων μογέοντες : yet another usage recurring in fifth-century Attic, foreign to the Epic. Elsewhere in the Epics μογεῖν means 'to work hard' (whether, as usual, transitively, or, as in *Il.* 11. 636, 12. 29, intransitively; LSJ need correction) ; it never means metaphorically 'to be distressed, fatigued', as it does here and in Aeschylus, *PV* 277, *Agam.* 1624, Eur. *Alc.* 849.

394 ἀπεκλελάθεσθε δὲ θάμβευς : ἀπεκ- is a combination unknown to the Epic (and extremely rare in classical literature of all kinds, ἐξαπο- being preferred). Cf. 222 above, the only example of ἐσκατα- in the Epic, again a great rarity in the Greek language. θαμβεῦς is unique: nowhere else is the genitive singular of a neuter in -ος contracted (whether spelt -ευς or -εος) in the unstressed half of the dactyl (even in the stressed half the contraction is very rare; Chantraine, op. cit. 58).

398 Ὀδυσεῦς : see Chantraine, op. cit. 34 ff. This contraction of the gen. sing. of a nominative in -ευς is absolutely contrary to Homeric law. (Some recent editions show that it is still necessary to point out that the form Ὀδυσεῶς would be equally unhomeric. The genitive of this name is exceedingly common, and takes three forms—Ὀδυσσῆος, Ὀδυσῆος, Ὀδυσσεος.)

402 οὖλέ τε καὶ μέγα χαῖρε: cf. the *Hymn to Apollo* 466, where alone this formula recurs; it and its verb οὖλειν are unknown to the Homeric Epics.

The above list is by no means exhaustive. Other points which have often been noticed and discussed include: 208 κλίσιον: it is not known from what level of society our poet exalted this word to the Epic vocabulary; it recurs nowhere in literature, and its meaning is a matter for conjecture. 222 Δολίος: see Ameis-Hentze (Anhang). We already knew two persons of this name, (1) the servant of Penelope, 4. 735, (2) the father of the wicked Melantheus and Melantho, 17. 212, 18. 322; our poet creates a third, the servant of Laertes. The composite individual into which all three are blent by some theorists is remarkably unlifelike. 231 αἰγείην κυνέην κεφαλῇ θέτο πένθος ἀέξων: 'he had a goatskin cap on his head, *thus* (or, *because he was*) *cherishing his grief*'—such must be the relation of the participial to the main clause. This comical sentence has naturally given great offence ('πένθος ἀέξων is said to explain the rudeness of his attire', Monro; 'an explanation of his curious dress, i.e. because he cherished his grief', Stanford. Such desperate remedies are certainly called for). 244 ἀδαημονίη: the adj. ἀδαήμων (*Il.* and *Od.* each twice) inspired our poet to create this irregular and unpopular novelty; the rest of Greek literature leaves it severely alone. 289–90: our poet has hardly done himself justice, or at least credit, in writing σὸν ξεῖνον δύστηνον ἐμὸν παῖδ᾽, εἴ ποτ᾽ ἔην γε, δύσμορον, and 301 ἐκβήσαντες ἔβησαν. 307 Σικανίης: 'Sicania' is not known to Homeric geography. 314 διδώσειν: this *monstrum rhapsodicum* has a parallel in *Od.* 13. 358.

(4) The fourth scene presents features of the same type as the third, only much fewer in number.

437 περαιωθέντες: this word belongs to the vocabulary of fifth-century prose; here only in dignified poetry (Comedy only Ar. *Ran.* 138).

465 Εὐπείθεϊ: the contracted dative in -ει in the unstressed half of the dactyl is absolutely contrary to Homeric law. (In 534 below τεύχεα at the end of the line has a few parallels: *Il.* 7. 207, 24. 7, 22. 322, al.; see La Roche, *Hom. Unters.* 146 ff.) Even in

the stressed half it is very rare (all Stanford's alleged parallels are of this irrelevant type). Chantraine, op. cit. 49.

491 μὴ δὴ σχεδὸν ὧσι: the Attic conjugation of εἰμί has invaded the Epic here and in a few other places: *Il.* 14. 274 ὧσι (in the Διὸς Ἀπάτη, a relatively late composition); 19. 202, *Od.* 8. 147, 163, 580 ἦσι (147 and 580 may represent original κ' ἔησι, ἵν' ἔησι); 7. 94, 19. 230 ὄντες, ὄντας; 19. 489 οὔσης. See Wackernagel, op. cit. 111.

497 ἐξ δ' υἱεῖς οἱ Δολίοιο: this modern usage of the article has very seldom invaded the Epics: *Il.* 20. 181, τιμῆς τῆς Πριάμου, is the only really close parallel, and that was athetized by Aristarchus. (*Od.* 24. 497 is not properly illustrated by examples in which the subject-noun is omitted, as in *Il.* 23. 348 τοὺς Λαομέδοντος, scil. ἵππους, 9. 342 τὴν αὐτοῦ scil. ἄλοχον; or by examples in which article+genitive is *followed* by adj.+noun, as in *Il.* 23. 375, *Od.* 3. 145 τὸν Ἀθηναίης δεινὸν χόλον. There remains only *Il.* 10. 408, where δαί may well be preferred to δ' αἱ.)

514 τίς νύ μοι ἡμέρη ἥδε, θεοὶ φίλοι: the Epic was very sparing of interjections (ὤμοι, ὦ πόποι): neither this expletive, θεοὶ φίλοι, nor anything else of the kind occurs elsewhere in the Homeric poems; Wackernagel, op. cit. 230. (Spohn, p. 206, writes: *omnis quidem haec sententia tam parum colore renidet Homerico ut Hermannum, quum puerili aetati adhuc proximus, ita quidem ut nondum iuvenibus annumerari posset, primum hunc locum legeret, vehementer offenderet.*)

535 θεᾶς ὄπα φωνησάσης: an abuse of an old Epic formula. In *Il.* 10. 512 ξυνέηκε θεᾶς ὄπα φ., 20. 380 ἄκουσε θεοῦ ὄπα φ., the accusative ὄπα is governed by ξυνέηκε (*Od.* 8. 241 ξυνίει ἔπος) and ἄκουσε (*Il.* 21. 98 ὄπ' ἄκουσε): our poet is so far from the tradition that he thinks ὄπα to be governed (directly or indirectly) by φωνησάσης, hence θεᾶς ὄπα φωνησάσης here, 'the goddess having *uttered her voice*'.

Among other points notice 416 μυχμῷ, a novelty, not elsewhere in poetry. 432 κατηφέες: the verb κατηφεῖν and noun -είη are at home in the Epic; not so the adjective, except in the irresponsible form κατηφών at *Il.* 24. 253. 485 φόνοιο ἔκλησιν θέωμεν: a new abstract noun; neither ἔκλησις nor any compound of -λησις occurs elsewhere in literature except ἐπίλησις once only in Pindar.

The phraseology is thoroughly unhomeric, like σκέδασιν θείη in *Od.* 20. 225. 486 πλοῦτος δὲ καὶ εἰρήνη ἅλις ἔστω: more unhomeric language; πλοῦτος in *Od.* elsewhere only 14. 206, a formula common to the *Iliad*; εἰρήνη not elsewhere in *Od.*, in *Il.* only (thrice) in the formular ἐπ' εἰρήνης. 499 πολιός: *grey*, meaning *grey-haired*, agèd, is characteristic of fifth-century Attic, especially Drama; the usage is unknown to the Epic. 511 τῷδ' ἐνὶ θυμῷ: the composers of *Iliad* and *Odyssey* finished their work without once having recourse to this obscure and unwholesome expression. 519: notice the artificial adaptation of this formula: it occurs eight times in the *Iliad*, where προίει is always 3rd person indic. (here of course imperative). 528 ἄνοστος: a useful word, if the Epic had known it. The alternative ἀνόστιμος occurs in *Od.* 4. 182, nowhere else in the Epics. 534 τεύχεα: for the monstrous misunderstanding of this very common word, see p. 113 below. 539 ψολόεντα κεραυνόν: see on 23. 330 above.

I suppress the names of those who have written such falsehood as the following: 'The evidence is, as regards both language and metre, so slight as to be negligible'; 'Language and metre, then, furnish no good evidence even for suspecting that 23. 297 to the end of 24 could not have come directly from Homer's hand.' It needs hardly to be said that the writers had not taken the trouble to find out what the evidence is.

The verdict of the Greek language is so clear and so emphatic that we are spared much troublesome and inconclusive dispute about general probabilities. We need not argue whether the earlier references to Laertes in the *Odyssey* lead us to expect a meeting between father and son before the end of the poem: it is certain that the meeting described in our *Odyssey* was composed at an era much later than the bulk of the *Odyssey*. Nor is any useful purpose served by trying to explain or excuse the structural fault of the scene; it is so obvious, and has been so often described, that a few words will suffice.[3]

Odysseus has killed the Suitors and made himself known to his wife. He now goes to make himself known to his father Laertes who lives at a distance in the country-side. There is no good reason why he should not at once explain who he is; and indeed time is pressing, for danger threatens at home. But instead he indulges in an aimless and heartless guessing-game; he pretends to be a stranger, unaware who Laertes is; he brings the name of Odysseus casually into conversation; and spins a long yarn such as we have already had from him on several other occasions, when deception had some purpose to fulfil. Here it has none. He plays upon his father's emotions until the old man is almost insensible from sorrow: then suddenly he springs the truth upon him. It is all very lively and amusing and decadent: taken by itself, as an independent idyll, it is a charming composition, in a highly individual style of Greek; only it pays no respect whatever to the story which it interrupts. Pope in his translation pleads that 'this procedure excellently agrees with the general character of Ulysses, who is upon all emergencies master of his passions, and remarkable for disguises and an artful dissimulation; this disguise has a very happy effect in this place; it holds us in a pleasing suspence, and makes us wait with attention to see the issue of the interview': the listener might, I suppose, wait with attention, 'in a pleasing suspence', first, to see whether this elaborate deception will in the end prove to have some purpose; secondly, to see whether Laertes will live long enough under this unfeeling treatment to recognize his son.[4]

Let us now briefly review the fourth scene, the last episode in the *Odyssey*. The relatives of the dead Suitors gather in the market-place; Eupeithes demands that Odysseus be punished for the murder of so many Ithacans; Medon and Halitherses speak in favour of Odysseus.

So far all is well enough: but at this point our poet, who has proceeded hitherto with dignified step at moderate pace, suddenly indulges in a moment of leap-frog followed by a gallop for the goal.

The enemies of Odysseus rush to arms, assemble in front of the city, put themselves under the command of Eupeithes, and suddenly we are all in heaven and Athene is talking to Zeus. There is no transitional phrase, not a word to indicate the change of scene.[5] One moment we are with Eupeithes in Ithaca, the next in heaven with Athene. We do not expect, and shall not find, anything like this elsewhere in the Homeric Epics: the poet has broken the most elementary rules of his craft; '*praefracta et horrida oratione ad Olympum abripimur, in concionem deorum mire sermocinantium, ne dicam garrientium*'.[6]

From this moment onwards the story rushes spasmodically and deviously to its lame conclusion. Listen to the sequence of events: Athene asks Zeus whether there shall now be fighting or friendship between the two parties. He tells her to do what she will, but advises that the proper course is to make a treaty of friendship, 'and there shall be wealth and peace in abundance'. Such is the will of Zeus, and Athene descends at once to earth—for what purpose? To do the will of Zeus, we suppose; for otherwise there was no point in telling us what his will was; and she made no objection. Our frivolous poet, however, has already forgotten this conversation in heaven: contrary to the will of Zeus, and contrary to what we were expressly told to expect, Athene goes her way as if Zeus had never spoken. She assumes the shape of Mentor, joins forces with Odysseus, encourages his party, actually incites them to join battle. Not until Eupeithes is dead, and his followers smitten with sword and spear, does she tell them to stop fighting, 'that they may separate *without bloodshed*': this ludicrous expression, 'without bloodshed', uttered at the end of battle, when men are lying killed and wounded, and the issue clearly decided, is greeted with silence or subterfuge[7] by those who detect the hand of 'Homer' even here.

In truth this poet is in a hurry to be finished, and does not stop to consider the meaning of his words: 'Thus spoke Athene, and pale terror seized them; and they were affrighted, and out of their hands flew their *suits of armour*.' Of course he meant 'weapons', not 'suits of armour'; no poet to whom the Epic language was a natural or even a familiar mode of expression could possibly use the word τεύχεα, 'the whole armour, or harness, of a man', when he meant 'weapons'.[8]

The last few events are crowded together most unhomerically and spurred into a brief and breathless gallop.[9] The enemy turns in flight toward the city; Odysseus swoops down on them like an eagle; Zeus flings a thunderbolt—aimed (if you can believe it) at the goddess Athene: she tells Odysseus to stop fighting, or Zeus will be angry with him; he obeys; and—so little does this poet know about the character and conduct of Homeric heroes—*rejoices in his heart* because the slaughter of his enemies is thus brought to a premature end. There had been a day when χάρμα expressed a different emotion. Athene at last makes the treaty between the two parties, *after* the one side has defeated the other. All this is composed in short perfunctory phrases, similar in style and quality to the conclusion of the *Battle of the Frogs and Mice* (285–93). Here is a minor poet, palely loitering in the shadow of the Greek Epic tradition. As Dr. Johnson said of an uninspired contemporary, we read him 'as one listens to a lecture—without passion, without anxiety'.

The events of this passage (24. 412–end) are clearly forecast in a singularly ill-conceived and ill-executed scene in the preceding Book (23. 115 or 117 to 170 or beyond), wherein Odysseus interrupts his interview with Penelope in order to take precautions against the kinsmen of the Suitors, and to bathe and put on fine clothes before resuming his attempt to persuade Penelope that he is her husband. This, the most inartistic of all interpolations in the *Odyssey*, was exposed in its true colours by Adolf Kirchhoff.

Odysseus' bath and robing could not easily be worse arranged. Instead of placing them *before* the interview with Penelope (the most natural course), the poet has chosen the worst possible moment—when Penelope has already admitted that this man (despite his rags) may be her husband, and is prepared to test him with secret tokens (108–10). The suspense of the action is rudely broken: meantime Penelope, in most unhomeric fashion, is supposed to remain seated where she was, ready to renew the conversation when Odysseus returns—not that we are ever told that (or when) he left her. And when he returns, what happens? Does he wait to see what Penelope will think of him now? Does he ask whether she now notices any resemblance to her husband? No: without waiting a second to see whether his bath and robing have had the desired effect, he repeats (168 ff.), in identical words, a reproach spoken by Telemachus a long time ago (100 ff.)

—a reproach which in the earlier passage arose naturally out of the action, and was adequately answered by Penelope: here its futile repetition serves no purpose but to warn us what kind of poet is at work. And then, to our bewilderment, we are led to believe that Penelope already knows him to be Odysseus and is only 'making trial of her husband'! (23. 174 ff., esp. 181 πόσιος πειρωμένη.) There is no more ruinous interpolation in the *Odyssey* than this: the suspense of the final scene of recognition is broken, ostensibly in order that Odysseus may convince Penelope by appearing before her clean and well-attired; yet when he returns neither party makes the slightest reference to this change in his appearance, and it plays no part whatever in the sequel. It is perfectly obvious that it was inserted in order to prepare the mind of the listener for the events of the last scene in the Twenty-fourth Book.

We now go back to the beginning. In the first of the four scenes that comprise the Continuation (23. 297–372) Odysseus recounts to Penelope the whole story of his adventures on the way home (310–43); next morning he goes with his son and servants to visit Laertes, while Penelope remains at home; precautions are taken to avoid contact with the kinsmen of the dead Suitors (344–end). This latter part is an introduction to the subjects of the second half of the following Book; with those episodes it must stand or fall.[10]

The earlier part, the brief résumé of the contents of Books V to XII of the *Odyssey*, has been much abused by modern critics. Unitarians and Dissectors join hands and chant dispraise in unison: 'strangely prosaic summary'; 'a straightforward prosaic summary, quite correct as far as it goes, . . . towards the structural culmination of the epic valueless'; 'not because it is a recapitulation, but because it is a bad one'; 'reads like a table of contents to Books V–XII. . . . Impossible to see that such a conscientious ἀνακεφαλαίωσις on 23. 310 κτλ. is useful or requisite in the economy of the poem. This summary is a smooth and fluent exercise in hexameters, with one redeeming feature, the vividness of v. 342'; 'the whole conception of such an allusive summary, no less than the skill with which it is done, indicates the lateness of its origin'.

This is all very well; it may be all very true. But my search for hard facts has led me to agree with Friedrich Focke, *mir ist ein durchschlagender Einwand nicht bekannt*; I have not come across any decisive objection to this passage.[11] True, the appearance of a long run of indirect speech is surprising: the Greek Epic prefers direct speech, whether of the poet or of his characters; it has nothing to show remotely comparable with the present episode in this respect. But, granted that a résumé of the adventures was to be given, there was no reasonable alternative. Odysseus must speak directly, at much greater length than this; or the poet must, as he does here, briefly tell us what Odysseus said. The new technique is forced upon the poet by the requirements of his story. We cannot be so certain as Paul Cauer would have us,[12] that only a relatively late poet would have conceived a plan which could only be executed in a long passage of indirect speech. It may be so, but we do not know it.

It is absolutely certain that modern scholarship would have identified the presence of a later poet or poets from 23. 344 onwards, even if the verdict of the Alexandrians had not come down to us. But it is very doubtful whether 23. 297–343 would have been included in the condemnation.[13] We remain where we started: the Alexandrians placed the end of the *Odyssey* before this passage, not after it. It would be very imprudent of us to contradict them without strong reasons; and we may as well admit that we have no such reasons.

It remains to consider the second of our four scenes, the most interesting and perplexing of them all (24. 1–204).

In a brief introductory passage (1–14) we are told that Hermes of Cyllene conducted the ghosts of the Suitors past the streams of Oceanus and the Rock Leucas and the Gates of the Sun and the Community of Dreams, down to the meadow of asphodel where the phantoms dwell in Hades: it has been recognized since remote antiquity that this poet has thrown overboard the standard Homeric beliefs concerning the passage of the ghost to the underworld; but the charge has seldom been correctly formulated, and has often been obscured by irrelevant detail.

The most casual reader or listener notices that the relatively late contracted form Ἑρμῆς,[14] instead of the Homeric Ἑρμείας, is employed; and that Hermes is here called Κυλλήνιος, a native of Mount Cyllene in Arcadia, contrary to the ideas and practice of the Greek Epic.[15] But these facts do not constitute the charge against this passage: indeed they are not even included in it, though they might be held to confirm it. The charge is that here, at the end of the *Odyssey*, the poet has suddenly been converted to an entirely new conception of the passage and entrance of the ghost to the Underworld; and the charge has not one count but at least three.

First, Hermes is described as Conductor of Ghosts to Hades. This function of Hermes, probably a very old one,[16] is elsewhere absolutely suppressed by the Homeric poets. Everywhere else[17]— and the occasions are very numerous—the ghost leaves the body at death and flies, without any guide, to Hades. Here too, in the last Book of the *Odyssey*, the same idea would have served the poet's purpose as well, or better; for Hermes has no further part to play. Why has the poet broken, at the last moment, the custom observed throughout both *Iliad* and *Odyssey*? It is specially unfortunate that the divinity in question should be *Hermes*: for the *Odyssey* has hitherto given him duties of a very different kind, as messenger between the gods in heaven and men on earth; though there was no reason, or at least none that we can comprehend, why the *Odyssey* should have contradicted the *Iliad* so roughly in this respect—in the *Iliad*, that office is assigned not to Hermes but to Iris.

Secondly, the ghosts are here conducted 'past the streams of Oceanus and the Rock Leucas and the Gates of the Sun and the Community of Dreams'. Now we have heard of many deaths in the *Iliad* and *Odyssey*; we have even been ourselves, with Odysseus, to the threshold of Hades; we have listened to the ghost of Elpenor, who made his own way thither. But we have never heard of anything like this before. Excepting the 'streams of Ocean', this is an entirely novel geography, and a very odd one. Who ever heard, before or since, of a Rock Leucas,[18] or White Rock, near the entrance to Hades across the river Oceanus? Who ever heard, in Greece, that the Sun issued through gates? Or that Dreams lived together in a settled community, fit to be called a *demos*?[19] Our poet is very far from the Homeric conception of the geography of Hades. And where his phrases may come from, we cannot tell; ἠελίοιο πύλας, Λευκάδα πέτρην, δῆμον ὀνείρων, are not, so far as we know, from the stock-in-trade of the Homeric bards.

Thirdly, we learn, to our intense annoyance, that the ghosts of the Suitors, whose bodies are not yet buried or burnt, nevertheless enter Hades without delay and mingle with other ghosts. Are we really required to be so short of memory and so slow of wit? To forget all about Elpenor, and all about Patroclus in the *Iliad*?—

> Bury me
> as quickly as may be, let me pass through the gates of Hades.
> The souls, the images of dead men, hold me at a distance,
> and will not let me cross the river and mingle among them,
> but I wander as I am by Hades' house of the wide gates.[20]

Thus Patroclus; and Elpenor told the same tale. If we knew anything about ghosts, it was this: that they cannot enter Hades until their bodies have had funeral rites.—

> nec ripas datur horrendas et rauca fluenta
> transportare prius quam sedibus ossa quierunt.—

These Suitors are not ghosts but gate-crashers; and this poet is not within the law of the Homeric tradition, but unaware or negligent of its most elementary customs. It is then a matter of relatively small importance that he should endow the ghosts in Hades with a voice to speak.[21]

This brief and most eccentric preface is followed by a dialogue between the ghosts of Achilles and Agamemnon, wherein the latter tells the former, at considerable length, what funeral rites were paid to him after death. Not the slightest attempt is made to adapt this dialogue to its position in the *Odyssey*. No reason is given or implied why the story of Odysseus' visit to his father should be interrupted by a lengthy discourse between two ghosts in Hades on the subject of Achilles' funeral ten years ago, a matter which lies entirely outside the scope of the *Odyssey*. I do not myself agree with those critics—devout Unitarians, both—who call these verses 'insufferable', and complain of their 'obvious poverty' : taken by itself the episode seems to me impressive, composed in smooth and highly conventional language, singularly free from such tokens of later Greek as abound in the scene which follows. The enormous irrelevance, the long interruption of the action of the story at a critical moment, may be defended by one excuse or another: I do not set foot on that shaky ground, for I observe that the text itself affords clear evidence that the conversation of Achilles and Agamemnon was not originally designed to stand where it stands today.

Consider 24. 13–15: Hermes is leading the ghosts of the dead Suitors down towards Hades, and 'swiftly they arrived at the asphodel meadow where dwell the phantoms of the dead. *And they found* the ghosts of Achilles, Patroclus, and others; thus they were consorting with him (Achilles).' Now who are 'they', who 'found' the ghost of Achilles? The ghosts of the Suitors, obviously. And yet, however obviously, certainly not. Look at 24. 99 ff.: *after* Achilles and Agamemnon have finished their long discourse, Hermes arrives on the scene, still leading down the ghosts of the Suitors; and Achilles and Agamemnon, when they see them, go at once to greet them. Clearly, according to this poet, the ghosts of the Suitors had not been there from the start—they had not already 'found' Achilles before the conversation with Agamemnon began; for he goes on to tell us that Hermes and his company of ghosts did not 'find' Achilles until the conversation was over.

Who then are 'they', who 'found' Achilles in 24. 15? There is no possible answer: the verb εὗρον is without any conceivable subject in our text. The poet has transferred this passage wholesale hither from some other source, and the faulty join at the very start has betrayed his artifice.[22]

The Suitors are now in Hades, and Agamemnon asks one of them, Amphimedon, what was the cause of their death. Amphimedon briefly narrates the history of the Suitors from their courting of Penelope down to their slaughter by Odysseus.

Agamemnon points the moral of the contrast between the virtue of Penelope and the vice of his own wife Clytemnestra. Thereupon the vision of Hades abruptly disappears, and all of a sudden we are in the Ithacan country-side, approaching the garden of Laertes.

The speech of Amphimedon's ghost is among the most perplexing of all mysteries in the *Odyssey*. The story of the return, revenge and recognition of Odysseus is now finished; we have heard the whole of it, in twenty-three Books of the *Odyssey*. Here it is briefly summarized by the ghost of Amphimedon: and the extraordinary fact emerges that the story as summarized here is in certain important respects fundamentally different from the story as it was told in the *Odyssey*; that which happened, according to this ghost, did not happen, according to the *Odyssey*—though it would have been more natural if it had happened. Let us consider the two[23] principal points which obtrude themselves; and, first, the story of the Web of Penelope.

The virtuous wife, awaiting the return of her husband, is beset by Suitors. She promises to surrender when she has finished a web which she is weaving, but secretly at night unpicks what she has woven by day; and the hour of reckoning seems thus indefinitely postponed. Suppose now that her deception is detected by the Suitors: they will compel her to finish her weaving and to fulfil her promise to surrender; but on the very day when the web is finished, when her wedding to a suitor is about to take place, behold, her husband is home, and she is rescued.

This is the story as told by the ghost, in accordance with the custom of universal folk-lore:[24] for three years Penelope deceived the Suitors; but then her deception was betrayed, and she was compelled to finish the web; 'and when she had woven the great web, and washed it, and showed it to us, *then it was* that an evil spirit brought Odysseus to the border of the land' (24. 147 ff.).

That is what the ghost says: and he lies in his teeth. The *Odyssey* did *not* employ the motif of the husband's return on the day when the web was finished. You might then very well judge that the *Odyssey* can have had no use whatever for the story of the web: for it would surely be a sad story-teller, who told us that

Penelope was caught unpicking the web and compelled to finish it, and yet that nothing whatever happened as a consequence— that the Suitors generously regarded the incident as closed, and allowed affairs to continue exactly as they were before the story of the web began. But that is what actually happens in the *Odyssey*: one of the Suitors, in the Second Book, and Penelope herself, in the Nineteenth, tell the story of the web in the same terms as those used by the ghost of Amphimedon; only they stop short, as they must, at the point where the deception is betrayed and the web finished. The incident was closed some time before the return of Odysseus; the Suitors did not require Penelope to fulfil her promise to surrender so soon as the web was finished, though the primary purpose of the story is frustrated unless they do so require her.

There are two problems here, not one. First, why has the poet included the story of the web in a version of Odysseus' return which deprives it of its purpose? More than one answer is at our disposal. We have already seen that the *Odyssey*, in stories which it tells, likes to include features of other stories which it is not telling, even at the cost of some inconsistency or even contradiction; and here the story gains more in portrayal of character than it loses in consistency of action. We must however reckon also with the fact that neither of the two previous accounts of the story of the web is well adapted or firmly attached to the place where it stands in the *Odyssey*. The Scholia say that Penelope's description of the stratagem in the Nineteenth Book was not to be found in the majority of their manuscripts, and was judged by Aristarchus to be an interpolation; and the description by Antinous in the Second Book sits in its present place so uncomfortably that many modern critics have supposed it to be a later addition to the text.[25]

Much harder is the second problem: what might induce a poet to say, at the end of a poem, that the climax of his story was reached by means of a certain device, when in fact that device was not employed? The same question is posed by the second of the two principal points which arise from the speech of this unlucky ghost.

9

We have come to the end of the *Odyssey*, and we have heard that Odysseus, having performed certain trials of strength and skill, and having slain the Suitors, at last makes himself known to Penelope. The recognition, that is to say, does not occur until the end, after the planning and execution of his revenge upon the Suitors. But here again we find that what happened according to the ghost is entirely different from what happened in the *Odyssey*. When Penelope announced her surrender and promised to marry the Suitor who should string a bow and shoot an arrow through twelve axes, she was acting of her own accord; she had not yet recognized Odysseus, and nobody had suggested to her that she should adopt this course of action. But according to the ghost this choice of a new husband by means of an ordeal with bow and arrows was dictated to Penelope by Odysseus: '*he craftily commanded his wife* to set for the Suitors the bow and the grey iron, as a trial for us ill-fated men, and the beginning of our slaughter' (24. 167 f.). That is what the ghost would have us believe: we, on the contrary, distinctly remember that the plan was (as in our version of the *Odyssey* it must be) Penelope's own (19. 571 ff.); the fact that Odysseus, when he heard of it, encouraged her to go forward, does not justify the poet in telling us now that she acted in accordance with a crafty plot concocted by her husband. Once more we ask, what might induce a poet to use, in a final summary, language which describes a course of action contrary to the truth, on a point of such importance? For not many points are more important than this: did Penelope recognize Odysseus, and act according to his instructions, from the beginning; or was she unaware of him until the end? Not until the end, says the *Odyssey*; from the beginning, grumbles the ghost.

Forms of expression must not be too strictly examined; every allowance must be made for momentary lapse and minor inaccuracy. But, in the present example, no such escape is open to us; for it has long been observed that there are other witnesses to the good character of this ghost; he is not, as we are too often told, meaning one thing and saying another. The *Odyssey* contains other unmistakable traces of a version of the story in which Penelope recognized Odysseus from the beginning, before the action against the Suitors began; and the decision not to adopt that version, or not wholly to exclude it, has caused the most serious of all the faults in the construction of the story—a fault which is apparently integral, not easily to be explained by any theory of interpolation or other alteration of an original text.

In the Nineteenth Book Penelope suddenly announces that she will wait no longer for Odysseus. This very day she will set an ordeal for the Suitors, and 'whosoever shall most easily stretch the bow and shoot an arrow through all twelve axes, him will I follow, forsaking the home of my marriage'. Now suppose that she has already recognized Odysseus, and has plotted together with him a means of killing the Suitors: then of course her announcement of surrender is a natural or even necessary development. As the ghost of Amphimedon said, Odysseus told her to arrange this business of the bow and arrows, knowing that he alone would be able to string the bow: he would then be armed with bow and arrows against men armed only with swords, and the doom of the Suitors would be swift and certain. But if, as it happens in the *Odyssey*, she has *not* recognized Odysseus, what motive can the poet give for this sudden surrender after ten years' waiting? It might have been made plausible, no doubt, by one expedient or another, whether by ancient poet or modern psychologist: but we are concerned with what is, not what might have been; and the fact is that the poet could not possibly have chosen a worse moment for Penelope's surrender—provided that she has not yet recognized Odysseus. Consider what has led up to this moment. First, Telemachus informed her, on that same day, that Odysseus was still alive; the first definite news she has ever heard. Secondly, the prophet Theoclymenus assured her that Odysseus was already at hand, in Ithaca. Thirdly, Odysseus in disguise has just told her that her husband was lately seen in the neighbourhood, and has sworn a great oath that he will arrive in the near future. Finally, Penelope herself has just dreamed a dream which she herself understood to portend the return and revenge of Odysseus. Never in the course of ten years has she known so great encouragement, so many tokens of hope in so short a period: and this, of all times, is the moment chosen by the poet, without a word of explanation, for her decision to wait not a day longer, to surrender at once to a new husband.

The fault in the construction is very great and very obvious. The poet is aware of a story in which Penelope recognized Odysseus *before* her surrender—in which her surrender was part of a plot concerted between her and Odysseus. He has nevertheless transferred the recognition to the other end of the story, thus leaving her surrender at this time deprived of all motive.

It is necessary at this point to consider, and if possible to pass judgement on, a remarkable scene in the Eighteenth Book, 158–304.

Athene suddenly inspires Penelope with the desire to visit the Suitors and promise her surrender. Since Penelope has more reason today than she has ever had before to *delay* surrender, it would be well if the poet explained why she must act thus contrary to expectation. And indeed the motive is expressed: '*That she might be more highly valued than before by her husband and son*' (18. 161 f.). What is the meaning of this? According to our *Odyssey*, Penelope is not aware that Odysseus is present; therefore this cannot be *her* motive for the action. May we then say—since Penelope acts as if she were a passive instrument of Athene's will —that the motive is *Athene's*? If we do say this, we must suppose that the poet has entirely forgotten (as we have certainly not) that husband and wife are now to meet for the first time after twenty years. What might induce Athene to believe that Penelope will be 'more highly valued by her husband', if the first words which he hears her utter are a promise of re-marriage?

The suggestion that the fault lies with momentary inadvertence on the part of the poet is the less acceptable since the implication of this passage (that husband and wife are already known to each other) is repeated later on. When Penelope tells the Suitors that the hour of her surrender is near, but that their proper course is to enrich her with gifts and to entertain her friends at their own expense, instead of consuming the substance of the royal palace, observe what words our poet uses of Odysseus, who is present in disguise: '*Odysseus rejoiced* because she was enticing gifts from them and beguiling their hearts with gentle words, *while her mind was set on other purposes.*' Consider what this means. Odysseus has not seen his wife for twenty years. He knows that she is in danger of being compelled to marry one of the Suitors. Here at last he sees her; and what are the first words he hears her speak? A statement that the time has come for her to re-marry. With what emotion does he hear this alarming news? *With rejoicing.* Because, we are told, he knows that she does not really mean it. How could he know that, why should he even suspect it—unless the two have already met and concocted the deception between them? But that is by no means all: for notice that this statement, 'her mind was set on other purposes', is, in this context, absolutely false.[26] Penelope's promise of re-marriage is made in good faith: there is no indication that she does not mean what she says. We have long looked forward to this moment, one of the most important in the poem, the first meeting of Odysseus and Penelope: and here we find an exceptionally muddled piece of composition. Odysseus cannot possibly know, and has no reason to suppose, that his wife is deceiving the Suitors; yet he rejoices, for he does so suppose; yet he is entirely mistaken, for she is not deceiving them. All this is the work of Athene, who does nothing to reassure Odysseus that Penelope is acting in his interest, but takes extreme measures (187 ff.) so to bewitch Penelope that her surrender to the Suitors shall *not* be feigned. It is not surprising that many critics, including some of the most faithful of the modern Unitarians, have finally abandoned the attempt to discover great art, or even good sense, in this procedure.

What is to be our judgement in general? First (what I take to be quite obvious), that whoever composed this scene (from 206 onwards) had in mind—and probably was altogether adopting— a version of the story in which Penelope and Odysseus were at this time known to each other; Penelope's promise of surrender was the first part of a prearranged plan. Secondly, that the scene is not organically connected with our *Odyssey*; it has been added to a context already substantially complete. Thirdly, that the earlier part of this alien scene has been largely modified, by a

relatively late poet, in order to adapt it to its new surroundings.[27]

   Can we take one step farther and point to a scene in the *Odyssey*
where this early recognition of Odysseus by Penelope is all but
described? It has been argued[28] that such a scene occurs in the
Nineteenth Book, where Odysseus, in the presence of Penelope,
becomes known to his old nurse Eurycleia, who sees and recognizes a scar on his thigh while she is washing his feet (19. 335 ff.).
This episode, it is said, is so designed that Odysseus' recognition
by Penelope seems not only likely to follow but also clearly intended to follow at once. This is the first meeting of husband and
wife; and the recognition of Odysseus by the nurse does in fact
occur in the presence of Penelope. It is followed by Penelope's
sudden announcement of her surrender to the Suitors—a surrender which runs absolutely counter to all that has preceded,
unless she has recognized Odysseus in the meantime, that is to
say, in the course of this interview. Clearly the conditions are
exceptionally favourable to the recognition of Odysseus by Penelope in this scene: but is there any objective evidence that the
whole purpose of the scene was to bring about such a recognition
—or, at least, that the scene in our text was closely copied from
an earlier scene which was designed for that purpose? One such
indication has been detected.
   Penelope commands her handmaidens to bathe Odysseus. He
declines the offer, *unless there is some very old person who will do him
this service*; and he accepts Penelope's suggestion that his old
nurse, Eurycleia, should wash his feet. Now, it is argued, Odysseus'
particular request for an old retainer, and his acceptance of the
service of his nurse, can only have one meaning: that he intends
to bring about his recognition, by means of the scar, in the presence of Penelope. For if he does *not* intend this, why did the poet
go out of his way to make him reject the service of those who could
not recognize the scar, and insist on the service of the only person
in the palace who is certain to do so? The ancient critics noticed
the fault in the construction of the story at this point; and so did
the poet himself, for he is careful to explain that Odysseus forgot,

until too late, that he had a scar by which the nurse would recognize him. Let us then put to the poet a simple and fair question: 'You cause Odysseus to make much ado about obtaining the services of his old nurse. You say, his purpose was *not* to bring about his recognition by means of the scar: kindly tell us what other conceivable purpose Odysseus could have had?' The poet will have no honest reply to this question, unless he pleads that, although *Odysseus* has no motive for what he did, *the poet* had a motive for making him do it.[29] The poet wished to create a moment of extreme suspense, to portray the recognition of Odysseus by the nurse, in the presence of Penelope but without her knowledge. The attention of the listener is strained to the highest pitch of expectancy, whether Penelope will or will not observe what happens. Eurycleia recognized the scar, and let fall his foot; and his leg fell in the basin, and the bronze vessel rang loud, and tilted over backwards, and the water was spilt on the floor. Joy and pain together took hold of her, and her eyes filled with tears, and her voice was stopped. She touched Odysseus' chin and said 'You are Odysseus'; and she looked toward Penelope to show her that her husband was there at home. But Penelope did not meet her eyes, or notice what came to pass, for her thoughts were turned elsewhere. And Odysseus felt for the woman's throat and gripped it with his right hand, and with the other dragged her close, and said 'Be silent; let no other person learn of this' (19. 468 ff.).

If there were nothing else to be taken into consideration, this would be a more than satisfactory account. It was unreasonable that Odysseus should go out of his way to ask for the one person who can defeat his purpose: but it was necessary to the poet that he should do so; and the means are justified by the end. It must however be admitted that the point cannot properly be considered in isolation. We have seen that the end of this episode, the surrender of Penelope, is unintelligible unless she has already recognized Odysseus—which she must have done, if at all, in this episode. We have found in the Eighteenth Book a lengthy passage which makes no secret of the fact that it has been bodily transferred from a version of the story in which husband and wife were known to each other from the beginning. The ghost of

Amphimedon told us plainly enough that the plot for the destruction of the Suitors was begun by Penelope at her husband's command. And now at last we understand why it is Penelope herself who requires the Suitors to allow the disguised beggar, Odysseus, to take part in the ordeal of the bow-stringing on which her destiny depends (21. 312 ff.).[30] It is thus proved beyond question that there was current among the Epic poets a version of the story of Odysseus in which he was recognized by Penelope before the action against the Suitors, not (as in our *Odyssey*) after it. And we can go so far as to say that there is a strong indication that the scene in our *Odyssey* where the nurse accidentally recognizes Odysseus, without Penelope's awareness, is an adaptation of an earlier scene in which the recognition by the nurse was intended by Odysseus and designed to lead at once to his recognition by Penelope.[31]

In summary: the following conclusions are surely proved by what is said and done in our text:

1. Whoever composed the Slaying of the Suitors in the form substantially represented by our *Odyssey* was aware of a version of the story in which Odysseus was recognized by Penelope at an early stage.

2. He preferred, however, a version in which the recognition was postponed to the other end: but did nothing to remove, or even to obscure, the consequent defect in the structure of the story. Penelope's pretended surrender to a new husband is left entirely without a motive; indeed it occurs, in our text, at a moment when she has more reason than she has ever had before to expect her old husband's immediate return. That is very well, if she has recognized Odysseus already; it is a serious fault in the structure if she has not.

3. A substantial fragment of the other version, in which the recognition occurred early, has been included, by chance or design, in the Eighteenth Book (158–304). And the Nineteenth Book includes a passage adapted by our poet from a scene in which the early recognition was actually described (19. 335 ff.).

4. Whoever composed the speech of the ghost Amphimedon, which occurs in a relatively late appendix to the poem, took his

facts from a version of the story in which Odysseus returned on the day when the weaving of Penelope's web was finished, and in which the recognition of husband and wife took place before the action against the Suitors began.

Finally, in general, we have seen that the verdict of the great Alexandrian critics is confirmed, beyond further appeal. The *Odyssey* ends, as they tell us it ended, at 23. 296, and all that follows is a later appendix, loosely attached to a poem already substantially complete.

This is the foundation upon which we could build, if only we had some bricks. We know that the Continuation is a later appendix: we should like to know when and why it was appended. These questions lie beyond my limits, not only now but always; for I do not see how certain or probable answers can be found for them. The question *when* depends partly (perhaps entirely) on our opinion about the manner in which a standard text of the *Odyssey*, in writing, was first created and circulated in Greece. The weight of evidence indicates that this most important step was taken at Athens in the earlier or middle part of the sixth century B.C.:[32] but we do not know in what form the Epic concerning Odysseus existed before that time. We may say, without hope of proof or fear of contradiction, that the probable date of the making of a standard text of the *Odyssey* and the probable date of the composition of our Continuation are much the same— about the middle of the sixth century B.C.

The question *why* cannot be answered except by guesses. I do no more than mention the line of approach which has hitherto proved to be the most popular and the least unpromising: the theory that our Continuation is a deliberate attempt to make the end of the *Odyssey* continuous with the beginning of another poem, the *Telegony*, which carried on the story of Odysseus from the point where the *Odyssey* leaves it.[33] There are difficulties in the theory, and it is improbable that our question will be definitely answered on the evidence at present available.

We have now passed in review the most serious of the obstacles to the belief that the *Odyssey* is substantially, in its present form, the work of a single author. The Visit to the Underworld and the Continuation are not parts of the original design, if there was an original design. The Journey of Telemachus and the Wanderings of Odysseus have suffered some interference at their beginnings. The story of the slaying of the Suitors reveals embedded in itself substantial fragments of different ways of telling that story. These are the minimum subtractions which would have to be made from a concept of single authorship. It does not at all follow that, when these subtractions have been made, we have finished our work. The creation of this poem may have been a very complex affair, far too complex for us to unravel at this distance of time. But it is my belief that we have now gone about as far as it is possible to go on solid ground: ahead there stretches a region of endless uncertainty, a quicksand thickly populated by theorists in every stage of submergence.

NOTES ON CHAPTER V

The earliest systematic inquiry is that of F. A. G. Spohn, *Commentatio de extrema Odysseae parte inde a rhapsodiae ψ versu ccxcvii aevo recentiore orta quam Homerico*, Lips. 1816. It may be necessary to warn the English reader that the articles by J. B. Bury in *JHS* 42 (1922) 1 ff. and by J. W. Mackail in *Greek Poetry and Life: Essays presented to Gilbert Murray* (1936) 1 ff. almost wholly ignore the extensive researches and results of their predecessors.

1. The notion of Eustathius (supported by Belzner, *Homerische Probleme* ii (1912) 202, 253, Bethe, *Hermes* 63 (1928) 81 ff., and Schmid-Staehlin I. i. 118), that the meaning is merely that the story of the *Odyssey* reaches its principal climax at this point—that the most important incidents here come to an end—has always been and always will be upheld by a very small minority; to the rest of the world it appears a transparent sophistry. But Bethe is surely right in denying that the last line of the *Argonautica* of Apollonius has any bearing on the question: many have held, and some still do, that Apollonius deliberately echoed, in his last line, what he took to be the last line of the *Odyssey* (23. 296); but there is no resemblance whatever between the two except that ἀσπασι- occurs at their beginnings.

2. On this question see Bethe, contradicting Wilamowitz, *Heimkehr* 72 ff., *Ilias und Homer* 12, Schwartz 151 f. So also T. W. Allen, *Origins and Transmissions*, 218 f., 'It seems probable that the Alexandrians had no documentary evidence before them. . . . The matter . . . rests undecided.'

3. All this, and more, is set out by Spohn 28 ff.

4. Eustathius explains that Odysseus wishes to break the news gently, otherwise his father may be overcome by the shock of recognition: Spohn (30) says all that is necessary in answer to this; it would be hard to devise a method of administering the shock *more* suddenly and severely—Odysseus waits until he has reduced the old man almost to insensibility (24. 315 ff.).

5. ' αὐτάρ (24. 472) . . . often marks a change of scene; cp. 20. 1, 22. 1', Stanford: the statement is incorrect, and the references inappropriate. αὐτάρ never 'marks a

change of scene', though it may of course stand at the beginning of a clause in which change of scene is described by other means, as in *Il.* 1. 430 αὐτὰρ 'Οδυσσεὺς ἐς Χρύσην ἵκανεν, 488 αὐτὰρ ὁ μήνιε νηυσὶ παρήμενος, 19. 40 αὐτὰρ ὁ βῆ παρὰ θῖνα. Thus in *Od.* 20. 1 the change of scene is clearly marked by ὁ ἐν προδόμῳ εὐνάζετο; in 22. 1 there is no change of scene.

6. Spohn 24. 24. 480 is particularly inept, since κείνους must denote *the Suitors.* Athene asked 'What is to be done about Odysseus and *the kinsmen of* the dead Suitors?' Zeus replies 'Why ask me? Was it not your own intention that Odysseus should return aṇd kill *the .Suitors?*' The inconsequence is perhaps not original: some manuscripts omit 479–80 (= 5. 23–24), to the great advantage of the sense; but see Monro, ad loc.

7. e.g. 'before *more* blood is shed', as the Penguin translator has it, despite the Greek.

8. It is not as if they were in the process of arming themselves: both parties are already accoutred (467, 500) and have for some time been fighting. The line is an unhappy adaptation of 12. 203 τῶν δ' ἄρα δεισάντων ἐκ χειρῶν ἔπτατ' ἐρετμά.

9. See especially Blass, *Die Interpolationen in der Odyssee* 218 ff.

10. 23. 310–43 (and 24. 1–204), were athetized by Aristarchus. This fact is of course not in the least inconsistent with his belief that the whole of the Continuation was post-Homeric. Athetesis here means what it always means: that the verses in question were believed to be later additions to a basic text; only here the basic text was, in Aristarchus' opinion, that of a poet other than Homer. Stanford (on 23. 296) has oddly misunderstood the position both in this respect and in his further comment that the Analysts 'find it difficult to explain how any poem could end with an antithetical οἱ μὲν ἔπειτα'. They have no such difficulty: for if 23. 297 ff. were added later, there is no reason in the world why the last line of the *Odyssey* should not have been adjusted to suit the first line of the Continuation. As Kirchhoff suggested, 295 may originally have ended οἱ δ' ἄρ' ἔπειτα . . . . I do not know what is gained, or even what is meant, by describing such a suggestion as 'nonchalant'. There is no certainty that 295–6 are the inviolate work of 'Homer'; notice the word θεσμόν, so common in later Greek, unknown to the Epics elsewhere.

11. Except the statement of Aristotle (*Rhet.* iii. 16. 7) that this résumé (23. 310–43) occupied *sixty* lines; since he is concerned to show how *short* it was, he is not likely to have almost doubled the true number. The natural inference is that more than one version of this résumé was current in antiquity: Aristarchus may then have judged that in a case where one version must be false, both must be held suspect.

12. *Grundfragen* 430 f. Cauer thinks that the skill displayed in the execution, together with the boldness of the plan, argues a relatively late stage of literary technique. I am not so sure about this: true, some skill is displayed in the variety of the verbs (Focke 373), but there is no avoidance of monotony in the tenfold ἠδ' ὡς, ὡς τε, at the beginnings of the lines. Granted that the thing is to be done, this seems to me a sufficiently unsophisticated way of doing it.

13. Thus Focke (372 f.) holds that the end of the *Odyssey* should be placed at 23. 343, not 296. One can only express general opinions about this: I find 296 a much more natural finishing-point than 343.

14. This contracted form occurs elsewhere only in the Θεομαχία, *Il.* 20. 72; in *Od.* 5. 54 and 8. 334, both athetized; and in 14. 435 (Ερμέᾳ *Il.* 5. 390).

15. But it was a common enough epithet for Hermes from the early sixth century, whatever the locality of the poet: Alcaeus fr. 308 χαῖρε Κυλλάνας ὁ μέδεις; *Hymn to Hermes* 2.

16. See Rohde, *Psyche* 9, 168; Farnell, *Cults* v. 12 ff.

17. Unless *Od.* 14. 207 is an exception: τὸν κῆρες ἔβαν θανάτοιο φέρουσαι εἰς Ἀίδαο δόμους. It looks like a misunderstanding of *Il.* 2. 302 οὓς μὴ κῆρες ἔβαν θανάτοιο φέρουσαι, which does not, or need not, imply transporting or conducting of ghosts to Hades. Rohde, op. cit., ch. i, n. 10.

18. See especially Radermacher, *Das Meer und die Toten*, Oest. Akad. d. Wiss., phil.-hist. Klasse 16 (1949) 308 ff.

19. δῆμος ὀνείρων is not merely 'land' of dreams: δῆμος in the Epic means not *regio* but either *regio ab hominibus habitata* or *ciuitas, populus*—either the land inhabited by a community or the community which inhabits a land.

20. *Il.* 23. 71 ff., translated by Richmond Lattimore.

21. This might be a legitimate artifice at any era, if the situation made it desirable. We are no longer in the position of having to maintain that one and the same poet took such elaborate measures in the Eleventh Book to enable his ghosts to speak but thought no measures whatever necessary in the Twenty-fourth. (The Homeric conception of the nature of the ghost contradicts the suggestion, which is still repeated from time to time, that although the ghosts need a stimulant to enable them to converse with a living man, they need none to enable them to talk among themselves.)

22. I suppose that in the original context the same persons were subjects both of εὖρον in 15 and of οἱ μέν in 19, the sense being: '*They* found the ghosts of Achilles etc. . . . Thus *they* [the same subjects as the previous "they"] consorted with him [i.e. with Achilles].' In our text, who are οἱ μέν, who 'thus consorted with Achilles'? Not the Suitors, for they are not yet on the scene; and not Patroclus, Antilochus, Ajax, for then ὥς would be meaningless. Another token of transference from a different context.

23. There are probably three: the story as told in our *Odyssey* probably once knew nothing of the removal of the armour from the dining-hall, mentioned by the ghost in 24. 165 f.

24. See Crooke, *Folk-Lore* 9 (1898) 121 ff. The idea of undoing by night what is done by day is common in folk-lore; the particular instance of *weaving* seems to be very rare.

25. (1) 19. 130–61: ἠθέτηνται λ'. ἐν δὲ τοῖς πλείστοις οὐδὲ ἐφέρον⟨το⟩, Schol. H on 19. 130. Porson altered λ' (= 30) to δ' (= 4), for two mistaken reasons: (a) '*136 et 139 agnoscit Aristarchus*'—i.e. Aristarchus commented on these two lines, therefore they cannot have been included in his condemnation. But it is incorrect to suppose that Aristarchus never commented on lines which he athetized. See, for example, Schol. on *Od.* 16. 287. (b) '*non coit sententia triginta tantum versibus expulsis, sed duo praeterea 160. 161 abigantur necesse est*'—i.e. the omission of 30 lines is impossible; the athetesis must be extended down to 161; therefore λ' cannot be correct. This overlooks the likelihood that 19. 153, omitted by a large number of manuscripts, was not in Aristarchus' text: λα' (= 31, Blass) is then at least as probable a conjecture as δ', though it is very far from certain that Aristarchus' text contained 31 (instead of 30) lines.

Bethe, *Hermes* 68 (1928) 90 ff., argued that the whole passage (19. 130–61) must be rejected on internal evidence. He observes how unnatural it is (a) that Penelope should talk about such matters in such detail to a stranger who has not yet even replied to her question what his name may be; (b) that Odysseus should entirely ignore all that she tells him here, not even alluding to the Suitors, or to the danger in which she stands (157 ff.), when he foretells the imminent return of her husband. I incline to the opinion that the external and internal evidence combine to make a strong case for regarding 130–61 as a subsequent addition to their present context.

(2) 2. 93–110: The resumption with ἡ δέ in 93 after δέ οἱ at the end of 92 is

jerky (not so the change from the present tenses of 90–92 to the past tenses of 93 ff. : that change follows naturally from the change in subject-matter; the present tenses are more or less inevitable from 89 to 92; the past tenses are required by the sense from 93 onwards). And the apparent contradiction between 89, 'The fourth year will soon be here', and 107, 'But when the fourth year arrived . . .', is exceptionally harsh. Focke (46, n. 1) follows Aristonicus and Eustathius in taking 89 to mean 'It is now three full years, and soon will be added a fourth full year (which is already in course)'; it is then not inconsistent to say that the web-incident occurred after the fourth year began. This seems to me very far-fetched (εἶσι does not mean either δίειοι (Aristonicus) or συμπληροῦται (Eustathius)): and I wonder if any listener ever understood 89 to mean anything but what it appears to mean, viz. 'It is now the third year, and a fourth will soon come', implying that we are now in the third year, and that the fourth year, though not far off, has not started yet.

A further point has been much debated: whether the description of the web-incident in the Second Book presupposes awareness of the description of it in the Nineteenth or vice versa. See Bethe, l.c.; Wilamowitz, *Heimkehr* 38 ff.; Schwartz 302 ff.; Von der Mühll 705, 735; Focke 45 f., 316 ff.; Merkelbach 62 ff. Bethe seems to me to have good reasons for saying that the description in the Second Book is intrinsically superior to that in the Nineteenth: 2. 106 ἔληθε δόλῳ (= 24. 141) is better than 19. 151 ἔληθον ἐγώ: 2. 108 τις ἔειπε γυναικῶν ἢ σάφα ᾔδη (= 24. 144) is much more vivid and appealing than the vague 19. 154 διὰ δμῳὰς κύνας οὐκ ἀλεγούσας; and 2. 109 ἀλλύουσαν ἐφεύρομεν (= 24. 145) has an effective accuracy of detail wanting in 19. 155 εἷλον ἐπελθόντες. There is therefore no particular difficulty in the relation of the one passage to the other: the later in sequence alters and adapts the earlier, sometimes for the worse, a natural state of affairs, whether one poet or more was at work.

Schwartz (302 f.) suggested that both 2. 93 ff. and 19. 130 ff. were added to the *Odyssey* after, and under the influence of, the Continuation (24. 128 ff.): 'a desperate notion, since the *Nekuia* [i.e. 24. 128 ff.] simply copies out the Second Book', exclaimed Wilamowitz (*Heimkehr* 39), applauded by Bethe and Focke. Whether Schwartz is right or wrong, the objection remains a manifest and monumental *petitio principii*.

26. It is therefore vain to argue either (a) that νόος δέ οἱ ἄλλα μενοίνα was already known to Odysseus from Athene's speech in 13. 381 (it would be very unlike the manner of the *Odyssey* to expect the listener to remember such a detail from so long ago; and I guess that very few listeners, or even readers, ever remembered it); or (b) that νόος δέ οἱ ἄλλα μενοίνα is merely a conventional formula associated with Penelope, especially with her behaviour toward the Suitors; that it is here simply descriptive of Penelope, not intended as an explanation of Odysseus' rejoicing: if this were so, it would make no difference to the main point at issue, which is that Odysseus' *rejoicing* is inexplicable unless he already knows that her encouragement of the Suitors is a sham; and in fact it is *not* a sham.

27. The earlier part of the passage is one of the few places in the *Odyssey* where tokens of relatively late composition are thickly clustered in contrast to their surroundings: 172 and 179 χρῶτα: this declension is foreign to the Epic (χρόα), except in the *Doloneia* 575; Wackernagel, *SUH* 146. 173 δάκρύοισι: one of the rare examples of this post-homeric prosody. 179 ἀπονίπτεσθαι: a very late formation; Wackernagel, op. cit. 74. 190 κλυντήρ: foreign to the Epic vocabulary (κλισμός). 190 τέῶς: also *Il.* 19. 189, 24. 658, cf. ἕῶς *Od.* 2. 78; the older Epic scanned τέος (τείος or τῆος). 191 θησαίατο: a monster, for θηησαίατο; rather a product of sheer ignorance than an ordinary *monstrum rhapsodicum* of the common type. 193 Κυθέρεια = Ἀφροδίτη: foreign to the Epic except in the relatively late lay about Ares and Aphrodite (*Od.* 8. 288). (This list is not exhaustive: notice further the abuse of language in

160 πετάσειε; the naming of the attendants Autonoe and Hippodameia, both here only (182) ; 192 κάλλεϊ apparently in a concrete sense, 'cosmetic'; the awkward dative in 199 φθόγγῳ ἐπερχόμεναι.) In the remainder of the passage, from about 200 to 304, the allowance of abnormalities is not above the average. There are some peculiarities in the vocabulary: 201 αἰνοπαθής, 224 ῥυστακτύς, 240 μεθύειν (also *Il.* 17. 390) and 246 Ἴασος: 269 γενειάω (cf. 176); all are foreign to the older Epic vocabulary. The prosody of πλέονες in 247 is unique in the Epic. 233–4 are feeble in sense and clumsy in expression. 265 ἀνέσει awaits elucidation. The natural inference is that the adaptation of the episode as a whole (158–304) to our *Odyssey* has led to some re-composing, by a relatively late poet, of the beginning only.

The earlier part of the scene has suffered further in a different way : things are said and done which may have been easily intelligible in some other context, but are not in this : (a) Penelope's 'futile laughter' (ἀχρεῖος γέλως)is downright meaningless in this context, and what she says to Eurynome is obscure and misleading. It is her heart's desire, she says, to appear before the Suitors and to tell her son not to consort with them so much. In fact it turns out that this reason for visiting the Suitors is not only feeble but also false. Her real reason is different and vastly more important—it is in order that she may announce that the time has come for her surrender. (b) Eurynome's reply is still more elliptical and obscure. She says in effect: 'Yes, go and talk to your son, *and beautify yourself beforehand*, for it is wrong to go on grieving forever, and your dearest wish—to see your son grown to manhood —is now fulfilled.' What is the meaning of this rigmarole? The sequel makes it clear enough : it is as if Eurynome knew that Penelope intends to announce her re-marriage. That is why Eurynome makes the proposal that she should beautify herself beforehand—a ridiculous suggestion in its present context, where Penelope is merely going to talk to her son in the presence of the Suitors, whom she hates (165). It is obvious enough (Seeck, *Quellen* 34 ff.) that this part of the passage (esp. 170–6) has suffered some mutilation, perhaps abbreviation (consider the lonely μέν in 175), in the course of a perfunctory and unsuccessful attempt to adapt the whole episode to its present surroundings. Nobody can seriously maintain that 163–76 are a free composition specially designed for this place, following readily on what goes before and leading naturally to the sequel.

Among other charges which have been brought against this episode, the most interesting is the flagrant breach of the Epic rule at 291–2 : in 291 the Suitors sent heralds to fetch gifts, in 292 the heralds return with the gifts. 'A considerable interval must be supposed, during which the action at the palace is at an absolute standstill. This is surely a violation of one of the most fundamental rules of Epic art', Monro, ad loc.

The question at issue is not seriously affected by the further problem whether Penelope's conversation with Telemachus (214–43) is a later addition to its context. See Wilamowitz, *HU* 30, and Monro, ad loc.: it is argued (a) that the speech of Eurymachus (244 ff.) follows so naturally after 212–13 that it must have been designed to follow *immediately*; (b) that 214–43, the removal of which leaves no trace, is 'irrelevant to the context, as it has nothing to do with the appearance of Penelope in the μέγαρον' ; (c) that this conversation ought to be held in secret, not in the presence of the Suitors. Opinions may well differ about the validity of these charges.

28. By Wilamowitz, *HU* 50 ff.; cf. Bethe 97 ff., Schwartz 107 ff., Woodhouse 75 ff., Merkelbach 1 ff. (Focke, 328 ff., takes the opposite view, but I cannot find in him any answer to what I take to be the most important parts of the argument: certainly he makes no, or too little, allowance for the fact that Wilamowitz's theory must (and does) hold that the episode in our *Odyssey* represents a deliberate

adaptation of an older source to present requirements. On the other hand Focke is clearly right in rejecting (331 f.) the very weak and subjective charges brought against 19. 395–466). On the treatment of this scene by P. W. Harsh (*A. J. Phil.* 71 (1950) 1 ff.; cf. W. Büchner, *Hermes* 75 (1940) 129 ff.) adequate judgement is passed by A. Lesky (*Homerforschung in der Gegenwart* 69): 'zuviel Interpretation zwischen den Zeilen.'

The case is little if at all strengthened by other arguments, e.g. that the whole course of Odysseus' interview with Penelope is designed to suggest the truth to her. (Wilamowitz, *HU* 52 ff., *Heimkehr* 44; Merkelbach 3 f.: 19. 298 f., Odysseus warns Penelope that her husband may return disguised—as *he* is; 225 ff., this knowledge of the detail of Odysseus' clothes is almost as good as a recognition-token; 306 f., Odysseus will return *today*. This is all too speculative. In particular the idea that 306 f. means, or could be understood by either Penelope or the poet's audience to mean, 'he will return *today*', is to be rejected absolutely. Merkelbach (3, n. 2) comments on Focke's view—viz. that 306 f. means 'tomorrow'—that it makes no difference, 'since, if Penelope takes the meaning to be "Odysseus will arrive to-morrow", the recognition must follow just the same'. I do not understand this; if the stranger says 'Odysseus will return tomorrow', he is obviously diverting Penelope's mind from the possibility that *he*, who has already arrived, might be Odysseus.)

The point is not seriously affected by the question whether 19. 346–8 are (as Aristarchus believed) an interpolation: in any case Odysseus rejects the services of other handmaidens, and accepts without demur the offer of Eurycleia's attendance. (It is clearly not true to say, as some have done, that Penelope's reply in 353 ff. *presupposes* Odysseus' having said 346 ff.)

29. Merkelbach (4, n. 1) thinks this explanation a mere subterfuge on the part of *die Modernen* (among them, V. d. Mühll 749, Focke 329; Hölscher, p. 69, has no difficulty in explaining the scene in terms of one of his *Typische Situationen*). But it is surely correct as an explanation of our text, and only becomes a subterfuge if used as a means of evading the main point. Whoever finally composed this scene, as it stands in our *Odyssey*, did precisely what *die Modernen* allege: he created a moment of great dramatic power by means of a motif which is very well suited to his purpose and very ill-suited to that of Odysseus. That is sufficient explanation of what he has done: but it leaves entirely open the question whether his use of this motif in this manner indicates that he is adapting to his own purpose a scene in which the recognition by Eurycleia did lead to the recognition by Penelope.

30. Schwartz 121 ff., Merkelbach 7 ff.

31. Merkelbach (1 ff.) brings this out very clearly, but states the conclusion too strongly for my taste: p. 15 'if you accept this explanation (of 158–304), then you are bound to explain all other passages in the same way'; similarly p. 6. I prefer to put it like this: the Niptra-episode independently offers evidence (not proof) of the theory that it was composed on the model of a scene which culminated in the recognition of Odysseus by Penelope before the action against the Suitors; common sense adds that that theory is confirmed by the fact that the existence of a version in which such a prior recognition occurred is proved by at least two other passages (18. 158 ff., 24. 167 ff.).

32. See Merkelbach, *Rhein. Mus.* 95 (1952) 23 ff., a most valuable and timely reaction against the fashionable practice of neglecting or despising some very awkward facts. See also Cauer, *Grundfragen* 112 f.; Bolling, *Ilias Atheniensium* 5 f.; Rhys Carpenter, *Folklore, Fiction and Saga in the Homeric Epics* 12 ff.

33. See Schwartz 148 ff., and especially Hartmann, *Untersuchungen über die Sagen vom Tod des Odysseus*, 1917. For the testimonia and fragments of the *Telegony* (a poem in two Books, by Eugammon of Cyrene), see Bethe, *Homer* ii. 185 ff.

(discussion 279 ff.). The most interesting recent discussion is that of Merkelbach, 142–53, 219–30: his theory would explain a lot (see esp. p. 150), but it depends to a considerable extent on a rather rough treatment of our meagre evidence about the *Telegony* at two points; (1) a special explanation has to be found for the fact that Proclus says nothing about an Underworld scene at the beginning of the *Telegony* (Merkelbach's explanation is at least not so unconvincing as Bethe's, op. cit. 284); (2) the alteration of εἰς 'Ιθάκην to εἰς τὴν ἤπειρον in Proclus (Merkelbach 146 f.), a change essential to one important aspect of the theory, seems to me entirely unjustified except by the requirements of the theory. But I do not pretend to have done justice to this very complicated and elusive topic.

VI

THE METHOD, TIME, AND PLACE OF THE COMPOSITION OF THE *ODYSSEY*

To the questions how, when, and where the *Iliad* and *Odyssey* were composed we can give none but vague answers, inspired partly by common sense and partly by our own judgement of their form and contents. There is not, and so far as we know never has been, any reliable historical record of these matters. The fact that tradition attached to both poems a single name, Homer, would be instructive if we knew what it meant. Taken literally, that tradition is certainly misleading: whether one man composed (substantially) either poem may be eternally disputed; that the same man did not compose both I take to be beyond question. The attribution of both *Iliad* and *Odyssey* (and incidentally a number of other Epic poems) to Homer may, for all we know, mean no more than that a poet of this name was preeminent among those through whose hands the traditional poems passed towards the end of a long period of development: we should still not know in what form the poems existed before him, or how much of their final shape and substance was his work.

It is proper to dismiss from the mind at the outset the prejudice, for which there is no confirmation in historical records, that the burden of proof rests upon those who deny unity of authorship, whether for *Iliad* or for *Odyssey*. Nothing was ever certainly known about Homer (at latest since the sixth century B.C.) except the name, and except the tradition which linked that name to the making of Epic poems in general, the *Iliad* and *Odyssey* in particular. When he lived, and where he lived, and precisely what he did, nobody ever knew in historical times: already in the fifth and fourth centuries B.C. widely different guesses were being made. Homer was a name without a history, though soon enough it acquired a fable.

10

I see no reason to doubt that a person, indeed a great poet, of that name existed and was remembered from the obscure past: but I think it certain that both the Wrath of Achilles and the Return of Odysseus were the subject of Epic poetry for (at least) several centuries; and that the two poems which we possess are not, in any ordinary sense of the word, original compositions, substantially the work of any one person. They are the final state of a long and continuous process of development. Suppose, if you will, that Homer was the name of the poet who created that final form: it is surely obvious that we, who do not possess for comparison any earlier form, have no hope of discovering what that process of development may have been, or what precisely its last great developer may have done—unless it should happen that the contents of the poems themselves give us some insight into their pre-Homeric form.

Now while I believe that the answers to our questions belong to the region of guesswork, not knowledge, I hold with equal firmness the opinion that such guesswork must be based on certain securely established foundations. I shall try, in this chapter, to summarize what I believe these foundations to be. What follows will be brief, dogmatic, and disappointing. In the vast desert of uncertainty, what green oases of comfort have been, or may still be, found?

I. If it is our desire to discover how the *Odyssey* was composed, to look into the minds and methods of Greek Epic poets in the centuries before the dawn of history, to understand and evaluate their achievement, it is absolutely necessary first to recognize how great a gulf divides two kinds of poetry—that which is composed and remembered in the mind, *without* the aid of writing, and that which is composed *with* the aid of writing. That the Homeric poems were composed and carried in the mind, and recited by word of mouth, and that this was the only method of their composition, and this for a long time the only mode of their publication to the audiences for which they were designed—the proof of these things is the outstanding achievement of an American scholar, Milman Parry,[1] whose premature death extinguished the brightest light that has been shed on the Greek Epic in our time.

In societies where the art of writing is unknown, the poet makes his verses out of metrical formulas—fixed groups of words, traditional phrases descriptive of particular ideas and readily adaptable to similar ideas; the stock of such formulas, gradually accumulated over a long period of time, supplies the poet at need with a whole group of lines, or a single line, or a part of a line, all ready-made. He cannot stop to meditate while he recites; he cannot read over—let alone change—what he composed a few hundred lines ago; he cannot plan in advance except in very broad outline. But whatever he wants to say, within the limits of certain traditional themes, may (and often must) be expressed in phrases long ago designed for that purpose, and immediately suggested to him by his practised memory. He may or may not be a good poet: he must be a good craftsman. There is a stock-in-trade, the vast number of traditional formulas, to be learnt only by long apprenticeship; and there is a technique, the craft of using and adapting formulas and systems of formulas, to be acquired only by long experience.

The Homeric Epic differs from all other Greek poetry, and from all poetry with which we (most of us) are familiar today, in just this respect: its elements are phrases, not words. It is largely composed of traditional formulas, fixed word-patterns, almost infinitely adaptable to the ideas suggested to the poet's imagination within the limits of his theme; and supplying lines, or parts of lines, more or less ready-made. In the *Iliad* and *Odyssey* this technique may be seen at a very advanced state of development, refined and thrifty, purified of superfluities, so that (in general) one formula cannot take the place of another, in the same part of the verse, without altering the meaning of what is being said. If the poet wishes to begin his verse with the thought 'But when they arrived . . .', he has one way, and one only, of expressing this, αὐτὰρ ἐπεί ῥ' ἵκοντο, 'denying himself all other ways of expressing the idea'.[2] The creation of the vast number of formulas, adaptable to almost all possible emergencies, must have been the work of many generations of poets; and from the refinement, thrift, and economy of the Homeric stock of phrases we are obliged to infer that we are at or near the culmination of a very long process.

Now the *Odyssey*, no less than the *Iliad*, is composed in this way: it reveals from start to finish the memory-technique of verse-making, the practice of composing from memory without the aid of writing. Whether the art of writing was known to its composers we may never know: what we do know, because we see it with our own eyes, is that the art of writing, if it was familiar, made little or no difference to the technique employed in the actual verse-making; that is still the formula-technique, the building of verses out of traditional phrases learnt by one generation from another and supplied to the poet by his practised memory at the moment required.

There is no longer any doubt about the fact; but one may well wonder whether it does not suggest some further questions of exceptional difficulty. Is not the complexity of the structure of the *Odyssey*—its blend of three stories into one; its blend of episodes within one story—beyond the limit of what is possible for a man who has nothing but his memory to assist him? And would not a poem thus composed be continually changing? Would it not differ from one recitation to another, and would it not become unrecognizably transformed in the course of a generation or two? Modern analogies confirm what common sense suggests—that 'the oral poem even in the mouth of the same singer is ever in a state of change; and it is the same when his poetry is sung by others'.[3]

These are difficult questions; I do no more than indicate the region in which their answer may be found. It is possible, or even likely, that the art of writing was practised (though not in general use) at the time when the first continuous *Odyssey* was composed. Now though that art played little or no part in the making of the poem, it might nevertheless be used to record the poem when made (or rather while making).[4] If this were so, the boundaries of the poet's powers would be greatly extended: he could then build, as nobody before such a time could build, a structure of considerable size and some complexity, if each development was preserved in writing; and his admirers or apprentices would be able to reproduce their master's voice much more faithfully than before, not because they could learn it from the written record—that was merely the architect's plan, not his structure—but because the version which they heard from the master was more or less unvarying. This does not imply that the master himself (and others after him) would cease to expand or otherwise alter his poem in the course of time: the written record is nothing more than an aid to memory, a tool of the trade. The text of a poem was still the spoken, not the written, word; the whole conception of a static poem in a standard text is entirely foreign to the memory-technique of verse-making and to the manner of its transmission from one generation to another.

This conception of an oral poetry, composed in the mind and designed for preservation by memory alone, has—or rather ought to have—revolutionized our understanding of the *Iliad* and *Odyssey*. It should be obvious that many of the principles of criticism applicable to a Virgil or a Milton have no place here. Virgil and Milton may be expected to choose a particular word or phrase because it most accurately represents their thought in a particular context. However much they may owe to the past, they are seldom limited by tradition to a particular mode of expression; they are free to form an individual style. In the Homeric poems, whatever the context and whoever the person may be, the same act, thought, or emotion is likely to be described in the same words; not because those words are particularly suitable to that person or context, but because those are the words which tradition supplies ready-made to the poet for the description of that act, thought, or emotion. His style is traditional and typical, not individual. He does not, as a rule, select or invent: he uses what his memory offers him, already adapted or readily adaptable to the part of his verse which he has to fill. It should be obvious too that the memory-technique of verse-composition and the employment of a traditional stock of phrases naturally impose severe limitations on the structure of the story and the characterization of the persons. It is very improbable that a poet who depends on nothing but his memory both for the making and for the preservation of his verses will so construct his plot that the true significance of an earlier part will emerge only in the light of a later part, and vice versa; except in very broad and simple conceptions integral to the main structure of his story. Delicate and subtle preparations *now* for what will follow in five hundred lines' time; veiled and indirect allusions *now* to what happened five hundred lines ago—such artifice lies beyond his power, even supposing that it lay within the bounds of his imagination. References backwards and forwards (over more than a short space) will be more or less explicit, and limited to the broad outlines of the story.

As with the plot, so with the characters. In poetry of this kind the characters will be—as indeed they are—envisaged in fairly broad outline. Their thoughts will be (for the most part) expressed in language which is traditional and typical, not specially designed for a given person in a given place; and the thoughts themselves (apart from their expression) will often be traditional and typical, not individual. Subtlety of soul, complexity of character, true portrayal of personality—for these we must wait until the practice of the art of writing affords the poet the necessary leisure and the necessary means for reflection, for planning the future in some detail, and for correcting the past.

Thus in answering the question how the *Odyssey* was composed we must start from the established position that this poem was composed in the mind, and destined for preservation by the memory alone, by a poet or poets highly skilled in the use of a traditional language which had been gradually developed over a very long period of time. Do not therefore suppose that little or no room is left for the exercise of an individual's poetic talent. A man may be either the master or the slave of the rules by which he lives; the conventions of an art have never yet confined genius and mediocrity in equal chains. The meeting of Hector and Andromache, the embassy to Achilles, the Doloneia, the ransom of Hector's body, the stories of Nausicaa and of Polyphemus (to give only a few examples) prove that those who worked within the limits prescribed by the Greek Epic tradition could attain the highest point of excellence in the poetic art. Only we have wholly misunderstood the nature of their achievement unless we recognize that they do, and must, work within those limits. They are not free (except to a very limited extent) to frame their own phraseology; they are not free (except, again, to a very limited extent) to invent new characters or to depict traditional characters in a mode contrary to tradition; they are narrowly limited in their choice of theme, in what their persons say and do; and there are some aspects of life and manners which they may not reflect at all. 'Homer' has often been highly praised for doing what had been done before him, and what he could have done in no other way. Intricacy of design and subtleties of thought wholly alien to the oral technique of composition have often been sought (and found) in him. The road is open (since Milman Parry found it for us) to a juster understanding of the distinction between the traditional and the non-traditional elements in the *Iliad* and *Odyssey*.

So much for the first of our fundamental facts. And here, with the utmost brevity, is the second.

The study of the language of Homer (and particularly its spelling) in our manuscripts proves beyond question that our manuscripts are the ultimate posterity of an *Athenian* parentage. The fact is certain: the detail of the genealogy is at many points conjectural. It appears probable that at Athens, in the sixth century B.C., there was made, and thereafter copied and circulated, a more or less standard text of the two poems; a descendant (or descendants) of this survived into the age of Alexandrian scholarship, when it was re-edited especially by Aristarchus, whose text became the standard for all succeeding ages. Fragments of the *Iliad* and *Odyssey* written on papyrus from the first century B.C. onwards for half a millennium have taught us that our Homer is Aristarchus' Homer, the direct descendant of his standard text; and that the poems have suffered no alterations of any importance since his time. Unfortunately we are unable to make the further comparison between the text of Aristarchus in the first century and the text of the Athenians in the sixth century B.C.: the former we know, the latter we do not know; evidence concerning its form and substance is meagre, mostly indirect, and often of doubtful reliability. For the *Iliad*, what can be done has been done by Professor Bolling; for the *Odyssey*, I must provisionally confine myself to the negative position that there is very little evidence to suggest that the text of Aristarchus differed substantially from the Athenian text of the sixth century B.C.; though we must reckon with a considerable number of minor additions and alterations.

The evidence of our own manuscripts proves the existence of a standard Athenian text of Homer; and history assures us that there is only one era in which this could have been made—the sixth century B.C., whether early, in the time of Solon, or later, in the time of Peisistratus or his sons. Now it happens that it was common knowledge, recorded for us from the fourth century onwards, that the recitation of the whole of Homer, 'exclusively and consecutively', was instituted at Athens for the festival of the Panathenaea in the sixth century; it was common knowledge too that the Athenians in that century had been able in some way to affect the text of Homer, inserting additional lines to which appeal might thereafter be made, as if their text, and no other, was generally acknowledged to be the standard. We are pleased to welcome this external evidence, though we did not really need it: the history of our own manuscripts had already proved essentially the same conclusion. As Professor Rhys Carpenter says, 'If antiquity had neglected to record for us the Peisistratean recension of Homer, we should have had to invent it for ourselves as a hypothesis essential to the facts.'

It thus appears certain enough that the creative phase of the Greek Epic, when poems composed in the mind were preserved in the memory, ended in what might be called an editorial phase, when the finally developed memory-poems were committed to writing in a particular form, and forever thereafter preserved in that form. It follows that in the study of the *Odyssey* we must make proper allowance for the possibilities that the editorial phase may have been the first full and continuous text ever made in writing;

and that the form in which it survived thereafter may have been very much affected by the conditions—unknown but by no means unimaginable—under which the Athenian text-makers performed their task. In short, our minds must be open to the fact that the text of our *Odyssey* may owe something, or even much, to two sources in particular—the persons who preserved the poems by memory for (at least) several generations, and the person (or persons) who made that standard written text at Athens in the sixth century B.C. which is the ultimate written source of our text today.

I touch in parenthesis on one other related topic.

Among those things which are certainly known is the following: that the making of Greek Epic poetry on the subject of the Trojan War reaches back beyond the dark ages to Mycenean Hellas. Our poems prove to us that their metre, phraseology, and subject-matter were long ago (to some indefinable extent) the property of poets composing in that dialect of Greek which was spoken by the Myceneans.[5] We are thus incidentally enabled to explain what would otherwise be a great mystery—how it could happen that the Homeric poems can accurately describe material objects which had not existed in the world since the downfall of Mycenean Hellas. The descriptions of such objects had come down to posterity embedded in an unbroken tradition of remembered poetry. But under what conditions did the Greek Epic survive and develop continuously throughout a period of three or four hundred years (or longer), an age of darkness during which the hands of men were otherwise idle, and their minds asleep, leaving no trace except the tokens of a rude and stagnant poverty? Can we point to any institution, itself continuously preserved throughout the dark ages, of a type favourable or necessary to the continuous preservation of the Greek Epic? I think we can.

When history dawns on the island of Lesbos in the seventh century B.C. we discover there a mode of government hardly distinguishable from that of Agamemnon at the siege of Troy, as portrayed especially in the second Book of the *Iliad*. The will of the sovereign power, Agamemnon himself, is not absolute: he must first summon a council of elders, and whatever they approve must be declared to an *agora*, an assembly of all lesser noblemen. In the seventh century B.C. at Lesbos the political constitution is exactly the same; and it happens that the sovereign power is still in the direct line of descent from the family of Agamemnon. From the poems of Alcaeus, written in the late seventh and early sixth centuries, and from Aristotle, for whom Alcaeus was the principal source, we learn that the descendants of Agamemnon's son, Orestes, were still in supreme power when the dark ages end, and that the state was still governed in the same way: the will of the sovereign must be sanctioned by a council and approved by an assembly of all men who rank as citizens.[6] In this place certainly, and in other places presumably, the royal family survived throughout the dark ages from beginning to end. At such a court, itself continuously preserved, the recitation and composition of Heroic poetry might well be continuously practised: the *Odyssey* itself portrays the professional poet as a member of the royal household—Phemius at the court of Odysseus at Ithaca; Demodocus at the court of Alcinous at Phaeacia.

II. When was the *Odyssey* composed? The meaning of this question I take to be: at what date did the traditional songs about Odysseus culminate in the continuous and unified narrative combining the Journey of Telemachus, the Wanderings of Odysseus, and the Slaying of the Suitors, substantially as represented in our text?

In the quicksand appears one tuft of solid ground: I nimbly leap upon it. Nobody in antiquity ever supposed that 'Homer' lived in what might properly be called the historical era. The contrast between the eighth and seventh centuries B.C. is in this respect most remarkable: from the eighth century little or nothing was handed down to posterity, except by word of mouth; from the seventh century there emerged a flood of literary and historical records. I suppose that there can be no serious doubt that the general use of the alphabet—I mean the art of writing as a common practice, however long the alphabet may have been familiar to some—was the efficient cause of this change, drawing the line which divides the one period so sharply from the other. And the composition of the *Odyssey* must be put back beyond that line: not because of its memory-technique of verse-making (that technique may have survived long after the general use of the alphabet) but because the absence of all information about these poems and their authors (except a mere name) would be quite incomprehensible if they belonged to an era in which so many other things were faithfully recorded—most of them much less interesting to the Greeks than the history of their greatest heirlooms, the *Iliad* and *Odyssey*.

The evidence of language and archaeology is less helpful than we hope: for that which is relatively late may have been added to the poem in the course of its transmission through the centuries; and that which is relatively early may have been derived from memory of the past, not from contemporary life. Miss Lorimer, in *Homer and the Monuments* (509 ff.), finds only two 'concrete objects mentioned in the *Odyssey* which cannot have found a place there before the seventh century'. One of these is the lamp with which Athene lights Odysseus and Telemachus when they remove the armour from the dining-hall (19. 34). Now a lamp is an object which we find in Mycenean chamber-tombs, in the remote past, and commonly again in the seventh century B.C.;[7] but never a specimen in the intermediate dark ages. It is enough for our purpose to note, with more satisfaction than surprise, that Athene's lamp illuminates one of those parts of the *Odyssey* which has come into the poem from some other source, the episode of the removal of the armour. The other object is the 'brooch or rather clasp which fastened the cloak of Odysseus when on his way to Troy' (19. 226–31; Lorimer, ibid. 511 ff.). This is a complicated matter, which I shall not now discuss. There is room for difference of opinion at more than one point; and, supposing that it were agreed that this passage describes an object which did not exist in the world before the seventh century B.C., it would remain possible that the passage was added to the poem in that century.

So much for the lower limit of date, which we confidently place about 700 B.C.: not many scholars have ever thought that the poet of the *Odyssey* was more or less a contemporary of Archilochus,

Callinus, and Alcman. As for the earlier limit, our information is equally meagre and much more inconclusive. The Greek language in the *Odyssey* reflects at many points a more advanced stage of development than in the *Iliad*, despite that general uniformity which is imposed on both by the use of a traditional stock of ready-made phrases: but this fact is not very helpful to us in our search for an approximate date. The chief archaeological arguments are stated and discussed by Miss Lorimer (ibid. 505 ff.). She (like others) finds the most solid ground under the feet of the Phoenicians in the middle of the poem (just that part where a poet of a continuous *Odyssey* seemed identifiable): 'The earliest documented appearance of the Phoenicians in the West is in Sardinia in the first half of the eighth century. There is no evidence that their ships had come even as far as the Aegean at any earlier date, though they were probably known in Crete and possibly in Rhodes.' It would, I think, be very imprudent not to allow a margin of error of half a century (or more) in respect of such an argument from archaeological silence: the most recent expert opinion requires a much earlier date for Phoenician activity in the west (Albright, *AJA* 54 (1950) 174 f.); and Miss Lorimer herself points to the warning given by the town of Citium in Cyprus, which is now known to have had a Phoenician settlement in the ninth century B.C., though until very recently nothing of the sort could have been inferred from archaeological remains.

Voluminous are the writings on this topic: what can be, has been, said. I have the doubtful comfort of reflecting that it is no longer possible even to make a mistake that is truly original. If we distinguish between what is reasonably certain and what is not, we shall find that the date of the culmination of the *Odyssey* cannot be defined within narrower limits than a couple of hundred years. It cannot be put so far forward as the seventh century: it would be very hard to justify a date so far back as the tenth. Whereabout it should be placed in the long interval we cannot tell. Our lips are sealed by ignorance, or opened only to utter interesting but unverifiable guesses. We shall be guided, in default of objective evidence, by impressions and indications, which, for what they are worth, with no very firm voice, tell in favour of a date somewhere in the middle of that obscure period.

III. Where was the *Odyssey* composed? To this question we can give an important negative reply: that the Odyssean poet lived in a region isolated from that in which the *Iliad* was composed.

The traditional vocabulary at the disposal of the *Iliad* is the product of a very long period of time and experience. The man who would so master it that it is at the disposal of his memory for the rapid making of verses (with or without the aid of writing) must devote many years of practice to his profession. Now it is a simple fact of observation that the traditional vocabulary of the *Odyssey* differs greatly from that of the *Iliad*, over and above such differences as may be necessarily connected with the difference in the subject-matter. Not only the extent but also the nature of the differences indicates that these two vocabularies could not have existed in the mind of a single poet—or of one school of poets, unless there was a long interval of time between the two poems. It would be absurd to suppose that one man might hold in his memory *two* traditional vocabularies, one for use in the *Iliad*, the other for use in the *Odyssey*. Moreover, so large is the content, and so gradual the development, of such treasuries of formular phrases, that there is no possibility that so great a change might have occurred within the lifetime of one man.

Many of the differences appear to be satisfactorily explained if we suppose that the *Iliad* was composed much earlier than the *Odyssey*; and that is the explanation most commonly accepted. There seems at first sight no need to argue that the place as well as the time must have been different. I conclude this chapter by expressing a few thoughts on this subject.[8]

That the *Odyssey* represents a traditional vocabulary at a later stage of development than the *Iliad* may be proved by a variety of observations. The topic requires, and would amply repay, a full investigation. I select from my notes a few points of interest.

A number of very old words and forms, common in the *Iliad*, re-appear seldom or not at all in the *Odyssey*. The old Aeolic adjectival ending -εννός survives in the *Iliad* in two words only, ἐρεβεννός and ἀργεννός, both preserved in traditional formulas and used in the *Iliad* commonly enough: in the *Odyssey*, which has abundant opportunity to use both words (whether in or out of their formulas) the latter adjective appears once only and the former not at all.[9] The old Aeolic prefix ἐρι- survives in the *Iliad* in eleven adjectives, most of them embedded in formulas: these are quite out of fashion in the *Odyssey*, which (while adding a twelfth to the list) has discarded four of them altogether and uses another five only once or twice each.[10] Specially noteworthy among these is the adjective ἐριβῶλαξ, ἐρίβωλος, which leaps to the mind of the *Iliad*'s poet on twenty-one occasions, whatever place is to be described—Troy, Thrace, Phthia, Tarne, Larissa, Lycia, Paeonia, Ascania; for the Odyssean poet, on the other hand, this is a word which, so far from being among his favourites, has almost disappeared from his vocabulary (ἐριβῶλαξ only 13. 235, ἐρίβωλος only 5. 34). The non-Ionic particle μάν occurs in the *Iliad* twenty-two times, in the *Odyssey* only twice.[11] Another non-Ionic particle, θήν, occurs thirteen times in the *Iliad*, in the *Odyssey* only thrice. The poets of the *Iliad* had at their disposal the convenient device of beginning a line τύνη δ᾽ . . . (τύνη δ᾽ ἔστηκας, τύνη δ᾽ εἰσελθών, ὡς τύνη κέκμηκας; six examples): not once is this to be found in the *Odyssey*—evidently τύνη had disappeared from its vocabulary, if indeed it ever existed therein. The useful adverb εἶθαρ (formular, εἶθαρ δὲ προσηύδα, εἶθαρ δ᾽ ὑπὸ γούνατ᾽ ἔλυσεν, and four other examples) suggests itself to the poets of the *Iliad* nine times, to the poets of the *Odyssey* never: similarly another old adverbial form, ὕπαιθα, familiar to the makers of the *Iliad*, has vanished from the Odyssean vocabulary. When the poet wishes to say 'of him', 'of himself', in the *Iliad* his favourite expression is ἕθεν (sixteen appearances); this form is wholly out of fashion in the *Odyssey*, where it barely survives in a single example.[12]

    This disappearance or decrease of the archaic (which may readily be illustrated by further examples) is balanced by the appearance or increase of the relatively recent. The *Odyssey* differs from the *Iliad* in the matter of abstract nouns,[13] not only in respect of quantity but also in mere vocabulary (only about one quarter of them are common to both poems). The *Odyssey* makes more use of the shorter form of the dative plural in -οις, -αις instead of -οισι, -αισι,[14] and of the freedom to leave a vowel short before a combination of mute and liquid (or nasal) consonants.[15] A long list of generally serviceable words might be compiled which are found in the *Odyssey* only: I select a few for special mention. (1) The *Odyssey* has at its disposal the noun χρῆμα, so common in all later speech and literature, to denote 'property' or 'possessions': not once is this useful word to be found in the *Iliad*, which, when it needs to express the idea represented by χρῆμα in the *Odyssey* (as it does quite often), employs an entirely different word (κτῆμα, common also in the *Odyssey*).[16] (2) Suppose that a poet's vocabulary included the common noun ὄνομα (or οὔνομα), 'name': how useful it would be; how often might he use it in the *Iliad*! But was it ever used by the makers of that poem? Probably not at all, just possibly once or twice: in the *Odyssey*, on the other hand, it is a common word, a normal element in the vocabulary.[17] (3) The *Iliad* has no substantive to express the idea of 'hope' or 'expectation', from the root of ἔλπομαι: the *Odyssey* has two, both so familiar as to be embedded in traditional phrases, ἐλπίς and ἐλπωρή.[18] (4) The combination of particles τοιγάρ is a normal tool of the trade for the Odyssean poet (eighteen appearances): it is not certain that it was ever used in the making of the *Iliad*, apart from the *Doloneia*.[19]

Since we are dealing with a traditional Epic vocabulary it is the phrase rather than the individual word which should attract our attention. What is the explanation of the fact that the *Odyssey* has a very large number of formular phrases which would be suitable to a very large number of contexts in the *Iliad* but never occur there? I give a few examples out of many: φρεσὶ (κακὰ) βυσσοδομεύων, ἀνδράσιν ἀλφηστῆσιν, τετληότι θυμῷ, ἤρχετο μύθων, ἀσπαστὸν ἐείσατο, ὀδὰξ ἐν χείλεσι φύντες, ὃ θαρσαλέως ἀγόρευε, μοῖρ' ὀλοὴ καθέλῃσι τανηλεγέος θανάτοιο, μεταλλῆσαι καὶ ἐρέσθαι, ἀληθέα πάντ' ἀγορεύσω, πολυκλύστῳ ἐνὶ πόντῳ, κατεκλάσθη φίλον ἦτορ, ἐπαρτέας ἔμμεν ἑταίρους, τῇ δ' ἄπτερος ἔπλετο μῦθος, ἔτι γὰρ καὶ ἐλπίδος αἶσα, νῦν δ' ἄχομαι, ἐπηετανὸν γὰρ ἔχουσι, λύθεν δέ οἱ ἄψεα πάντα, γόον δ' ὠίετο θυμός, παλίντιτα ἔργα, Κακοΐλιον οὐκ ὀνομαστήν, τερψιμβρότου ἠελίοιο; how long a time would be required to create so great an addition to the stock of formular phrases? Surely they were not yet at the disposal of the *Iliad*: or are we to believe that a poet whose memory had in store such expressions as ἤρχετο μύθων, μοῖρ' ὀλοὴ καθέλῃσι, λύθεν δέ οἱ ἄψεα πάντα, τετληότι θυμῷ, Κακοΐλιον οὐκ ὀνομαστήν, ἀληθέα πάντ' ἀγορεύσω (to mention only a few) never once thought of them in 15,000 lines? So great is the difference between *Iliad* and *Odyssey* in their stocks of phrases that we may begin to wonder whether any reasonable lapse of time will account for it. Certainly the lifetime of one man could not possibly suffice. We have hitherto considered the relation between the two poems to be that of father and son: is it not much more probable that they are elder and younger brother, living in different places and developing in different ways? I suggest that this is so, and that it can be proved to be so. The Odyssean poet is not only later in time than the *Iliad*: he is also entirely isolated from the *Iliad*; he does not know things which he must have known if he was familiar with the *Iliad* in anything resembling its present form.

There are certain words which are common in the *Iliad*; which remain common in all later Greek literature; but which never occur in the *Odyssey* although the scope for them is very wide. I draw particular attention to two examples which seem to me to preclude all but the remotest possibility that mere chance might be the cause of this remarkable by-passing of the *Odyssey*.

Consider first the common Greek word for the flame of fire: there is the familiar noun φλόξ, used nineteen times in the *Iliad*; there are two adjectives, φλογεός and ζαφλεγής, another noun φλέγμα, two verbs φλέγω (with its compounds ἐπι- and κατα-) and φλεγέθω, bringing the total of usages of this root in the *Iliad* up to thirty-two. Not once in the whole of the *Odyssey* is any of these words, or any other word derived from this root, to be found. Why not? In the *Iliad* the use of these words is naturally suggested to the poet by a context in which a fire is burning: are there no fires burning in the *Odyssey*? I count more than fifty.

What is the reason why these words, φλόξ and its fellows, so common in the *Iliad* and in later poetry, are absent from the *Odyssey*? There are (I suppose) two theoretically possible reasons: it must be either because the root from which all these words are derived was wholly unknown to the Odyssean poet; or because of mere chance. And you will naturally ask, how likely is that chance? One can only judge from the commonness of this root in other substantial volumes of poetry. The proportions are such that, if the length of their works were the same as that of the *Odyssey*, this root would be found 25 times in Hesiod, 40 in Pindar, 42 in Aeschylus, 20 in Sophocles, 22 in Euripides; and even in Aristophanes (the words are largely confined to dignified poetry) about 12 times. It seems clear enough that the chance, even if this were an isolated example, could cheerfully be left to those who back horses at about 25 to 1; but it is not an isolated example.

The principal theme of the *Odyssey* is the Return and Revenge of Odysseus: the second half of the poem is primarily concerned with the payment to be exacted by Odysseus from the Suitors for their misconduct in his palace. Now few if any words in the Greek language are so appropriate to this theme as ποινή and its cognate ἄποινα, 'the price of injury', 'compensation', 'the penalty paid'. These words are common in the *Iliad* (ποινή 10 times; ἄποινα, ἀνάποινον, 26) and remain current throughout later literature: they exist in our minds so soon as we have read through the *Iliad* once; if they existed in the mind of the Odyssean poet, to whose theme they are so peculiarly suitable, what is the explanation of the fact that he never once thought of them in the course of 12,000 lines? And yet he did know a word from this root, and thought it specially applicable to the conduct of the Suitors—νήποινος, a word which does *not* occur in the *Iliad*, and which *never* had a life of its own in literature after the *Odyssey*;[20] he could use this obsolete word with special reference to the conduct of the Suitors, but not once did the common words ποινή, ἄποινα suggest themselves to his lively mind. In my submission there is only one possible excuse for him: ποινή and ἄποινα simply did not exist in his vocabulary. Or have we again to admit the operation of mere chance? There may be some excitement, but there is not

as a rule much sense, in backing horses at odds of 25 to 1 : to back
several such horses in the same race indicates that whatever your
interest in the matter may be, it is not the desire to be guided by
reason.[21] If there are, as indeed there are, common Greek words,
found in the *Iliad* and continuing into later Greek literature, but
excluded from the *Odyssey*, though specially appropriate to its
theme in general and to many of its passages in particular, then I
see only one rational explanation of the fact : that the traditional
vocabularies of *Iliad* and *Odyssey* diverged at an early date, and
went their separate ways; and that the words which we have
been considering came to exist in the one but never came to exist
in the other.

Arguments derived from single words are not all of equal
weight. The poet of the *Iliad* has constantly in his mind the words
φόβος, 'flight' (36 times), ἕλκος, 'wound' (21), κλόνος 'turmoil'
(with κλονέω, 26) : not once does any of these common words
occur to the poet of the *Odyssey*. You will say that they are all
much more readily suggested by the subject-matter of the *Iliad* :
true, but candour will compel you to admit that there is abundant
opportunity for their use in the *Odyssey* too—is it again *by mere
chance* that none of them came into the poet's mind in the composition of 12,000 lines? Mere chance already wears a strained
and haggard look : now add something to its discomfort. The
Odyssean poet often needs an adjective to signify 'swift' : we,
who know the *Iliad* only moderately well, think at once of its
formular words, λαιψηρός and καρπάλιμος;[22] the Odyssean poet
never thought of them. However often the idea of 'defend', 'ward
off', or more generally 'assist' may be present, the favourite verb
of the *Iliad*, χραισμεῖν (19 appearances), is never in our poet's
mind. Is it really nothing but mere chance which deprived the
Odyssean poet of such generally serviceable words, all known to
the *Iliad*, as κύρω (with κυρέω, 4 appearances), μαρμαίρω (9),
ματάω (3), οἰκτείρω (5), ὀρθόω (6), παμφαίνω (8), παρεῖπον (6),
πηδάω (3), αἰχμή (36), ὀμίχλη (4), ἀφρός (with ἀφρέω, 5), κρουνός
(3), λοίγος and λοίγιος (25), ὄκνος (with ὀκνέω, 5), ὄφελος (3),
πάταγος (with πατάσσω, 7), πέτρος (4), ἀλίαστος (7), ἀμείλιχος

and ἀμείλικτος (5), αὐτόματος (4), ἄφαντος (2), δήιος (46), διίφιλος (17), ἐᾱνός and ἑᾱνός (10), ἐλεύθερος (4), εὔζωνος (7), ζάθεος (7), ἵλαος (3), κωφός (3), μαλερός (3), μαρμάρεος (3), μέρμερος (6), νηπίαχος (3), νηπύτιος (9), ξυνός (with ἐπίξυνος, ξυνήιος, 6), σφεδανός (3), τέλε(ι)ος (4), and many more? Was it by mere chance that the whole of the *Odyssey* was composed without a single one of the following formular expressions ever coming into the poet's mind—φρεσὶ πευκαλίμῃσι, ὑπέροπλον ἔειπες, λαμπρὸν φάος ἠελίοιο, δέμας πυρὸς αἰθομένοιο, οὐκ ἀλεγίζω οὐδ' ὄθομαι, ἐρεβεννὴ νύξ, μοῖρα κραταιή, οὐκ ἀμέλησε, ὄσσε φαεινώ, μή νύ τοι οὐ χραισμῇ, ἠὼς μὲν κροκόπεπλος, βάσκ' ἴθι, μέγα σθένος, αἰσχροῖς ἐπέεσσιν, πυκινὸν ἔπος, τὸν δὲ σκότος ὄσσε κάλυψε, βρότον αἱματόεντα, and dozens more such recurrent phrases which are firmly fixed in our minds, and quickly supplied by our memories, so soon as we have merely read the *Iliad* once or twice?[23] How could it happen that not one of them suggested itself to the poet in the making of a poem so long as the *Odyssey*? If you are still backing horses at long odds, your paddock is already congested with unpromising cattle: let us now inspect an outsider of curious colour. Let the *Odyssey* be later in time than the *Iliad*; let mere chance have more room than it has a right to. What is to be said about the fact that the *Odyssey* alone preserves a number of immensely ancient words and forms, some of them at least so ancient as to be already of uncertain meaning at the time when they were used in the *Odyssey*? σὺ δὲ τηυσίην ὁδὸν ἔλθῃς, ἀνδράσιν ἀλφηστῇσιν, προμνηστῖναι ἐσέλθετε, βυκτάων ἀνέμων, καιρουσσέων ὀθόνων, πόδες δ' ὑπερικταίνοντο, ἀσπαίροντα λάων, Ἴασον Ἄργος, θεὰ δασπλῆτις Ἐρινύς, πανθυμαδὸν ὀκριόωντο, ἀδευκής, ἀμφουδίς, ὀλοφώια? From what source did these and their brethren come to the Odyssean poet? Not from any familiarity with the *Iliad*, as we see with our own eyes. Certainly they were not recent creations, first formed in an interval of time between the two poems. Obviously they go very far back; they belong to a remote period in the development of the traditional vocabulary. But if the *Odyssey* is later in time than the *Iliad*, and these words and phrases were not preserved by the *Iliad*, how were they preserved? Once more: either their absence from the *Iliad* is the effect of mere chance; or we must conclude that the Odyssean vocabulary diverged from that of the *Iliad*, preserving some things which the *Iliad* discarded, and discarding some things which the *Iliad* preserved. The stream of the Greek Epic divided, at an early date in the dark ages, into two reaches: the main flood was more or less equally distributed between the two, but the courses which each followed, and the tributaries which ran into them, were different.

Now if we conclude that *Iliad* and *Odyssey* were created in separate regions, each with its own treasury of traditional phrases, what, if anything, can we say about the period of time, probably a couple of hundred years, during which they were handed down to posterity by word of mouth? Here is a remarkable fact which may be brought up to reinforce our general argument. As time passed, and generation after generation recited the poems, relatively modern words made their way into them—words common in later Greek, but not included in the traditional phrases of the older Epic. Some of these words are common to both poems, but a surprisingly large number entered the one but not the other. In the *Odyssey* we meet for the first time such common and useful words as ἀνθεῖν ἀπιστεῖν ἥδεσθαι θεραπεύειν θηρεύειν λακτίζειν μακαρίζειν στερεῖν; ἀνίη βολή δάφνη ἑορτή εὐχή ζωή λέσχη μορφή φήμη χοή; ταχύτης; νεανίας (and -ίς); θεσμός κοῖτος (and -ή) μῶμος οἶστρος σποδός (and -ιή) ὕμνος ψάμμος; εὖρος πάχος; ἄθυμος βίαιος γνώριμος δῆλος εὔθυμος ἥμερος ἴδιος λυπρός σφοδρός τίμιος χρόνιος; ἐπιστήμων μνήμων ἀτελής τάλας; ἅπαξ ἡνίκα πέλας πλήν, and many more of the same generally serviceable type. Most of these occur once only or very seldom in the *Odyssey*: no doubt they have not come from the source but have entered the stream farther down; the point of interest at present is that not one of these words, all of them so useful and most of them so common in later Greek, ever entered the stream of the *Iliad*. The *Iliad* has its own store of such words, absent from the old formula-vocabulary but continuing into later literature—only by-passing the *Odyssey*: ἄκοσμος βοηθόος γενναῖος ἐρατός ἐραννός ἡσύχιος ἱμερτός κρυπτάδιος μιαρός σκολιός τυφλός ὑγιής; ἀμύσσειν ἀφρονεῖν διαφθείρειν ζητεῖν μαραίνειν μισεῖν; ἀνδράποδον καῦμα ὄφις σκέλος χαλινός; δεῖ ἐνταῦθα μέσφα μεταξύ μέχρι. Again, most of these occur once only or very seldom in the *Iliad*: they may well have entered the stream a long way down its course; but, again, not one of them ever entered the stream of the *Odyssey*.[24]

Thus the evidence strongly suggests not only that these two poems were largely created by persons possessed of two divergent stocks of phrases, but also that they were transmitted to posterity by persons whose own language developed differently or at different paces, or who differed at least in respect of what was deemed admissible in Epic verse. The *Odyssey* has so much that the *Iliad* must have used if it was known; the *Iliad* has so much that the *Odyssey* must have used if it was known. The differences cannot be explained in terms of the priority in time of the one poem over the other: they point clearly enough to the conclusion that the two poems were composed and transmitted in separate regions of Hellas.

How little the one region knew or cared about the ideas and conventions of the other may be illustrated by the fundamental differences between the two in their conceptions of Olympus and the gods; in their social and ethical relations; and in numerous other ways. Not the least remarkable of such conflicts is the difference in their ideas of the proper material for poetry: to the one, it is the more or less historical record of the past, the story of the Trojan War, the faintly remembered splendours of an earlier civilization with its great events and glories; to the other, it is the folk-tale and the fairy-tale, the wicked giant, the beautiful sorceress, the goddess with the magic wand, the virtuous wife, the return of the rightful king. And so little regard have the Odyssean poets for the sanctities which invest the great heroes of the *Iliad* that they transform one of the greatest into a figure of folk-tale. Such an Odysseus, so far removed from his natural setting, is capable of speaking as follows (8. 215 ff.): 'Well do I know how to handle the polished bow. I should be the first to shoot and strike my man in the throng of foemen, however many comrades might stand beside me and shoot their arrows. Only

Philoctetes surpassed me in archery in the land of Troy, when-soever we Achaeans used bow and arrow; of all others I declare myself to be the best by far.' Picture the scorn and indignation of a poet brought up in the tradition of the *Iliad*: is this fellow so profoundly ignorant as to be unaware that no first-class hero in the *Iliad* ever deigned to use the bow in warfare?[25] The bow is a weapon reserved for the barbarian enemy, for your own rank and file, and for a few eccentric outsiders like the Locrians: whoever heard of Achilles, Agamemnon, Ajax, Menelaus, Odysseus using a bow in battle? Were this truth and this blunder the work of one and the same person, or even of one and the same branch of the Epic art?

Consider finally that the *Odyssey*, although it presupposes the story of the siege of Troy, '*never repeats or refers to any incident re-lated in the Iliad*' (Monro, *Od.* ii. 325). It is as if the Odyssean poet were wholly ignorant of that particular story which is told in the *Iliad*. Nowhere is there any allusion to the wrath of Achilles or to the death of Hector, or indeed to any other incident, large or small, described in the *Iliad*. Yet the *Odyssey* often pauses to nar-rate some part of the Trojan story and refers freely to a variety of older and contemporary Epic poems—*always excluding the Iliad*. There is Helen's tale of Odysseus' entry into the city of Troy in disguise (4. 235 ff.); there is Menelaus' story of the wooden horse (4. 266 ff.); we hear of Odysseus' valour in battle over Achilles' corpse (5. 309 ff.), and of the rivalry between Odysseus and Ajax (11. 543 ff.); Nestor tells at some length of a quarrel between Agamemnon and Menelaus (3. 103 ff.); Demodocus sings of a quarrel between Odysseus and Achilles (8. 74 ff.). Are we seriously asked to believe that a poet (or poets) who knew the *Iliad* might compose a poem of 12,000 lines concerning one of the *Iliad*'s greatest heroes without ever showing the slightest aware-ness of that poem? The purpose of the Odyssean references to the Trojan story is almost uniformly to illustrate more brightly the virtues of Odysseus: could the poet find no such material in the *Iliad*? Or is it again *by mere chance* that the *Iliad* is so consistently ignored? We do not expect the Odyssean poet to re-tell what was already told in the *Iliad*: but is there any conceivable reason why he should absolutely exclude it from his thought, why he should debar himself from the slightest allusion to the greatest of the poems about the greatest of his heroes? This curious fact, that the *Odyssey* shows no awareness of the existence of the *Iliad*, is generally thought (by the few who notice it) to afford a problem, for which no very pleasing solution is suggested: to me it affords no problem, but only comfort and corroboration—the reason why the *Iliad* is ignored by the Odyssean poet is simply that the *Iliad* was unknown to him.

Suppose that the region of the *Iliad* was the Ionian part of the eastern Aegean sea: where was the region of the *Odyssey*? It is worth while to reflect on the possibility that it might have been on the mainland of Greece: but I think it much more likely that it was in some other centre of Ionian life in the eastern Aegean. The one region might be on the coast, the other on one of the islands, in which the Epic art might be practised more or less in isolation during the dark ages.

There was a story told in the second century A.D. that the ghost of Homer, when interviewed in the after-life about the interpolated passages in the *Iliad* and *Odyssey*, replied that he personally wrote every one of them. I do not believe him. But I do believe that somewhere in the dim-seen past there lived a great poet, who fashioned from traditional songs an *Odyssey*. If he saw his poem today, he would remark that somebody has inserted a Visit to the Underworld in the middle of it; he might wonder why somebody has interfered with the beginning of the Journey of Telemachus, and composed a new prologue for the Wanderings of Odysseus; he would notice that chaos reigns here and there in the middle of the poem; and he would read the Continuation with deepening gloom. There are many smaller things that he might find unfamiliar, but he would regard all such additions and alterations as accidents natural to his profession: had not he himself dealt as he wished with the work of earlier poets? And his poem remains essentially unspoilt—in the Eleventh Book improved—by the hands of time and chance. It has ranked

for twenty-five hundred years among the great masterpieces of
the mind; and it will be found still in that company when—in
the words of his only superior—

> When time is old and hath forgot itself,
> When waterdrops have worn the stones of Troy,
> And blind oblivion swallowed cities up.

NOTES ON CHAPTER VI

1. The Homeric writings of Milman Parry are conveniently listed by A. B. Lord,
AJA 52 (1948) 43 f.; cf. also Wade-Gery in *The Poet of the Iliad* (1952) 81. Much
that I might have added here will be found in the first chapter of Rhys Carpenter's
Folk Tale, Fiction, and Saga, &c. (Sather Classical Lectures XX), 1946, and in
the second chapter of M. I. Finley's *World of Odysseus* (1954).

2. Parry, *Harv. Stud.* 41 (1930) 89: the examples on p. 88 are very impressive
and instructive.

3. Ibid. 43 (1932) 15.

4. See Wade-Gery, op. cit. 9 ff.: but I cannot find any reason (let alone evidence) for the supposition that the alphabet was '*invented* [my italics] as a notation
for Greek verse'.

5. This is the certain conclusion to be drawn from the old Aeolic and Arcadian
elements in the Homeric dialect. The distribution of races and dialects in historical
times proves that Arcadian was among the dialects predominant on the mainland
at the traditional date of the Trojan War. There is no other way of accounting
for the fact that the island of Cyprus, where the Myceneans settled, shows in historical times, despite centuries of separation, a dialect so closely related to Arcadian
that their original identity must be inferred. There could be no more satisfactory
proof that the small state of Arcadia, as we know it in the archaic and classical
eras, penned into the interior mountains of the Peloponnese, is the relic of the
kingdom of Agamemnon. In the north of Greece the predominant dialect in
historical times is Aeolic, which is much more closely related to Arcadian than to
any other member of the Greek family. Indeed it is likely that the differences
between the two in the Mycenean era were slight; and that what we call Arcadian
words in the Homeric poems, mainly because we find them in Arcadian prose
inscriptions (and nowhere else) in historical times, were in truth shared equally
by both dialects in the earlier period.

The fact that very numerous old Aeolic–Arcadian words and forms are firmly
embedded in the predominantly Ionic dialect of the Homeric Epic proves that
poetry in the metre (and concerning many of the subjects) of the *Iliad* was composed at the time when (and in the places where) the natural dialect of the poets
was Aeolic–Arcadian; and it is now obvious that the Aeolic of the Epic is enormously older than the Aeolic of Alcaeus and Sappho at the beginning of the sixth
century B.C.

Among other features the most clear and certain are: the modal particle κε;
the pronouns ἄμμες, ὔμμες, for which the Ionic forms cannot (as a rule) be substituted; adjectives with the prefix ἐρι-, mostly preserved in stereotyped formulas,
and always in words which are foreign to the Ionic dialect; the termination -εννός,
preserved by the Ionic poets if the word itself was foreign to their dialect, altered
to -εινός if the word itself existed in their dialect. μάν, a useful companion to Ionic
μέν; κεκλήγοντες, which could not be replaced by Ionic κεκληγότες; ἔμμεναι, an

invaluable double for εἶναι; patronymics in -ιος (Τελαμώνιος); κάτ, πάρ, beside Ionic κατά, παρά.

(On Aeolic forms in the Greek Epic see Meillet, *Aperçu d'une histoire de la langue grecque* (3rd ed. 1930) 162 ff.; Witte, *RE* s.v. Homeros 2214 ff.; Cauer, *Grundfragen* 148 ff.; Parry, *Harv. Stud.* 43 (1932) 27 ff., 43 ff. (but his treatment of the Lesbian–Aeolic dialect is mistaken). On the Arcadian element, see H. Weir Smyth in *Transactions of the American Philological Association* 18 (1887) 59 ff.; Hoffmann, *Die griech. Dialekte* i (1891) 276 ff.; Bowra, *CQ* 20 (1926) 168 ff.; Parry, l.c. 26.)

6. Some detail on this topic may be found in my *Sappho and Alcaeus* (1955) 177 ff.

7. See especially Beazley, *JHS* 60 (1940) 22 ff.

8. In the notes which follow I have distinguished the *Iliad* as a whole (even including the *Doloneia*) from the *Odyssey* as a whole (excluding only the Continuation, 23. 297–end, which is not in the main stream of the Epic tradition). The facts and figures would of course be still more favourable to my argument if I transferred from the account of the *Iliad* to that of the *Odyssey* those parts of the *Iliad* which are so much at variance with their surroundings in the *Iliad* and so remarkably Odyssean in style: notably 9. 507–605, the story of Meleager; 10 wholly; 11. 670–*c.* 760, the Pylian story; 14. 135–360 and 15. 1–77, the Διὸς Ἀπάτη; 21. 328–525, the Θεομαχία; 23 and 24 wholly; and some other shorter passages.

Not until my own work was done (in this chapter I give merely a few specimens) did I consult the work to which Ebeling's Lexicon makes such frequent reference, L. Friedländer's 'Zwei Homerische Wörterverzeichnisse', in *Jb. Class. Phil.*, suppl. iii, 1857–60 (no. 13) 713–830. So important is the class of words which he deliberately omits (p. 789) that his lists are, from the beginning, of limited value: moreover, his figures are not reliable, and there are some extraordinary mistakes in the word-lists (e.g. μηχανάομαι should be transferred to the Odyssean list; εὔζωνος should be deleted from the Odyssean list) and unintentional omissions (such as φλόξ, ἕλκος, αἱματόεις) sufficient to render the lists inadequate for his purpose and almost useless for mine. The student who tries to make use of his lists of ἅπαξ εἰρημένα in *Iliad* and *Odyssey* will quickly discover that there are many additions and subtractions to be made.

9. ἐρεβεννός eight times in *Il.*, not in *Od.* ἀργεννός five times in *Il.*, *Od.* only 17.

472. The Ionic form -εινός is represented by ἀλεγεινός and φαεινός, about equally common in both; by κελαδεινός, *Il.* only; by ἐλεεινός and ἐρατεινός, twice as common in *Il.* as in *Od.*; and by αἰπεινός, twelve times in *Il.*, once only in *Od.*

10. ἐρι- in *Il.* only: -βρεμέτης, -τιμος, -αύχην, -θηλής; ἐριβῶλαξ (-ος) very common in *Il.*, twice only in *Od.* Once only in *Od.*: -μυκος (2 *Il.*), -ούνιος and -ουνης (6 *Il.*), -σθενής (3 *Il.*). Common to both: -ηρος, -κυδής, -(γ)δουπος. Where the word as a whole exists in the Ionic dialect, the poets changed ἐρι- to Ionic ἀρι-: -γνωτος (2 *Il.*, 4 *Od.*), -δείκετος (2–7), -ζηλος and -δηλος (6–1: the only one of these words which recurs in classical prose), -πρεπής (5–4), -σφαλής (0–1), -φραδής (2–5).

11. The Attic form μήν is found seven times in the *Il.*, thrice in *Od.*

12. *Il.*: ἕο 5, εἷο 1, εὗ 6, ἕθεν 16; *Od.* ἕο 8, εἷο 1, εὗ 0, ἕθεν 1 (+23. 304); the *Odyssey* prefers αὐτοῦ to all other ways of expressing 'of him'.

13. This subject needs careful handling, and has received it primarily from Paul Cauer, *Grundfragen* 437 ff. (correcting the signal errors of J. A. Scott in *CR* 24 (1910) 8 ff., an article already severely handled by G. M. Bolling in *C. Phil.* 14 (1919) 328 ff.). I have been over the whole of the ground afresh, and find that Cauer is correct in all essentials, though there will always remain room for argument about minor points.

Abstracts in -τύς (excluding βρωτύς, ἐδητύς, common to both, and semi-concrete in meaning): *Il.* 6 (of which 5 not in *Od.*), used 9 times; *Od.* 10 (of which 9 not in

Il.), used 17 times. In -οσύνη and -φροσύνη: *Il.* 16 (9 not in *Od.*), 25 appearances; *Od.* 22 (15 not in *Il.*), 33 appearances. True abstracts in -σις and -τις: *Il.* 19 (11 not in *Od.*), 34 appearances; *Od.* 17 (9 not in *Il.*), 23 appearances. In -ίη: *Il.* 51 (29 not in *Od.*), *Od.* 50 (28 not in *Il.* In this class it is particularly important to distinguish between what really is 'abstract' and what is not: as Cauer says, 'the number of true abstracts . . . is not only relatively but also absolutely greater in the *Odyssey* than in the *Iliad*').

When the great difference in length between the two poems is taken into account (*Il.* = *c.* 15,700 lines, *Od.* 1–23. 296 = *c.* 11,500) it becomes at once obvious that the *Odyssey* has advanced considerably beyond the *Iliad* in the number and the use made of abstract nouns; that is the immediate impression made on the reader of the poems, and the statistics merely confirm what we had already recognized.

14. In both poems the dative plural of the first and second declensions in nouns and adjectives normally takes the longer forms, -οισι, -αισι. The shorter forms, -οις, -αις (-ης), are occasionally admitted as follows:

(1) At the end of the line: only 15 examples in *Il.*, of which 7 are in the word Ἀχαιοῖς. 23 examples in *Od.*, of which 7 are in the formula πολιὴν ἅλα τύπτον ἐρετμοῖς; among the remaining 16, two others show a tendency to become formular, κεφαλῇ τε καὶ ὤμοις (twice) and περὶ στιβαροῖς βάλετ' ὤμοις (twice). None of the *Iliad*'s examples shows a tendency to become formular except Τρωσὶν μὲν ∪∪–∪∪–∪∪ αὐτὰρ Ἀχαιοῖς (twice); considering the immense convenience of Ἀχαιοῖς at verse-end, the restriction on both amount and manner of its use is remarkable. The *Odyssey*, on the contrary, shows a marked tendency to construct formulas including this rare licence.

(2) The demonstrative and relative pronouns τοῖς, τῆς (οἷς, ἧς, cf. *Il.* 2. 180 σοῖς) stand 14 times before a consonant in *Il.*, always (with one exception) at the beginning of the line; of these 14 examples, 5 are in the Catalogue of Ships; of the other 9, two have a slight tendency to become formular, τοῖς δ' αὖτις μετέειπε (twice), τοῖς δ' ἅμα (twice). In the *Odyssey* there are 18 examples, including marked formular tendencies: τοῖς δ' αὖτις μετέειπε (twice), τοῖς δ' Ὀδυσεὺς (Ἀγέλεως) μετέειπε (4), τοῖς δὲ δολοφρονέων μετέφη (3). The *Odyssey* has several examples in positions other than at the beginning of the verse (3. 113, 490 = 15. 188, 12. 425); the only such example in *Il.* is 24. 201, ἧς τὸ πάρος περ|.

(3) (From this category I exclude χρυσέοις δεπάεσσι (*Il.* 4. 3, cf. 8. 162, 12. 311), perhaps earlier -οισι δέπασσι; ἀγανοῖς βελέεσσι (-οῖσι βέλεσσι); and τρητοῖς λεχέεσσι (-οῖσι λέχεσσι).) Within the line, before a consonant, the shorter forms -οις, -αις are occasionally admitted (*a*) in adjectives, (*b*) when a noun taking the longer form, -σι (of whatever declension), follows—or precedes—in agreement with such adjective: *Il.* 1. 89, 5. 641, 12. 297, 14. 180, 24. 25, 796 (in all these the adj. stands before the noun), 1. 179, 22. 442 (noun before adj.). In 20. 292 it is the adjective which has the longer, the noun the shorter, form (ἀθανάτοισι θεοῖς); in 24. 442 both forms are in nouns (ἵπποισι καὶ ἡμιόνοις). If the general rule is stated thus, that the shorter form before a consonant within the line occurs only in conjunction with a longer form in the same line, then the whole of the *Iliad* will afford only ten exceptions: 1. 238, 2. 137, 4. 253, 5. 606, 11. 132, 779 (athet. Aristarchus and Aristophanes; earlier perhaps ξείνων for -οις, cf. *Od.* 9. 268), 16. 766, 20. 394, 23. 478, 24. 664. The *Odyssey* has much the same number of examples, but much less restriction to the conditions (*a*) and (*b*) above (only 9. 86 = 10. 57, 17. 221, 21. 137 = 164; short noun preceding long adjective, 4. 755, 7. 279, long noun preceding short adjective, 4. 683 = 20. 213, 19. 490). The shorter form *not* in conjunction with a longer form occurs in 4. 239, 11. 242, 603, 13. 424, 14. 528 = 15. 61 (unique example of two shorter forms in the same line), 19.140, 20. 65, 374, 22. 288, and μεγάροις 13 times. There is a marked tendency to

include -οις, -αις, in formular phrases: περὶ στιβαροῖς βάλετ᾽ ὤμοις (2), ἐνὶ μεγάροις γεγάασιν, sim. (often), θοῆς παρὰ νηυσίν (2), σφίσι δ᾽ αὐτοῖς (2), ἐυξέστης σανίδεσσιν (2). Here again the *Odyssey* tends to use as a normal tool of the trade that which is alien to the traditional vocabulary.

(The material was assembled—not quite completely—by G. Gerland, *Kuhns Zeitschrift* 9 (1860) 36–68; the most recent treatment is that of H. J. Mette, *Der Pfeilschuss des Pandaros: Neue Untersuchungen zur 'Homerischen' Ilias* (1951), init.)

15. On the prosody of naturally short vowels standing before mute+liquid (or nasal) consonants see especially La Roche, *Homerische Untersuchungen* (1869), where the material is fully assembled and well arranged.

(1) Where both vowel and consonants stand within the same word (e.g. ἀφρο-δίτη): The vowel may remain short only if the word cannot otherwise be used in this metre, either absolutely (ἀφροδίτη) or in that form (ἀλλόθροων). To this general rule there are very few exceptions: in the *Iliad*, only 8. 323 φαρέτρης and (in proper names) 19. 287 πατρόκλε, 20. 383 ff. thrice ὄτρυντ-; perhaps 3. 414 σχέτλιη ought to be added; in the *Odyssey*, 19. 122 δάκρυπλωειν, 23. 110 κέκρυμμενα, and four examples in which the vowel in question is the syllabic augment, 5. 488 ἐνέκρυψε, 11. 583 προσέπλαζε, 19. 470 ἔκλιθη, 21. 138 and 165 προσέκλινε (none of these is protected by metre against what is called emendation).

(2) Where the vowel is terminal, the consonants initial (e.g. ετοιμᾶ προκειμενα): The general rule that such vowels are lengthened by position admits of certain exceptions; the vowel may remain short (a) if the following word cannot otherwise be used in this metre (προκειμενα cannot be used unless a short vowel precedes); (b) if the following word, though not itself intractable, belongs to a family of intractables (βροτῶν βροτοῖς βροτούς demand a preceding short vowel: the privilege is naturally extended to other declension-cases, βροτοί βροτοῦ βροτῷ &c. which do not make the same demand); (c) if the following word is a monosyllable beginning πρ- (short before πρός, *Il.* 12, *Od.* 6; before πρό, 4–1; before πρίν, 2–2); and in the *Iliad* there seems to be no objection to a short vowel before πρόσ(σ)ω (4 examples) and the name Πριαμίδης (7 examples).

Apart from these exceptional classes, breach of the general rule is very rare in both poems, noticeably less rare in the *Odyssey* than in the *Iliad*: *Il.* 4. 329 ὅ πλησιον, 5. 462 ηγητορι θρηκων, 9. 382 (= *Od.* 4. 127) οθι πλειστα, 11. 69 δὲ δραγματα, 11. 697 ειλετο κριναμενος, 18. 122 τινὰ Τρωιαδων, 20. 121 δὲ κρατος, 23. 186 δὲ χριεν, 24. 795 γέ χρυσειην; *Od.* 3. 320 τινὰ πρωτον, 4. 127 (= *Il.* 9. 382) οθι πλειστα, 5. 422 πολλὰ τρεφει, 8. 92 κατὰ κρατα, 8. 353 οιχοιτο χρεος, 10. 234 μελὶ χλωρον, 11. 527 ωμοργνυντό τρεμον, 12. 99 τέ κρατι, 12. 215 τυπτετέ κληιδεσσιν, 13. 410 νεσσι τρεφει, 14. 529 δὲ χλαιναν, 17. 275 σῦ πρωτος, 20. 92 αρὰ κλαιουσης, 23. 106 τί προσφασθαι. If the difference in length of the two poems is taken into account, it appears that this very rare licence is to be found nearly twice as often in the *Odyssey* as in the *Iliad*. It is, however, in other respects that the difference between the two poems is most clearly marked.

(i) The *Odyssey* makes enormously greater use of the *Iliad* of the exceptions defined under 2 (a) (b) above: this is only to a very limited extent to be explained by the *Odyssey*'s greater need to use certain otherwise intractable words; e.g. ∪ τραπεζα (*Il.* 7, *Od.* 28) and ∪ θρον- (*Il.* 3, *Od.* 20); the same explanation will not serve for ∪ βροτ- (*Il.* 22, *Od.* 47), ∪ προς αλληλους (*Il.* 10, *Od.* 21), and others.

(ii) The *Odyssey* introduces words and forms, unknown to the *Iliad*, which necessarily demand the liberty in question, though alternative words and forms *not* involving that liberty were at its disposal: ∪ κλιθηναι (*Il.* κλινθηναι); ∪ κλυδων (*Il.*—and also *Od.*, in the same sense—κυμα); ∪ κρυφηδον (*Il.* λαθρη); ∪ κρεων (*Il.*—and *Od.* too except at 15. 98—κρειων); ∪ κλεηδων (= φημη).

(iii) Unless we rewrite all our manuscripts 'with preposterous and frantic outrage', the *Odyssey* has several examples of a liberty absolutely unparalleled in the *Iliad*—the short syllabic augment, not only without compulsion but even without the slightest apparent need (see 1 above).

16. As Ebeling observes, a distinction may generally be drawn: χρήματα = *omnia quae possides*, κτήματα = *res pretiosae*; the one merges imperceptibly into the other in some contexts; the *Iliad* uses κτήματα to cover both.

17. ὄνομα does not occur in the *Iliad*; οὔνομα only (i) in 3. 235, a line not found in Pap. Brit. Mus. 126 (saec. iv–v p.C.) and omitted by two thirteenth-century manuscripts, and (ii) in 17. 260, athetized by Zenodotus ('with good reason', as Leaf says). οὔνομα twice in *Od.*, ὄνομα 18 times.

18. ἐλπωρή (always | ἐλπωρή τοι ἔπειτα . . .) is used with an infinitive and without ἐστί. ἐλπίς only *Od.* 16. 101, 19. 84 ἔτι γὰρ καὶ ἐλπίδος αἶσα.

19. *Il.* 1. 76 is the apparent exception: Allen (*Homer's Iliad*) prints τοὶ γάρ.

20. νήποινος Pindar *Pyth.* ix. 58. νηποινεί survived here and there in ordinary or official language.

21. It is impossible to say just where the line should be drawn between what might be fortuitous and what could not possibly be: but it is sometimes possible to say on which side of the line (wherever drawn) a particular fact falls. Does anybody believe that it is *by mere chance* that neither of the Epics employs κίνδυνος, μόχθος, νόμος (and νομίζω), ὀργή, σεμνός, τύχη, φέγγος?

22. Though the adverb καρπαλίμως was constantly in the Odyssean poet's mind.

23. Notice further the rarity in the *Odyssey* of ὄσσε (49 *Il.*, 13 *Od.*), σθένος (37–4), αἱματόεις (19–1), λαμπρός (11–1), αἰσχρός (9–1), θοῦρος (37–1), (ἐν)ορούω (23–1), ἐρείπω (27–1). Another very common word with which the Odyssean circle was barely familiar is the verb ῥήγνυμι, 57 times (including compounds and verbal adj.) in *Il.*, only thrice in *Od.* (12. 409 ἔρρηξε, 9. 481 ἀπορρήξας, 8. 137 the compound with συν-, which does not occur in *Il.*). While difference of subject-matter accounts sufficiently for the disparity between *Il.* and *Od.* in use of the stem of κόρυς (65–4), θώρηξ (35–0), θωρήσσω (39–3), τάφρος (36–1), φάλαγξ (34–0), χάζομαι (46–3); yet it remains very surprising that so useful a verb as ῥήγνυμι should be so rare, and that such generally serviceable words as αἰχμή (*Il.* 36), δήιος (46) should not make a single re-appearance in the *Odyssey*.

24. There is much more that might be said. How else are we to account for the fact that the same thing may be denoted in the *Iliad* by one word, in the *Odyssey* by another? e.g. αἰδοῖα (*Il.*) = μήδεα (*Od.*). Conversely the same word may denote different things—e.g. δνοπαλίζω in *Il.* 4. 472, *Od.* 14. 512. [Leumann, in *Homerische Wörter* (1950), has many observations which bear on this point; but I remain entirely unconvinced by the most important part of his argument. Cf. (for an example) op. cit. 167: ἀπριάτην is used (properly) as an adjective in *Il.* 1. 99, (improperly) as an adverb in *Od.* 14. 317; the suggestion that the Odyssean poet's source was none other than that passage of the *Iliad* presupposes what we certainly do not know and have no reason whatever to believe—that the *Iliad*'s phrase ἀπριάτην ἀνάποινον (or the like) could not have been known to the Odyssean poet from the traditional stock of phrases common to all poets, and existed nowhere in the world but in that one line of the *Iliad*.]

The Odyssean use of ἄρτος (17. 343, 18. 120) for σῖτος, κυνηγέτης (9. 120) for θηρητήρ, ὑπόδημα (15. 369, 18. 361) for πέδιλον, may be explained simply by the lateness of the poem relative to the *Iliad*.

25. See Lorimer, op. cit. 289 ff. Teucer (*Il.* 13. 313 f.) is an exception. Our poet, who gives the palm to Philoctetes, has (as always) not the *Iliad* but some other branch of the tradition in mind. In the *Doloneia* Meriones gives Odysseus a bow and quiver, forgetting that these are not the weapons for a hero in the *Iliad*, and that their utility *at night* is likely to be very restricted.

APPENDIX

To this Appendix I relegate certain matters which have played a considerable part in discussions of the 'Telemachy'.

It is convenient to begin by stating briefly certain principles which nowadays one may hope to take for granted:

(1) That if a line, or part of a line, or group of lines, recurs (identical or adapted) in more than one place, no question of borrowing or interpolation or the like arises automatically; and if of two identical or similar passages one is the better adapted to its context, it does not follow that the better adapted one was composed earlier than (let alone that it is the source of) the less well adapted. Homeric diction consists for the most part of a limited number of phrases adapted in endless variety to the poet's requirements; the repeated phrase is a means of making the verse, not an accident or ornament of it. (Parry, *Épithète traditionelle* 91 f., *Homer and the Homeric Style* 78.) Occasional imperfections in the adaptation of a traditional phrase to its context are to be expected (and are found often enough); they have no bearing on questions of authorship or priority, unless the fault is exceptionally grave or unless some additional fault is to be found, unconnected with the mere fact of repetition.[1]

(2) That allowance must be made for the addition, to a basic text, of isolated interpolations, usually on a small scale: even the most conservative text of the most confirmed Unitarian admits this in principle, bracketing at least a few lines, here and there; opinions differ about the extent, not about the fact.[2]

(3) That there are few, if any, extensive passages of the *Odyssey* which do not present uncommon words, forms, features of style and syntax (including usages peculiar to, or specially characteristic of, the Attic dialect), though there are very few passages in which anomalies are thickly congregated by contrast with their surroundings: moreover, that there are sentences, and parts of sentences, which appear to be

[1] The repetitions in the First Book are listed in Kirchhoff's *Odyssee* 165–78. Fault is easily found with 97–101 (= *Il.* 5. 746 ff.); 148 (= *Il.* 1. 470, al.); 185–6 (185 = 308); and of all these lines it is attested that they were wanting in ancient texts (almost all were athetized by Aristarchus). In addition to these, 139–41 (= 4. 55 ff.) and 171–3 (= 14. 188 ff., 16. 57 ff.) have the stigma of omission or athetesis in antiquity. A few other repetitions remain more or less suspect, but their number is not above the average.

[2] The number and quality of suspected interpolations in the First Book, over and above those listed in the preceding note, are certainly not more significant than one might find in most other passages of comparable length.

deficient in sense or deplorable in style; but these again occur sporadically throughout the poem, very seldom closely congregated. It is consequently imprudent, as a general rule, to draw from the language, in
relation to an isolated passage, inferences which would not apply with
more or less equal force to a considerable number of other passages;
though there may be a few exceptional places. If we make allowance
for the further possibility that superficial damage may have been done
to the language of the Epic in the course of a long history of transmission, it becomes clearer still that it would be imprudent, as a rule,
to draw from linguistic peculiarities any inference about date or
authorship of a particular part of the poem.[1]

I. On the extent of the interference in the First Book

Is the interference in the First Book more or less confined to Athene's
address (269–305) and Telemachus' premature action thereon (374 ff.),
or does it extend more generally throughout the Book?

First, the question whether 1. 1–268 affords internal evidence of the
activity of more than one composer, or of subsequent addition to a
basic *Odyssey* (or part thereof). I forbear to discuss the matter at any
length, since the arguments hitherto advanced, so far as I know them,
are for the most part of a type which seems not to distinguish what
might be from what is; to select one explanation where others would
serve as well; and to draw, not always correctly, conclusions from subjective impressions dogmatically asserted and incapable of proof.
A brief sample must suffice.

(1) Athene appears in the First Book as the Taphian king, Mentes,
in the Second as the Ithacan, Mentor; and the part she plays in both
guises is essentially the same. Are we to believe (the writer asks) that

---

[1] The First Book has a few abstract nouns and other linguistic features, and a
considerable number of other words, unknown to the *Iliad*; but very few which do
not recur in the *Odyssey*. Nothing in the language is more surprising than the
appearance of the word λόγος, foreign to the Epic (except *Il.* 15. 393, an uncomfort-
able passage). ἔπειτα seems meaningless in 65 and 106. I sympathize with those who
think it very odd to say that a person lives 'in an island, *where is the navel of the sea*'
(50); the sea had no 'navel', least of all in such a site as Calypso's island. And I am
not convinced that it is merely modern taste which finds 215–16 a most improbable
statement in the context. The casualness of the references to iron (184, 204), and
the allusion to poisoned arrows (260 ff.), are remarkable, but have no apparent
bearing on questions of multiple authorship. In the category of the very obscure,
if not quite senseless, is 318, σοὶ δ' ἄξιον ἔσται ἀμοιβῆς. Among the linguistic peculiarities are specially to be noticed 390, a clear example of a 'genitive absolute'; 337
οἶδας, here only in the Epic for οἶσθα; αὐτοῖσιν in 109 and 143, αὐτῶν in 308;
ἔκτοθεν prepositional, 132 (not elsewhere in *Il.* or *Od.*; adverb in *Od.* only, twice);
the form κλιθῆναι in 366 (elsewhere only 18. 213, the same line; the Epic form is
κλινθ-).

one and the same poet purposefully made both fictitious names so similar? Further (he continues) the name Mentes, together with the half-line in which it first appears (1. 105 Ταφίων ἡγήτορι Μέντῃ) is 'borrowed' from the *Iliad* (17. 73 Κικόνων ἡγήτορι Μέντῃ). We thus stand before a dilemma: either one and the same poet 'borrowed' Mentes from the *Iliad* and then invented 'Mentor' on that model; or a second poet, having a first poet's Mentor in front of him, deliberately 'borrowed' from the *Iliad* a name which resembled it. The decision (he concludes) is easy: *aber ohne Mentes ist kein a*—if Mentes is to be eliminated, what is left of the First Book? Mentes must have been invented after, and in imitation of, Mentor, and so the First Book, in which Mentes plays an integral part, must have been composed later than the Second.

The dilemma before which we stand is one of our own making, and if we care to stand somewhere else we are free to do so. It is obvious that the poet requires Athene-Mentes, to whom the situation in Ithaca is to be explained, to be a stranger to those affairs; whereas Athene-Mentor must be a friend already familiar with those affairs. We are not asked to believe that a poet could not require his goddess to perform both functions; but we are asked to believe that he could not call the one person Mentes, the other Mentor. We are under no compulsion whatever to agree with this dogma. We shall of course observe the resemblance between this pair and that other, the nurses Eurycleia and Eurynome: but we shall be told that they are not available as defence-witnesses; the prosecution has reserved them to give evidence of multiple authorship at a later stage. As for the 'borrowing' from the *Iliad*, we no longer believe in such concepts, at least in a case of this kind (see Parry, *Épithète traditionelle* 92, *Homer and the Homeric Style* 142).

(2) In 1. 259 Athene-Mentes says that Odysseus went to Ephyra to fetch poison for his arrows; in 2. 327 the Suitors suggest that Telemachus may go to Ephyra to fetch poison to put in their wine. We are to believe (what the *Odyssey* does not suggest) that Ephyra in the First Book is an hypothetical place, in the Second a fixed geographical location; and that a jocular suggestion made in the Second Book is converted into grim reality in the First. 'Can the borrowing be more obvious, can it be clumsier?' I make no comment.

(3) In 22. 331 Phemius is said to be *holding* a lyre in his hands; but in 1. 154 a herald *puts* a lyre into his hands. Why? Because (we are told) the composer of 1. 154 was under the mistaken impression that Phemius was *blind*, and so needed a herald to hand him the lyre, on the model of 8. 62–82, where a herald must take care of the blind Demodocus. This and the following may serve as examples of that

nimia in minimis diligentia which has done so much more harm than good in the study of the Homeric poems.

(4) 1. 437: Telemachus sits down on the bed and takes off his tunic. This, we are instructed, is impossible: 'Who can take off, while sitting down, a tunic that reaches to his feet?' And why is this young man so tired that he must undress sitting down? This is not (as one might have thought) argued in jest: the questions are asked by Kirchhoff, and reiterated by Wilamowitz, with every appearance of solemnity.[1] This is a kind of discussion to which there is no end. Different opinions are held, none of them demonstrably correct, some of them demonstrably incorrect. The list could be prolonged, but not with profit. There is still nowhere to turn for proof, or even a strong argument, derived from the text itself, that the bulk of the First Book was composed later than what follows, or that the interference in 1. 269–302 extends, to any noticeable degree, backwards.[2]

Much more interesting is the question of the abnormal theology of 1. 28–43:[3] it is an entirely novel idea, not to be found elsewhere, that a man's crimes may be the outcome of his will contrary to his destiny, ὑπὲρ μόρον,[4] and that the gods may generously send a messenger to

---

[1] The above samples are to be found in Wilamowitz, *HU* 6–27, together with more of the same kind; (3) and (4) also in Kirchhoff. I have said this much to explain why I take elsewhere so little notice of Wilamowitz's two books on the *Odyssey*: it is not easy to preserve a balanced judgement, when an author displays so much arrogance and anger; but I find it hard to believe that there is much of value in these works. A very characteristic example of his reasoning is to be found in his treatment of the relation of Circe to Calypso: I withhold what I had written, for the refutation by Focke (*Odyssee* 261 ff.) is sufficient, though it might be considerably strengthened. For further criticism of Wilamowitz's opinions on the Telemachy see Hölscher, op. cit. 4 ff., Klingner, op. cit. 8 f.

[2] I do not now enter into the debate about the *prooemium*, 1. 1–10, of which the salient feature is its limitation to the contents of Books V–XII, the wanderings and adventures of Odysseus; there is not a word to indicate the action of the whole of the second half of the *Odyssey* (or indeed of the first four Books thereof). In the detail the points most criticized are (1) that v. 3, '*he saw the towns and knew the minds of many men*' is a far from obvious way of describing the return journey of Odysseus as depicted in our poem; (2) that half the *prooemium* should be devoted to the relatively unimportant subject of the death of Odysseus' companions. The *prooemium* ends, and the continuous story begins, at vv. 10–11; not until the *prooemium* is finished do we hear anything about the subject of the second half of the *Odyssey*; and the phraseology in vv. 16–19 is obscure and negligent (the meaning seems to be 'when the time came for him to go to Ithaca, not even there (οὐδ' ἔνθα) was he free from troubles, *even* among his own friends', or '*and* among his own friends'; but, if so, the language is certainly not distinguished by elegance or clarity).

[3] See Jaeger, *Sitzb. Berl. Akad.* 1926, 73 f.; Pfeiffer, *Deutsche Lit.-Zeit.* 1928, 2364; Dodds, *The Greeks and the Irrational* 32 f., with further references 52, n. 22.

[4] I take this to mean that since the gods sent him warning, he could have refrained from the act. It was therefore not an act which he was bound by destiny

warn him against the consequences of wrong-doing, before he does it (though they take no further step to prevent him from doing it). Homeric gods do not elsewhere put on to mortal shoulders the burden of blame; nor do they kindly intervene to warn the prospective sinner before the event. It remains, however, quite impossible to use this novelty as evidence for a date of composition within a century or more; and its bearing on the question of multiple authorship is therefore very indefinite.

Secondly, what follows (1. 303–444). Here we find at least one firm support: the speech of Telemachus in 368–80 is (as we have seen) wholly interpolated, and there must have been some modification (at least) of the surrounding context. Apart from that passage there is no proof and not even much suspicion of interference. The narrative is straightforward in itself and coherent with what follows in the Second Book. The usual allowance must be made for isolated additions and modifications on a small scale,[1] and for peculiarities of style and language of a type from which no extensive passage is entirely free; but the general statement that the remainder of the First Book is an integral part of the same composition as the Second Book cannot be refuted by internal evidence. It is finally to be observed that Athene's visit to Telemachus in the First Book, on the day before the assembly in the Second Book, is explicitly mentioned in 2. 262–5:

κλῦθί μευ ὃ χθιζὸς θεὸς ἤλυθες ἡμέτερον δῶ . . . .

II. On the relation of the Second Book to the Third and Fourth

The common opinion is that the Second, Third, and Fourth Books form a coherent whole. In the Second Book Telemachus announces to the Suitors his intention to sail to Pylos and Sparta; makes his preparations, and sails; and the story of his travels is told in the Third and Fourth Books. The Second Book thus forms a prologue to the two following and is generally thought to be an integral part of the 'Telemachy'.

to do; and his doing it was in that sense ὑπὲρ μόρον, beyond what was allotted to him. This is not a normal usage of μόρος in the Epic; but then there is nothing normal in the context.

[1] 356–9 would have offended our taste even if we did not know that they were absent from the 'better MSS.' in antiquity and regarded by Aristarchus as interpolated (Schol. on 356). 422 ff. have probably suffered local interference: (1) the text is exceptionally unstable at 424 (see Bolling, External Evidence 221); (2) 425–6 are very odd; they are much the same as 14. 5–6, but there the expression περισκέπτῳ ἐνὶ χώρῳ is appropriate to the site of Eumaeus' hut, whereas it seems an absurd description of Telemachus' bedroom, presumably in the precincts of the palace.

This opinion has been contested, especially by Bethe in 1922; and since he now has a formidable ally in Merkelbach (1951) it is necessary to consider afresh, however briefly. It is their contention that (1) all references to the Journey of Telemachus in the Second Book were inserted by the last editor of our *Odyssey*; (2) the assembly of Ithacans, which is the central theme of the Second Book, was originally the introduction (or part thereof) to a poem in which Odysseus was already, from the start, about to take vengeance on the Suitors. Let us examine the latter point first.

In the course of the assembly of Ithacans in the Second Book Telemachus called upon the gods to redress his wrongs: thereupon two eagles, sent by Zeus, flew above the assembly and looked down upon the heads of the assembled, and death was in their eyes, and they tore their necks and cheeks with their talons, then darted away to the right across the city. Up rose an old man, Halitherses, skilled in augury, to interpret the omen thus: the Suitors, he declared, will have good cause for grief. 'Odysseus will not be long away from his friends; *even now he is somewhere near, plotting death and doom for all these Suitors.*' Now, says Bethe (and Merkelbach agrees), this can only mean one thing: to say that Odysseus is *somewhere near* means that Odysseus is *already in Ithaca*; not until he is there does he begin to plan the destruction of the Suitors; at such a time, of course, there can be no question of travels to Pylos and Sparta. We are not to suppose that this seer has been specially introduced in order to talk falsehood or nonsense: it is his business to give an accurate interpretation of a heaven-sent omen; if so, we must abide by what he actually says—that Odysseus is at hand, and that he is at this moment engaged in devising a plan to destroy the Suitors.

The observation is shrewd and interesting; and (for the Unitarian) there is only one honest way of avoiding the inference which is drawn from it. We must frankly admit that the poet has here (contrary to normal practice) allowed the interpretation of an omen greatly to exceed the limits of the truth, and actually to include in its detail matters which are false: to say that Odysseus is 'near' is a pardonable exaggeration of the truth (he is at the penultimate station on his journey home, and his twenty years' absence has reached its last few weeks); but to say that he is at this time plotting the destruction of the Suitors is simply false.

For my own part, believing as I do that the assembly-scene is a specially composed prologue to the Journey of Telemachus as a separate recitation, made up without reference to the detail of what we call the First Book, and without any more reference to the remainder of the poem than the general pre-supposition of a return and revenge of Odysseus, I see no cause for wonder if my poet has reminded his listener, in these general terms, that his story has a wider background; so long as it is not included in a continuous *Odyssey*, but serves merely as a general reminder of extrinsic events, the seer's interpretation of the omen is blameless enough—for the facts which convict it of falsehood exist only in the continuous poem, not in the separate recitation. It is important not to exaggerate the meaning of ἐγγὺς ἐών, 'being *near*'; this does not mean or imply 'being *in Ithaca*'. If Odysseus were in Ithaca, of course Telemachus cannot now go sailing to Pylos and Sparta. But if he is told that his father is 'somewhere near', there is no compelling reason why he should not at once set forth to find him; though it certainly seems unnatural that he should go so far afield as Pylos and Sparta. I think we must candidly admit that this poet has made his prophet say things which are not true in relation to the continuous *Odyssey*, and which do not have their natural consequence even in the separate recitation of the Telemachy.

The second main point was that all references to Telemachus' journey in the assembly-scene are interpolations. Here the argument centres on the lines in which Telemachus first announces his journey to the Suitors, 2. 208–23. If, as it is maintained, this passage is demonstrably a later addition to its context, there would be good reason to suspect the same of all subsequent mentions of the journey in this scene, even though little if any intrinsic fault were to be found in them.

The context is (briefly) as follows. After Halitherses has interpreted the omen Eurymachus addresses the assembly. He makes fun of the augurer, declares his conviction that Odysseus is dead, and threatens that the Suitors will continue their disorderly conduct until Penelope marries one of them. Telemachus, who speaks next, asks for a ship to take him to Pylos and Sparta in search of his father, and adds that if he discovers that his father is dead he will return and give his mother in marriage to one of the Suitors. There follows at once an address by Mentor, an old friend of Odysseus, who, without referring to Telemachus' speech, rebukes the assembled citizens for their ingratitude and their connivance at the ruin of Odysseus' property. He is answered by Leiocritus, who observes that the citizens do well not to interfere, and that the Suitors would make short work of Odysseus himself if he should return; he adds that Mentor and Halitherses shall assist

Telemachus to prepare his journey overseas. And that is the end of the assembly.

Bethe and Merkelbach assert (1) that Telemachus makes no answer to what was said by the preceding speaker; (2) that Telemachus' own speech is ignored by the speaker who follows him; (3) that, if you simply omit Telemachus' speech, the passage runs much more coherently than if you do not omit it. It will then follow that Leiocritus cannot originally have referred to Telemachus' journey, since no such journey has been mentioned; and all subsequent passages in the Second Book which attest the Suitors' awareness of the journey are involved in the same condemnation. Let us consider the alleged facts and the inference drawn from them.

In 139–45 Telemachus had requested the Suitors to leave his house. Eurymachus replied that they would not do so until Penelope should marry one of them. Very well, says Telemachus, I shall not repeat my request, ταῦτα μὲν οὐχ ὑμέας ἔτι λίσσομαι: give me a ship and I will go in search of my father; if I find that he is dead I shall return and give my mother in marriage. It is surely incorrect to say that this statement follows incoherently on what has gone before; and still more surely incorrect to say that it makes no answer to the preceding speech—the last sentence, 220–3, is in fact a direct answer to Eurymachus' statement that the Suitors will not depart until Penelope yields; she shall yield, says Telemachus, if I return convinced of my father's death.

It is admitted that Mentor, who speaks after Telemachus, takes no notice of what Telemachus has said. Here the alleged fact is true; but is the inference compelling? 'One would really expect him to support the request for a ship', says Merkelbach; I am not so sure. If it were one of the *Suitors* now speaking and ignoring all that Telemachus has said, there would be good cause for surprise: we do expect the first Suitor who speaks after Telemachus to mention this matter of a ship for the journey; and, behold, the first Suitor does mention it—he says that Mentor and Halitherses shall promote the journey, though he adds that he does not believe that it will ever take place.[1]

I do not think that Bethe and Merkelbach have established a good case on this particular point; but I do agree (on other grounds;

---

[1] The part (an important one) of Klingner's book, *Die vier ersten Bücher der Odyssee*, which I find least satisfactory concerns the speech of Telemachus at 2. 208 ff. Telemachus' request for a ship at this point 'drängt sich wunderlich in das sonst einheitlich zusammengeschlossene Gebilde, kann sich aber darin nicht entfalten' (p. 20): it may not unfold itself therein, but it follows very naturally thereupon (especially as we have all been waiting for something of the sort since 1. 88 ff.).

pp. 61 ff. above) that the whole matter of the Suitors' knowledge of, and attitude towards, Telemachus' journey is hopelessly confused as it stands in our *Odyssey*. About the fact there is no doubt whatever; about the reason for it we can only speculate.

As usual there is much subsidiary argument.

(1) According to Bethe, Telemachus' reference to his journey in 2. 214–16 is a copy of 1. 281: quoting the former passage, where Telemachus says that he will go to Sparta and Pylos νόστον πευσόμενος πατρός, Bethe comments, 'That is false; what he is able and eager to inquire about is not *the return*, but whether anyone *has any news* of Odysseus, whether Odysseus *is still alive or not*.'

I suppose I need make no special comment on this.

(2) Bethe denies that there can ever have been any prior intention of travelling to Sparta. Telemachus goes to Pylos, and Nestor, who cannot help him, naturally advises him to try elsewhere: but Athene must have known from the start that the journey to Sparta was all that mattered; if Athene prescribes the journey, she must say 'go to Sparta', not 'go to *Pylos and* Sparta', for the visit to Pylos is a waste of Telemachus' time: i.e. either he had no intention of going to Sparta until Nestor told him to, or (if his instructions came from Athene) he had no intention of going to Pylos.

This is all much too severely rational. The primary purpose of the journey of Telemachus is to tell the story of the return of the great kings from Troy; a visit to Nestor was worth including, and therefore prescribing, in such a narrative even at the cost of greater inexactitudes than this.

(3) Bethe argues (and Merkelbach agrees) that the character of Telemachus portrayed in the Second Book differs from that portrayed in the Third and Fourth Books: in the former he is bold, resourceful, manly; in the latter he is shy, awkward, impressionable. I find no substance in this. I do not particularly expect that his behaviour in the market-place towards his enemies will be similar to his behaviour as a guest in the palace of Nestor and Menelaus.

(4) Bethe argues further that Mentor's indignation against the Ithacans and his exhortation to them to rise against the Suitors are 'not very intelligent', since Telemachus has just come to an understanding with the Suitors. This seems to me special pleading of a type about which it is vain to argue.

(5) It is suggested that the stranger about whose identity the Suitors inquire in the First Book (405 ff.) was, in an earlier form of the story, Odysseus himself in disguise, present in Ithaca from the start. This is

12

merest speculation; and, since the lines in question are perfectly appropriate to their present context, in which the stranger is Athene-Mentes,
not Odysseus in disguise, I do not see anything to recommend it.

III. *On the references to the Suitors in the Third and Fourth Books*

Was the Journey of Telemachus a self-contained poem, a *Kleinepos*,
or does it presuppose the sequel of our *Odyssey*, the return of Odysseus
and the killing of the Suitors? That is (in effect) how the question is
commonly formulated: to me it appears obvious that a separate lay
might include allusions to events beyond its own immediate concerns;
but I meet the argument on its own ground.

The Third and Fourth Books (3. 1–4. 620, to which, for the sake of
the argument, I shall confine my attention) include references to the
misconduct of the Suitors and their impending doom; but several
scholars (including Bethe and Merkelbach) have tried to prove that
all such passages are later additions to their contexts, inserted into the
Telemachy after its conjunction with the main Epic.

It has often been said that the notion of a 'Telemachy' independent
of an *Odyssey* is in itself unacceptable; that the journey of Telemachus
has not sufficient substance or significance to form the theme of a self-
contained poem. I do not believe that this observation has any value
at all: it is useless to make positive assertions of this kind about what
might be, or not be, a proper theme for an Epic lay. We know so little
about the matter; and I see nothing improbable in the idea that, when
an *Odyssey* already existed, a poet might compose a Journey of Telemachus separately, presupposing in his audience a knowledge of that
Odyssey.[1]

There is perhaps only one question to which a useful answer can be
given more or less objectively: whether the four passages in the Third
and Fourth Books which connect the 'Telemachy' with the *Odyssey* by
referring to the misconduct of the Suitors and its requital can be
proved to be later additions to their contexts.

(1) 3. 195–228. The evidence here is decidedly in favour of the
prosecution. There is a fault in the vulgate text both at the beginning
and at the end of a short passage which includes references to the

---

[1] Nor do I find anything helpful in statements of opinion of the following type:
'That in a story in which Suitors are wasting the royal substance and wooing the
queen, Telemachus cannot undertake journeys abroad; he must stay at home and
protect his property'; or 'That the object of Telemachus' journey is to inquire
about Odysseus' fate, not to complain about the Suitors; and if he had indeed left
such disorder at home, he must ask Nestor and Menelaus for advice and assistance,
and this they must provide for him.'

Suitors. It is a reasonable inference that the passage as a whole was designed and added later specially to introduce those references.

(i) Telemachus told Nestor that he had come to inquire about Odysseus, and asked him whether he had any news (83 ff., 97 ff.). It is remarkable that Nestor, in the course of his long reply, makes no direct answer to this question; indeed to the question whether he has *heard* anything he makes no reply at all. And yet he ends his discourse in a manner which leaves no doubt of his intention to make such a reply. 'Thus I came home,' he says, 'not knowing who were saved and who were lost. But what I have heard as I sit here at home I will tell you. Safely, they say, the Myrmidons came home, and safely Philoctetes, and Idomeneus brought all his companions to Crete; and of Agamemnon you yourselves have heard, how he returned to die at Aegisthus' hand; but Aegisthus paid the penalty—so good a thing it is that a son be left when a father dies, to avenge him.' And now, what about Odysseus? What purpose has this list of safe arrivals served except to culminate in the statement 'But of Odysseus I have heard nothing at all'? In place of this we find two lines, most unhappily transferred from a better context (1. 301 f.), here marked as an interpolation by Aristophanes and Aristarchus: 'You too, friend, for I see that you are both handsome and tall, be valiant, that you may be praised even by them that are born hereafter.' Telemachus must surely reply, 'Thank you for this unexpected compliment; but I think you had not quite finished what you were saying?'

I think that we should have to be very prejudiced to deny that the list of those of whom Nestor *does* know must once have led to its obvious conclusion—the mention of the one of whom he does *not* know, about whom he was particularly asked (and here we have waited in suspense for his answer)—Odysseus.

(ii) It is difficult, perhaps impossible, to make sense of the vulgate text from 216 onwards. Nestor says to Telemachus, 'Who knows, but Odysseus may return and pay the Suitors out, whether he alone or all the Achaeans? Would that Athene might love you as she loved your father at Troy; if she would so love you and take care of you, the Suitors would soon forget their courting of Penelope.' The incoherence is plain enough: 'Odysseus may well return and kill the Suitors; if Athene loved you as she loved him, you would soon dispose of the Suitors.' Coherence is restored at once by the readings of Zenodotus at 216–17, ἀποτείσεαι and σύ γε: according to this, after Telemachus had said 'If only I had power to deal with the Suitors', Nestor replies 'Who knows, but you may go home and pay the Suitors out? If

Athene loved you as she loved your father, you would succeed quickly enough.'

So far, so good. But what follows is absolutely opposed to this solution. Telemachus now replies to Nestor, 'Your word will not be fulfilled; what you say is too much; I am dumbfounded; never could this come to pass within my hope, not even if the gods willed it so.' Thereupon Athene-Mentor comments, 'Telemachus, what have you said? *A god can easily rescue a man, if he will, even at a distance.*' This comment of course presupposes that the possibility which Telemachus had denied was the return of Odysseus, and that in turn presumes that Odysseus was the subject of Nestor's discourse in 216–17. Sense can only be restored in the one place at the cost of nonsense in the other.

But now there is a further reason why the problem must remain finally insoluble; it arises out of the vulgate text, which is utterly unreliable at the critical point. Zenodotus again had something different: in his text Telemachus said 'These things will never be, *unless the gods will have them so*'—a much likelier sentiment, I suppose, than the vulgate's '*Not even if* the gods will have them so'. What Athene replied is unknown, except that Zenodotus' text did not include the line 'A god can easily rescue a man, if he will, even at a distance'. Thus the text of Zenodotus made coherent sense from start to finish. Our manuscripts, on the contrary, do not. Moreover, the remainder of Athene's speech, 232–8, was held by Aristarchus to be an interpolation. Thus the evidence indicates three discrepant versions of the text: that of Zenodotus, that of our manuscripts, and that which Aristarchus believed to be correct.

Whatever the solution of the textual problems may be, it is now apparent that the vulgate text is in a muddle both at the beginning and at the end of this passage; and therein lies the force of the contention that that which intervenes between the two faults is, as a whole, an interpolation, and that the interpolation is the cause of the faults. It is prudent to admit that a good case has been made out here; if the case against the other references to the Suitors in the Telemachy were as good, or nearly as good, the cumulative effect of the evidence might be decisive enough.

(2) 3. 313–16. Nestor relates what happened at Mycenae. Orestes killed Aegisthus, who had murdered his father Agamemnon; Menelaus arrived home on the day of Aegisthus' death. He continues: 'So do not you, my friend, wander a long time far from home, leaving your properties, and men thus insolent in your house, lest they divide and

devour your properties, while you go a fool's errand. I bid you go to Menelaus, who has lately come from a strange land,' &c.

The charges brought against this passage are exceptionally weak. First, it is alleged that the thought is incoherent: having told Telemachus that he must not wander long at a distance from home, Nestor cannot at once continue 'But proceed from here to Sparta'. As if a few days at Sparta might reasonably be called 'wandering a long time far from home'; and as if it were proper to scrutinize the Epic so exactly. Secondly, Nestor has not been informed of Telemachus' intention to go to Sparta; we must therefore expect that Nestor will expressly tell him *why* he should go there, viz. because Menelaus may have news for him. This would be plainly desperate pleading even if its premiss were true; but in fact Nestor does explain why he recommends the visit to Sparta, 327-8, 'Implore Menelaus to tell you the truth'.

(3) 4. 163-7. Nestor's son Peisistratus, friend to Telemachus, addresses Menelaus and alludes to the troubles at Ithaca: 'Telemachus wanted to see you', he explains, 'in the hope that you might suggest some advice or action. A son has many troubles at home when his father is abroad, if he has no other helpers; and so it is with Telemachus—his father is gone, and he has nobody to defend him from injury in Ithaca.'

It appears that Aristarchus was aware that some of his predecessors had judged these lines to be interpolated, though that was not his own opinion (τὸ δὲ ἦθος οὐ συνιέντες τινὲς ἠθέτησαν τὰ ἔπη). Here at least it is easy to understand the objections. First, it is contrary to Heroic custom that a man should give the reason for his visit before he is asked for it. Secondly, the reason given here is not the true one: Telemachus has come to inquire about his father, not to consult Menelaus about his difficulties in Ithaca. And thirdly, Menelaus takes no notice whatever of this request for 'word or deed': on the next morning (312 ff.) the proper order of events is observed, and the proper reason given; as if the present passage had never occurred, Menelaus invites Telemachus to say why he has come, and Telemachus replies: 'To inquire about my father.' I have great sympathy with the opinion that the lines spoken by Peisistratus are a later addition to their context.

(4) 4. 318 ff. Menelaus asks Telemachus why he has come. Telemachus replies: 'I am here in the hope that you may tell me some report of my father. My home is being devoured, my rich lands are ruined, my house is full of enemies—the Suitors of my mother, with insolence beyond measure—who are for ever slaughtering my sheep and cattle. Therefore I am now come to your knees, hoping that you

may be willing to tell me of his lamentable death, if you saw it with your own eyes, or heard from some other,' &c.

The charge made here is that two different matters are set down side by side without any formal or intrinsic connexion. First, the request for information about Odysseus; secondly, the description of the disorder at Ithaca, after which the former topic is resumed more urgently and at greater length. I find it hard to take this very seriously: Telemachus' journey in search of his father is most closely and necessarily connected with the fact that the troubles at home have come to a climax; it is certainly untrue to say (as Bethe does) that there is no *intrinsic* connexion between the two statements made here—'I came to inquire about Odysseus' and 'At home, disaster threatens'.

Menelaus begins his reply with a long outburst of the liveliest indignation against the Suitors (332–46): what fault can be found with this? The charge as stated by Merkelbach runs as follows: First, that Menelaus' indignation is not enough; he *must* give advice, if not assistance. Secondly (quoting Bethe, p. 27, with approval) the passage is 'dragged in just as disconnectedly, and breaks off just as abruptly, as the other references to the Suitors in the Journey of Telemachus'. Moreover, like all those other references, it contributes nothing to the story of the journey, but rather distorts the otherwise straightforward lines of development.

It seems to me that we have now descended too far down the scale of what is required as evidence to prove a point. At this level we are merely expressing opinions, and one can only be countered by another —for example, that since the sequel has no use whatever for intervention by Menelaus in Ithaca, it is not surprising that the poet was satisfied with an outburst of indignation by Menelaus; and that the statement that 332–46 are disconnected at the beginning and abrupt at the end appears to me to be the reverse of the truth.

In summary: a very strong case has been made out against 3. 198 ff., and a good one against 4. 163 ff.; but the charges against the other two passages fail altogether. That is to say, it is impossible for us to prove that the Journey of Telemachus ever existed in a form which did not presuppose the sequel of the *Odyssey*, the return of the hero and the overthrow of his enemies. Of course we must admit that 3. 313 ff. and 4. 315 ff. may be interpolations, even though we cannot prove them to be such: the style and materials of Greek Epic poetry, and the circumstances of its transmission, are such that it was very easy to insert lines and groups of lines without leaving any trace by which the insertion could be detected. Of the four passages, two are condemned; it is perfectly possible that the other two are equally guilty, acquitted only because not caught in the act. But I do not see the use of speculating about what might be, if there is no means of discovering whether it was or not. And it must be remembered that even if all the passages in question could be proved to be interpolations, it would still not follow that the Telemachy was ever independent of the *Odyssey*; nor (on the other hand) if all or any were integral, would it follow that the Telemachy was *not* independent of the *Odyssey*—it might be an independent lay presupposing knowledge of the *Odyssey* in its audience.

IV. *On the Ambush at Sea*

The theory that the Telemachy existed independently of the *Odyssey* has a further question to consider. The *Odyssey* relates that the Suitors dispatched a party to lie at sea in ambush, in order to waylay Telemachus on his approach to Ithaca after the journey to Pylos and Sparta. The ambush of course presupposes the journey; it links the journey of Telemachus to the events in Ithaca, and consequently to the whole of the second half of the *Odyssey*. It was the opinion of Kirchhoff (adopted and elaborated by a long line of followers, including Wilamowitz, Bethe, Schwartz, Von der Mühll, and Merkelbach) that this story of the ambush was invented and composed (or at least expanded, modified, and re-arranged) by an editor whose purpose was to link the journey of Telemachus to the remainder of the *Odyssey*.

The facts are briefly as follows. The *Odyssey* tells of two different plans for the murder of Telemachus. First, the Suitors attempt to waylay him on his return from Pylos to Ithaca; secondly, when that plan has failed, they discuss a plan for catching and killing him 'in the country, far from the city, or on the road'. The second of these two plans (first proposed in 16. 383 ff., postponed in 20. 241 ff., and mentioned in 22. 53; in 17. 79 f., 595, there are references to the danger in which Telemachus stands) presents no intrinsic difficulty, since it does not necessarily presuppose a journey to Pylos and Sparta. Such difficulty as there may be arises out of the first plan, the ambush at sea, and out of the relation of the first plan to the second.

The ambush at sea is mentioned in the following places: 4. 625 ff.; 13. 425 ff.; 14. 181 ff.; 15. 27 ff.; 16. 342 ff. and 462 ff. (it is vaguely anticipated in 2. 367 ff.). It must be admitted that this is a sad collection: the second of these passages coheres with the magical transformation

of Odysseus, a fragment of a different version of the story (pp. 88 ff.);
the third (14. 174–84) is obelized in cod. M as an interpolation;
the fourth occurs in a context which has almost certainly suffered
some interference; and the fifth (16. 342 ff.) is exposed to criticisms
which we shall consider in a moment. It appears very probable that
this matter of the ambush has been enlarged by means of rather
unskilful additions to the text in the course of time; but I do not think
that it is possible to prove that it was ever altogether absent from the
poem. I offer no more than a few observations on three passages.

(1) 16. 342 ff. Here, as often, we have to listen to arguments which
differ greatly in degree of respectability. First, an example at the
lowest level. When Eurymachus observes that the ambush at sea has
failed, he says 'Let us launch a vessel and get together fishermen as
rowers to go with all speed and tell the ambushers to come home'.
'That', says Wilamowitz, 'is not very intelligent; it would have been
quicker to send *one* fisherman in a boat'—as if one man might row
faster than a crew. Next, one or two points of detail: (*a*) When
Amphinomus sees that the ambushers have already returned we are
told that he '*broke out into merry laughter*'—to explain, indeed to attach
any meaning whatever to his mirth at this moment, a little special
pleading (or more than a little) would be of service. (*b*) It is unnatural
that the Suitors should go, as they do, *to the place of public assembly*, εἰς
ἀγορήν, to discuss the failure of their murder-plot and to devise another.
In the whole of Ithaca there was no more unsuitable site. The poet
himself is aware of the absurdity. He would disarm criticism by adding
that 'they did not allow any other man, young or old, to sit among
them': then what was the object of going there at all?

These are small points, but not without significance when joined by
larger ones.

(*a*) It is remarkable that Amphinomus should be introduced at
length and in detail at 394 if he had already appeared and spoken a
few lines earlier (351). This plain breach of the Epic convention is a
good point in favour of the opinion that the earlier part of this scene
is a later addition, or at least has suffered some interference.

(*b*) The latter part of Antinous' speech (364–92) and the advice of
Amphinomus which follows are not well adapted to the general situation. The Suitors have failed in their attempt to murder Telemachus.
Antinous now suggests that they should try again, but blunts the edge
of his advice by suggesting that the Suitors may prefer to return to
their homes and allow Telemachus to live in peace while they court
Penelope in a proper manner. Since murder was attempted a little

while ago, the proposal of this innocent alternative rings false enough. Then Amphinomus declares: 'I am not in favour of killing Telemachus; it is a serious thing, to kill a king's son. Let us first consult the gods, and kill him or spare him according to their counsel.' Thus spoke Amphinomus, and the Suitors approved.—Since they have already plotted and attempted the murder of Telemachus, without misgiving, indeed without discussion, these scruples are seriously belated; nor is it easy to take in earnest the suggestion that the Suitors thought that the 'oracles of great Zeus' might well give their blessing to the proposed assassination.

We may temperately judge that the first of these two points is sufficient to taint the whole context with a doubtful colour; and that the second point reinforces our suspicion—the passage as a whole is certainly not of high quality. If the Ambush at Sea depended on this passage, I should have little faith in it.

(2) 16. 462–75. Telemachus asks Eumaeus whether the Suitors are still maintaining or have abandoned the ambush at sea. Eumaeus replies to the point at some length. I find no intrinsic fault in this place; drastic measures, warranted only by a pre-conceived theory, would have to be adopted to dislodge the Ambush at Sea from this context.

(3) 4. 625 ff. There are blemishes enough in this passage, throughout to the end of the Book, but it is doubtful whether their number is increased by any matter concerned with the Ambush at Sea. I mention only the statement of Bethe and Merkelbach that in the Fourth Book 'Penelope's inactivity [when she hears of the murder-plot] is incomprehensible'. I do not understand what is meant by calling her inactive. She at once demands that a messenger be sent to Laertes in the hope that he may take action to protect Telemachus. That is the most effective measure in her power. The story does not allow the proposal to be carried out, so Eurycleia dissuades her; she then formally prays to Athene to protect her son. These are sensible measures; what better could she do? Complain to the Suitors, as she does in the Sixteenth Book?—a vain gesture, destined from the start to the failure in which it ends. (The theory which we are discussing attributes considerable importance to the argument that the scenes in 4. 625 ff. and 16. 409 ff. resemble and repeat each other to such an extent that the one must be a copy, by a different hand, of the other; and it has often been maintained that the Sixteenth Book has the original, the Fourth the copied, version. I find no convincing evidence for this. In both places Penelope is informed by a herald, Medon, that the Suitors intend to kill her

son: the scene in 4 is much longer than that in 16, and Penelope's conduct is quite different in the two places. We should need much stronger evidence than that which is actually adduced to convince us that the two scenes could not have been composed by the same poet as integral portions of an Epic.[1])

Nobody who carefully considers this matter is likely to conclude that the case against the Ambush at Sea is negligible. The means at our disposal do not enable us to dislodge it from 16. 462–75; but it may well be more than mere chance that all other references to it occur in contexts of doubtful (or more than doubtful) colour.[2] It seems quite probable that this episode was first introduced into the poem at a relatively late stage of its development; but, if so, the fact would not necessarily have any bearing on the question whether the Telemachy was integral to or originally independent of the *Odyssey*.[3]

---

[1] We are not obliged to agree with Bethe when he tells us (p. 44) that the scene in the Fourth Book is 'disproportionately extended, and wanting in power'. Nor am I convinced that 16. 346 f. is the original, 4. 663 f. the copy, on the ground that ἐτελέσθη is more aptly used in the former place, after the whole journey has been accomplished.

[2] Consider particularly this question: when did Odysseus, Telemachus, and Eumaeus first learn about the Ambush?—Odysseus at 13. 425; Telemachus at 15. 28; Eumaeus is aware of it at 14. 181. I can well understand the satisfaction of those who believe in an independent Telemachy when they find that all three of these passages occur in contexts which are, for other reasons, rightly judged to be, or to include, the work of poets at a late stage in the continuous tradition.

[3] Because the episode might have been added to a poem in which the Telemachy was already combined with the return of Odysseus. But of course the fact, so far as it goes, is one of the more useful (and legitimate) instruments in the hands of those who would prise the Telemachy altogether out of the *Odyssey*.

INDEXES

I. LINES AND CONTEXTS FROM THE *ODYSSEY*

II. GREEK

III. ENGLISH